Our America:
Discovery
Through Our Civil War

Our America:
Discovery Through Our Civil War

Sandi Ludwa

Copyright © 2019 Sandi Ludwa

All rights reserved.

ISBN: 978-1-7335778-0-9

Cover Design and Cover Photography by J. David Anderson

Interior Photos by Sandi Ludwa

All rights reserved. No part of this book may be reproduced or transmitted in any form or by any means, electronic or mechanical, including photocopying, recording, or by any information storage and retrieval system, without permission in writing from the copyright owner.

Dedication

Without Dr. J. Edward Lee, of Winthrop University, this book would not exist. I am guided by his continued optimism, encouragement, and support. He has inspired me and thousands of others with the spirit and pride that exists in all of us for this great country of ours. I sincerely appreciate the patience and understanding given to me by my husband Michael and daughter Nicole, while I pursued the passion of publishing this work.

Contents

Dedication..v

Forward/Introduction... xiii

Chapter 1 **Discovery** 1
    Setting the Foundation   2
    Columbian Exchange   10
    Hawaii   16
    A Word About the French   16
    Summary   18

Chapter 2 **Settlement** 20
    Conditions in Europe   21
    Sir Walter Raleigh   24
    Summary   26

Chapter 3 **Fort Jamestown** 28
    The Establishment of Jamestown   29
    The Headright System and Indentured Servants   32
    1619 Was an Important Year   34
    Summary   35

Chapter 4 **Religion comes to the colonies** 37
    The Pilgrim Separtists   38
    The Puritans Non-Separtists   40
    Salem Witch Trials   42
    Slavery and the Labor System   46
    Let's talk about slavery   47
    Bacon's Rebellion   48
    Summary   49

Chapter 5	**Shedding Our Roots**...	51
	Religion in New England	55
	Great Awakening	55
	Stono Rebellion	59
	Summary	60
Chapter 6	**Becoming Americanized**...	62
	Tariffs, Acts, and Distrust	63
	Summary	66
Chapter 7	**The American Revolution: The Road to Americanism Continues**	67
	The American Revolution	68
	The Declaration of Independence	71
	Summary	77
Chapter 8	**Building Our Own Nation**	78
	Ordinances, Laws, Compromises	80
	Shay's Rebellion	79
	Getting to Know George Washington	81
	Summary	83
Chapter 9	**The Constitution and Bill of Rights**..................................	84
	Amendments (Bill of Rights)	86
	The State of the Nation	88
	Summary	89
Chapter 10	**Politics and the Election of 1800**	90
	Who is this man called Alexander Hamilton?	92
	John Adams becomes our second president	95
	Let's visit Patrick Henry's final speech	96
	Summary	98

Chapter 11	**Politics, Discontent, and Another War?**	99
	Thomas Jefferson – A Renaissance Man	99
	Hamilton and Burr	104
	James Madison	106
	Highlights	108
	Summary	109
Chapter 12	**America is changing once again**	111
	James Monroe	112
	Vesey's Rebellion - that never happened	113
	Summary	114
Chapter 13	**Corruption and the Presidential Election of 1824**	115
	Andrew Jackson's inauguration	117
	Who was John C. Calhoun?	118
	Jackson and Native Americans	120
	Nat Turner's Rebellion	122
	Summary	125
Chapter 14	**Sectionalism – Discontent Arises from the Embers**	127
	Are we Two Separate Nations?	127
	Martin Van Buren	127
	William Henry Harrison	128
	John Tyler/His Accidency	129
	Summary	130
Chapter 15	**The Many Roads that Led to War**	132
	The Mexicans and General Antonio Santa Anna	134
	Remember the Alamo	135
	The Lone Star Republic	136
	Summary	137

Chapter 16 **Technology, Immigration, Factory Life, and "Yes Marie, We Have Leisure Time."** 136

    Factory Life in New England   144
    Education   147
    Summary   148

Chapter 17 **The Rumble of Thunder and Lightning Approaches** . 149

    James K. Polk   150
    "Spotty" and The Spot Resolutions   151
    Zachary Taylor   151
    Henry Clay's Last Compromise   154
    Millard Fillmore   155
    Going West with the Hopeful Family   158
    Summary   159

Chapter 18 **Approaching War - More Fuel is Added to the Fire** .. 162

    Franklin Pierce   164
    Bleeding Kansas   166
    The Crime Against Kansas   167
    Stormy Waters   169
    Summary   170

Chapter 19 **From Compromise to Secession** 168

    James Buchanan   171
    Dred Scott   173
    Honest Abe   175
    Summary   177

Chapter 20 **So, What Exactly is this Peculiar Institution?** 178

    Summary of what went before us   183

Chapter 21 <u>Over the Edge to War</u> 185
    Who was Abraham Lincoln?   185
    Who was Jefferson Davis?   186
    Summary   187

Chapter 22 <u>WAR!</u> 194
    The Civil War   195
    The Civil War - What Was It? Many Questions   198
    Johnny Clem - The Drummer Boy of Chickamauga   202
    Belle Boyd - Spy   204
    Summary   206

Chapter 23 <u>The War Continues: 1863-1865</u> 208
    The Battle of Gettysburg   209
    The Gettysburg Address   212
    The Horrors of War - Prisons   214
    Summary   215

Chapter 24 <u>The Tide Turns and It's Total War</u> 216
    The Assassination   218
    Summary   220

Chapter 25 <u>A Broken Nation- Where do we go from here?</u> 221
    Hopes and Dreams to be Rebuilt from the Ashes
    The Situation in the American South   222

<u>Prologue</u> 223

  Bibliography 225

  Endnotes 245

Forward/Introduction

I Guess I'm a late bloomer. Thirty-two years after receiving my B.S. in Business Administration, college once again knocked on my door. I was a grandmother of four, working for many years in jobs ranging from secretarial and managerial to jitney driver on a major railroad. My own guess is that I had about twenty different occupations during my lifetime, so far. Nevertheless, I went back to school and two years later, received my M.A. in History.

My life changed. Soon, I wrote a thesis, published a book, taught at a junior college, and composed my second book which is presented to you today: *Our America*. I'm continually receiving rejections and being asked questions. "Why are you writing another history book?," or "isn't it too scholarly, overly commonplace, too entertaining, or just a why?"

I can't respond to these statements and questions in one sentence but will try and make this concise. My aim is for YOU to read and understand our American hi-STORY. Our forefathers and foremothers were each unique individuals who made a difference in his or her own way. Many did not become legends. They were living and breathing people who had dreams, emotions, aspirations, goals, loves, and beliefs in a greater power. As humans, they had thoughts and feelings like us and often battled fears, greed, and powerful desires, leading to deeds for personal satisfaction, often disregarding others in society.

We all have dreams. Some are very personal and some aspirations are to change the world. Observe, look, and listen to our past and understand what our predecessors hoped to accomplish. How can we not marvel at the Washingtons, Lincolns, and unsung individuals who made this great country? How many of us have unrealized dreams? Can we overlook flaws and realize what has been accomplished? We are living in the twenty-first century, and during these troubled yet exciting times must rekindle our innate patriotism, nationalism, pride, and regard for others. We can do this through knowing about our past, understanding what it was like to live in those forgotten times, and internalizing the memories and lessons learned.

***

My information is drawn from multiple lectures, notes, experiences, and photographs that I accumulated throughout the years. Since most of it is classified as 'common knowledge,' I have kept footnotes to a minimum, to avoid any distraction. When necessary, I have cited the source that has provided information or can furnish additional information, just in case you want to read a little more. There is also a Bibliography which lists cited and recommended sources that I have consulted but may not have used their materials.

Many of the books were written in the nineteenth and twentieth centuries and can be found in university libraries. Just to hold an old book that many others have experienced a century or so before is a thrill to me. I often wonder what type of persons read it, what were their thoughts after reading it, and did it influence them? Times have changed, and the world moves on. Our judgment and views centuries ago would be somewhat different than today. We wouldn't have the advantage of the internet, which I have also used in research. Modern technology has become the wave of the future.

When we research, we find hundreds of sources which differ in views on some of the numbers and statements of events. I have taken the best consensus of opinions and my perception, in this text. It is understandable that most readers are not too concerned to know an exact number or specific date, and an overall approximation is adequate. The language is simple and in terms that you or I would use if we were speaking or writing to one another. There are no confusing fifteen letter words that would send you to an on-line collegiate dictionary. This book is fun, interesting, and not intended to be an ultimate scholarly textbook but enjoyed and not homework!

The bottom line is to judge by past standards and not those of today. Try to have some understanding of conditions during these periods and once again, place yourself at the scene, witnessing the events as they occur. Walk in the shoes of our predecessors, experience the moments, and ask yourself, "What would I have done?"

Take a deep breath. Take my hand, pack your imagination, and join me as we tour *Our America* through the centuries. America is ours and I hope after passing through the centuries with me, you will share my patriotic pride in being an American.

Let's get started on our journey. We will vicariously live events and become better Americans when we understand our past and the people who went before us.

Chapter 1

Discovery

Coming to America...When we look at pictures of the Pilgrims and observe their stern expressions, if we weren't depressed before, we are now. No one seemed happy. Why weren't they happy? After all, they came to this wonderful land of ours. I think everyone will agree that over the past thousands of years, people migrated, immigrated, emigrated, traveled, wandered, and voyaged for thousands of different reasons. When some came to our land for religious freedom and the intention of spreading the Good Word of God, others came for the promise and hope of a better life. Yet, many came for the adventure, to seek their fleeting fortunes, greed, or to escape from hostile and unbearable environments. However, there is one exception. There were those who came in chains, both physical and mental.

A large part of American History involves the slave trade which climaxed at the Civil War. To set things in perspective, the following will clarify my previous paragraph involving those enslaved who were brought to this country unwillingly. According to the *Transatlantic Slave Trade Database*, over 10 Million people came against-their-wills to both North and South America, and the Caribbean, because they were enslaved. Estimates state this figure could be closer to 12.5 million. Of this, figures show 305,326 coming to North America from 1500-1875.[1]

Slave importation was forbidden on January 1, 1808 when the Slave Trade Act was passed. Twenty years before, the 1787 Constitutional Convention compromised to calm down the Southern plantation owners and voters. There was a clause that stated importing slaves from Africa was legal, only for another twenty years. When the earliest feasible date arrived, importation was banned. Unfortunately, slaves were still illegally brought to America because the ban wasn't strictly enforced.

The enslaved had children and death rates were lower in North America than in tropical areas where crops such as sugar cane were so intense, that people died after a few years of enslavement. Natural procreation kept slavery alive until emancipation. It also put the freed men and women at a disadvantage to establish themselves in America on an equal basis with whites, after living subservient for their entire lives once liberation was achieved. Laws, cultures, prejudices, jealousies, fear, and human nature seemed to stand in the way as people always wanted some persons or class to exist below their own.

Today's world is complex and frightening, but the same motivations to become American are apparent. People willingly come to America and struggle to somehow pass through its gates, legally or illegally. Gone are those days when millions were chained and involuntarily forced through its portals against their wills. Few are fleeing from our land, and for many, America is the final destination from a long and perilous journey. America, despite criticisms, is the best country in the world! As we travel through the centuries, meet those in the history books, witness events, and become one, we will understand what our country is all about and take pride in the land in which we live. This is not only my country, but our country, so let's take the first step and start our journey…

Setting the Foundation

Life in this new world was not easy and the struggle for survival remains today. Once we satisfy our basic needs, we look for further well-being, which can be expressed in many ways. There are those who believe self-fulfillment comes through altruism, while others believe it comes from material wealth and power. Keep motives in mind when thinking about some of the people in this great story, which is America. Wealth came through gold, salt (yes salt, which was needed to preserve food), minerals, owning human beings, or whatever means it took. For the majority, wealth took on the desire for assets of worldly goods while for others it was a spiritual peace. With the greed and desire for riches came a thirst for power and often overwhelming exploitation. History in the year one AD or 2019 AD, are related. In humans, there is always a desire for something more.*

Let's start at the beginning with a clean slate. There was a time when there were no people on this land we now call America. First, some clarity just to put a time-line in place. You will note, the designations BC, BCE, AD, and CE. The use of BC means before Christ, while AD is at the time of Christ. Using the terms BCE and CE take away the name of Christ but mean the same thing as BC. Christ's birth is designated by year one, which can be AD or CE.

Come with me on this journey through the ages and become involved. Live vicariously and pretend you are there and living in the era I describe. You can be a silent observer or take the role of one of the main actors and live the role in your mind. People create or react to events. Yes, both you and I create history.

((((

Since the 1800s, most historians believed the first people came over to North and South America on a land-bridge, often called Beringia, that went from Siberia to our present-day Alaska and Canada. This was as early as 40,000 BC or BCE, however you want to write it, or as late as 15,000 BC or BCE. Some eventually migrated a very long distance, to present day South America. They, and more migrants from Europe (Eurasia), came from the Bering Strait since most of the water was glacier. The ice mass moved at less than a snail's pace, lowered the ocean levels, and created a 0-600-mile bridge between Asia and America. Again, historians disagree on the distance. Zero miles or 600 miles, nevertheless, people moved across glaciers and ended up in this new world.

Today, theories are plentiful, and some believe people came from the old world on boats that crossed either the Atlantic or Pacific. Scientists continue their quest through radiocarbon dating, digging, and whatever means necessary, but it is still disputed. Did people come from Asia, Europe, or perhaps they originated somewhere in this country? No, I'm not going to ponder the Garden of Eden and where man was first created. I will leave that to your own discretion.

At any rate, if people migrated, there are thousands of legends on why they did so. For example, the Tuscarora Indians of North Carolina passed along stories of a famine approximately 13,000 to 7,000 BC which caused them to seek new territory. There were several huge migrations and the third may have been about 3,000 BC. Then, migration stopped and the world was segregated. Why? The glaciers melted, and our Western Hemisphere was once again inaccessible from the rest of the world. It is difficult to imagine in today's technological world, a land mass cut off from the rest of the world.

Nevertheless, early people on this continent thrived and did not become extinct. Their instincts, spirit of survival, organization, and the hope and anticipation that kept them waking up every morning is apparent. We look at artist renditions and often think of early men as Neanderthals, but we must consider that they persevered, survived, and flourished. Man has never been a solitary animal. To continue to exist, people came together, formed groups, and established tribes. Teamwork, mutual cooperation, solidarity, and camaraderie were apparent and individuals became part of united and cohesive communities. After all, two are better than one!

Let's look at the animals that inhabited this continent. They were here before humans and there are hundreds of theories about their development and where they came from. By no means, do I want to venture into the origin of man, animals, and plants, so once again, I will leave that to the scientists and religious scholars to ponder.

We are back in a time when we would need to catch, hunt, grow, or pick our food in order to eat. We can't call and order a pizza, drive or walk to a supermarket, go to a restaurant, or do a fast-food drive through. We've got to establish some ground-rules and figure out our roles in this establishment of early society and learn what we need to do, in order to have things run smoothly.

First, roles were clearly established out of sheer common sense. Men became the hunters, fishermen, and gatherers because physically they were more muscular than women and could handle the heavier tasks. Envision animals that were hunted down to extinction or were extinct before humans arrived. There were Mastodons, giant horses, early bison, an American lion, and an animal called the dire wolf, to name a few. Visit the La Brea Tar Pits in Los Angeles wherein there are the remains of over 1,600 dire wolves!

While men were busy hunting and fishing, women were more homebased and gathered wild foods, cared for children, and organized a communal life. Ladies, please take note that there is absolutely no reason to think that in all cultures women were considered inferior. Certainly, there were gender roles based on strength and lifting heavy objects and physical characteristics such as being able to bear children, but there was no inferiority in being born a female. Women were never the "weaker sex" so-to-speak as far as their roles in the community.

Often, trade existed between the tribes and traditions were established. There were religious rites, burial customs, social formalities, and family structures. These established methods were passed along from generation to generation with changes being made when and if they were necessary. It was trial by error and learning from what worked and what did not. In every society, some structure and leadership was needed, so social behaviors and hierarchies developed. Climate, environment, and sheer luck sometimes changed the course of life.

Montezuma Castle National Park 1

Hundreds of very different tribes existed in North America and each had their very own history. Some tribes were stationary, while others were nomadic. Just as we have a variety of housing to choose from today, they lived in caves, tepees, or small homes which were built with materials accessible in the area. Leaders could be warriors, women as well as men, elders, or councils. Each-and-every tribe was unique, just like every family, church, or small town may be unique with all of its residents abiding by the customary rules.

We learn about individual tribes through pictographs, petroglyphs, or stories that were passed on from generation to generation. We often consider ourselves and our families unique, and the same holds true for tribal groups. Traditions changed but were no different from how we live today. Think about it, how many customs are passed along from one generation to the next? Great, great aunt Josephine's bread recipe may be passed along and changed for generations to come as well as new family traditions being added to the mix. How about the way we celebrate special occasions, and the rites we repeat year-after-year just because they are habits and common-practices?

Northerners utilized natural resources and fished, hunted, chopped timber, planted, and drew water from streams and rivers. Southerners, on the other hand, were blessed with a long growing season, a variance of soil, and embraced agriculture. Some societies treated women as equals, and consisted of both patrilocal and matrilocal make-up, meaning a young couple would live with the male or female's family after marriage. There were no nuclear families. Families were extended, meaning they could be extremely large, and together that worked for survival.

The most important thing was that these early Native Americans lived close to the earth and they knew that everything in the universe was related. Many tribes, such as the Lakota Sioux, used the circle as a symbol of this unity and their strong bond. A circle is forever and endless and always comes back to the same point. Time also is circular and always comes back to the same place. Life starts with birth and the years pass to youth, maturity, death, and again back to new birth. The seasons change and so do the movements of the sun, moon, and stars, but everything interconnects to the never-ending cycle.[2] Think about history repeating itself. It is a circle and we often find ourselves thinking that we or our parents had the same or similar issues many moons ago.

Such was the world when Leif Erikson, (Eric's son --- son or sen at the end of a name designates "son of"), came to America. This was before Columbus in AD 1001. He came from either Iceland or Greenland. His father was expelled from Iceland, and he lived with family and they owned slaves. Leif landed in Labrador, Canada but also called some of the land he explored Vineland, which may have been present day Cape Cod. He converted to Christianity after visiting King Olaf of Norway who accepted him.

Some in America observe Leif Erikson Day on October 9 but why isn't he given the credit for discovering America? After all, he came here 500 years before Christopher Columbus.

Yes, Leif may have been here but he never created a colony. The world wasn't ready for settlement when Leif Erikson and the Vikings explored. However, a lot can happen in 500 years, and by 1492 there was ship-building, sailing, safer weapons, detailed maps, the magnetic compass, and measuring tools such as the quadrant and the astrolabe which calculated by the stars.

However, these early mechanisms were still very basic and undeveloped. Columbus did originally venture out to find a route to the Indies but ended up discovering a new world, and he colonized it. Hence, although Columbus didn't actually arrive on our East Coast, he arrived in the Americas and he colonized. Therefore, we celebrate Columbus Day.

When Christopher Columbus arrived, 70 million people, equal to all of Europe's population, lived in North and South America. Most of them lived South of what is today the Mexican border and somewhere between seven and eighteen million lived in the land that is our present-day U.S. and Canada. Each belonged to their own tribe. They had different languages, dialects, histories, and ways of life evolving in different forms according to the climate, land, fauna, and wildlife.

To reiterate, when Columbus arrived, the Americas were already inhabited with this 70 million people on the continents of North and South America which was equal to the population of ALL of Europe at that time. Great civilizations thrived in the Americas such as the Aztecs and Mayans in South and Central America and the Plains Indians, Puebloan, and Mound builders in North America to name a few.

When Columbus sailed to America, it was not a fun-touristy voyage. Ferdinand of Aragon and Isabella of Castile united their kingdoms and sanctioned Columbus. They had turned him down repeatedly and he was frustrated. We can all relate to Columbus because sometimes after too many tries, we give up our dreams. However, he didn't give up. Nothing has changed in history and it's always about money. Sanctioned still meant he needed a money-sponsor. He got that from many businessmen including his main sponsor, Luis de Santángel who was wealthy, powerful, and a member of the Templars.[3] The Order of the Knights Templar was an order of military and religious who were protected by the Pope, and were the financial bankers of most of Europe. They wanted a new world order or Utopia and believed they alone could lead and accomplish this through every and any means necessary.

De Santángel, was a Jew who converted to Christianity, and later in his life was involved in a plot with Queen Isabella's maid to poison Isabella. Although the scheme failed because of insufficient poison being put into her food, and De Santángel's death in 1498, the Templars tried again.

In 1504, after years of suffering, Isabella died. In 1492, however, De Santángel was well-respected and the financial guru of the court of Ferdinand

and Isabella. He put-up his own money after convincing the court that this would be an advantageous venture for all of them.

Columbus was not a saint. He was close to 6 feet tall, which was taller than the average male in the fifteenth century, and the red-haired Columbus was ambitious, arrogant, fearless, and a product of his time. He was undeterred and knew he wouldn't be swallowed by the seas, monsters, or fall off of the edge of the earth because he knew the world was not flat. Columbus was also very smart, ruthless, and did what he had to do in-order-to accomplish his own goals. The Reconquista had just occurred, and Muslims and Jews were driven from Spain. The Spanish were no longer forced to show allegiance to their Muslim rulers. For over 700 years they endured Muslim domination and were treated as second-class citizens.[4]

Spain returned to Christianity and this was a prime time for him to set sail. Columbus didn't intend to convert the world, but to find riches and earn the prestige he craved. He searched for a direct water route to the riches of Asia. Gold, silver, and spices were the lure and he tried to persuade the crown to give him ten percent of any loot he acquired. However, Ferdinand and Isabella were desperate for revenue.

After driving out the Muslims, Spain was putting together a kingdom which was still a combination of loosely-knit regions and had its hands full keeping the Muslims from attempting to take power again. There was not any Spanish unity or patriotism. To get soldiers, they needed to pay them in metal, and gold was a necessity. Gold was the most sought-after metal and greedily pursued by the conquistadors.

In August 1492, Columbus set out on three ships, the *Nina*, *Pina*, and *Santa Maria*. His crew consisted of seamen and a few convicts who were given amnesty if they went with him. After seventy days and 3,000 miles, they landed in the present-day Bahamas on the Island of San Salvador. It was not easy going and Columbus' men were terrified. They almost mutinied when running low on food and were ready to throw Columbus overboard.

On October 10, Columbus told them if they didn't reach land in two days they would go back to Europe. Imagine his relief the next morning when they reached land, and on October 12 went ashore. In-order-to keep up morale, Columbus kept two sets of logs. One contained the true distance they traveled, and another held the incorrect and shorter distances. He never even considered that the journey would take as long as it did.

Our America

Columbus absolutely believed he reached Asia (the Indies) so he claimed the land for Spain and called the people Indians. He had no idea where he really was – perhaps Japan, China, or India? Columbus was somewhat naïve on two beliefs. First, he believed the old folklore of rivers of gold being abundant. As a result, 40 men were left on Hispaniola which is the present-day Haiti/Dominican Republic. Although we offer Columbus credit for colonization, he never found these glorious cities of lore in North America. Spain and Portugal became rich because of the settlements in Central and South America, and the gold and silver sent back to Europe.

The second reason why Columbus was naïve, was he thought the Indians could be enslaved and converted to Christianity quickly and easily. He never understood Native Americans, their long history, and their entrenched culture. Columbus possessed tunnel vision and saw things one way, that Europeans knew best, other cultures were primitive, and they were to be conquered. When we look to the antebellum South, 350 years in the future, this belief was primary in the minds of the rich planters. They believed slaves were children with underdeveloped brains and as a result, these gentry adopted a warped and paternalistic state-of-mind.

When Columbus died in Spain in 1506, he still believed he found Asia. The Treaty of Tordesillas, authorized by the Pope, divided the world to address discovery. An imaginary line was drawn 1000 Miles from the Cape Verde Islands. It gave the West to Spain and the East to the Portuguese. Spain got the Americas and Portugal acquired Brazil and most of Africa. Keep in mind, Spain and Portugal won it all. There was nothing for England or anyone else!

By the middle of the sixteenth century, both Spain and Portugal were what we today would call uncontested superpowers. When the pope gave them this vast territory, which was even greater than they knew, none of the other world powers questioned it. The Dutch, English, and French had their own privateers or private warships authorized by their own governments, which easily took the cargo from the Spanish ships, in particular. It is ironic, as the Spanish exploited and stole from natives in Mexico and South America, their galleons in return were plundered by other countries. Was there a difference between pirating, privateering, and authentic trade?

After 1492, the majority of African-Americans arriving in the Americas came as slaves. Most were from Africa's

Western Region. There were large cities such as Timbuktu where the population was around 70,000. These are small cities by today's standards and are often names we have never heard of. Examples are Mountain View, California or Kenner, Louisiana or my own residence in Rock Hill, South Carolina with an estimate of close to 73,000.[5] These were highly developed societies and cities. Most people practiced Islam which dominated Africa in about the Eleventh Century. The population consisted of skilled workers, those in trades, artisans, merchants, or farmers.

Let's look a little further back into Africa. The richest man of ALL time, who makes Bill Gates and Warren Buffett look like small fish in big waters, was Mansa Musa (Mūsā) I of Mali (The king of Timbuktu). I understand the spelling can be Musa or Mousa, also called Kankan Mūsā or Mansa Musa. He lived in the late thirteenth and into the fourteenth century and died in the 1330s. His wealth came from salt and gold and he had 72,000 slaves and servants. He spread so much gold around to the poor and needy in his travels, that he devaluated the economy of various countries.[6]

Africa aside, back in the present-day Americas, society was quite different from European culture of the time. There was also gold, which was a natural resource. Families were clannish. Religion worshipped nature and the spirits who inhabited the physical earth. Written and oral history were passed along from generation to generation. Columbus never understood the people and the value of their knowledge and experience, which played a huge part in establishing our great Nation.

So, what did America look like at the time of Columbus? Sparsely populated areas, as well as large cities existed. I can write about the great civilizations in the Americas, such as the Aztecs, Incas, or Mayans, to name a few because histories and cultures overlap, but our journey is on North America. Conditions in both America and Europe changed as South American gold flooded the nation, and illness became the major concern.

In 1972, Alfred W. Crosby wrote a book which created the term, the "Columbian Exchange." The words, Columbian Exchange stuck and this exchange truly changed the world. In plain language, it is swapping or exchange of everything from plants, animals, diseases, trade, and customs between the old and the new worlds. This occurred after there was contact between the Europeans and the Americas. We will continually see this, as the voyagers, fortune hunters, and trailblazers overcame Native Americans.[7]

This is a simplified version because there is much more to the Columbian Exchange. I suggest reading *Guns, Germs, and Steel, The Fates of Human Societies*, by Jared Diamond for a brilliant study on the subject. It is from this publication, that the following information is brought forth.[8]

I have broken down the various concepts. Most of us can relate to food, disease, and culture but have we ever thought about how they came about? The first and one that we are all concerned about, is disease.

Disease: In 1492, when Columbus landed in Hispaniola, it was inhabited by thousands of natives. Nonetheless, by 1600, over 90 percent died. To furnish labor, the Spanish then resorted to Africans as their slave labor. As a result, the entire Caribbean population was now black. In the meantime, in the old world, Europeans also increased their own population by leaps-and-bounds.

So what diseases caused this dramatic change? Let's look at Chickenpox, Smallpox, malaria, measles, typhus, yellow fever, and even influenza or the flu. Since the Europeans brought more animals, many endemic diseases were spread from animals to humans. One example was the bubonic plague which is spread by rats. Disease among the Native Americans spread 100 percent faster than it spread among the European population and wiped out entire communities. Germs were exchanged and Natives got the short end of the deal. Natives had no prior exposure and lived in isolated communities, but many diseases were airborne or transmitted just by touching someone. Europeans and their slaves usually had some prior exposure, which offered some immunity.[9]

In Europe, germs that had evolved to spread quickly, were hardy, left antibodies, and stayed in the human population. These germs didn't survive amongst the tribes because they died before they spread. Think about the flu season today and how germs have mutated and spread quickly. How many of us stayed away from crowds during the past winters attempting to stay healthy and not contract the deadly virus? Did you stay home from work because of the flu? The 2017-18 winter brought about millions coming down with the flu, thousands of hospitalizations, and thousands of deaths even though many were vaccinated.

Epidemic diseases also rapidly spread in animals, like cows and pigs. When we humans started domesticating animals, the diseases mutated and latched onto us.[10] Some examples are:

Riderpest started in cattle and is closely related to measles. It is deadly and has an indirect effect on humans.

Tuberculosis was another disease that started with cattle.

Why do you think this disease is called cowpox? It came from cattle and became smallpox.

And yes, influenza came from pigs.

Pertussis came from pigs and dogs and became whooping cough.

There is controversy about malaria. Did it start from chickens or chimps?

The bottom line is that these diseases came from Eurasia and because people were living so closely together, they co-evolved. Natives in the Americas did not have many domesticated animals, other than some coyote dogs, and thus germs and antibodies did not co-evolve here. As a result, they never developed resistance, while the Europeans had the advantage of being exposed to it all and didn't suffer to the extent the Natives endured.

When humans walked over land bridge from Asia in small groups, any diseases that might have been in their group died out because of lack of hosts during the frigid crossing. Believe it or not, our primate ancestors, such as chimps and gorillas never lived here. Columbus reintroduced deadly pathogens to the New World. These included smallpox, measles, whooping cough, bubonic plague, malaria, yellow fever, dysentery.

Later, when blacks were brought to America, they were highly immune to some forms of malaria and more suited for the hot southern climate. However, this sickling trait worked against them causing other problems such as a greater incidence of miscarriage and joint abnormalities. Yet, they were more highly susceptible to respiratory illnesses than Europeans.[11]

The Native American population, (used interchangeable with Natives, Native Indians), was unlike Europe and didn't have enough adults surviving these diseases to reproduce enough children to survive the diseases, grow-up, and continue the race. The Native American death rate from disease was often one-third to one-half of their population which was like that of Europeans. This was the reason Europeans had so many children, besides the fact that effective birth control was not yet in the picture. Think about how we react to epidemics today. Ebola terrified and continues to terrify the globe. When diseases killed millions of Native Americans, survivors were horrified. People halted any social or political relationships. Yet, diseases spread along trade routes, years before permanent European settlement and people believed that most of this New World was uninhabited during the seventeenth Century.

However, there were bacterial and viral diseases already in the Americas before Columbus came. One major disease Europe did not have or didn't document was Syphilis. Could it be that this mutation was different in Europe? There were recorded symptoms and examinations of bones and bodies, going back centuries to Egypt. There is proof that this disease may have existed in different forms, but there is a strong case that Syphilis originated in America. Remember, how is Syphilis transmitted? As I stated earlier, Columbus and his men were no angels. There were no women on their voyages and Native women were routinely raped.

Animals: European animals, pigs, horses, goats, were introduced. Animals overwhelmed the North American and Caribbean environment. Let's look at wild boar or pigs. There are over a million in America today and they are the result of domesticated pigs left loose to graze in the South. They are everywhere, including Hawaii. We'll look at fence and grange laws in a few more centuries!

In the islands these 'pigs' ate shellfish and even iguanas, which made these native species almost extinct. They remain a threat to domestic livestock, multiply rapidly, and pollute our waters through defecation, which also spreads disease. To maintain their size, which can exceed 200 pounds in North America, they eat everything and anything, eliminating food sources for other animals. Since they have no natural predators and can birth up to twelve piglets at one time, their numbers are overcoming many areas. Don't underestimate the wild boar's intelligence. They are smart, difficult to kill, and dangerous. Boar understand sound and one shot from a rifle will scatter the sounder of boar.

Cattle thought they died and went to heaven when they discovered the grasslands which covered much of the new world. Keep in mind, the square mileage of all of Europe is about 4 million square miles while the square mileage of North America alone is around 9-1/2 million square miles! Add South America and we have another 6.9 million.

Horses also experienced a huge population explosion. The grasslands in the western United States (remember, no fences, corrals), contributed to their going wild. Along the Outer Banks of North Carolina, we now have "herd managers" who are administering birth control through darts to the wild horses who are believed to be descendants of the Mustangs brought to the area centuries ago.[12]

Rats, cats, and dogs, also went wild in this new environment. The introduction of these species helped the Spanish in their later conquests. For example, Cortez fed his army Cuban horse meat and they went on to conquer Mexico. We do think Native Americans did domesticate dogs, but our pets of today are not the same, and it is believed that European canines replaced the early pets.

If we travel to the Western United States today, we can observe the wild horses and donkeys. Nevada has the largest population. There is not enough food to support them. Horses alone number over 72,000 and their population is increasing despite lack of food. They are extremely fertile! Perhaps adopt one.[13]

So different from the Old World was the new. When the Europeans saw hummingbirds, they thought they were bees or a cross between some unknown insect and a bird. Natives still lived close to mother earth while. Europeans had gotten away from nature. Europeans developed a society that they believed to be superior to that found in the Americas. How about honeybees? They are not native to America.

There is more on Foods and Calories. Both people and animals enjoyed new world tastes. The Europeans took maize back to Europe, but it was the potato that was a real hit. Sweet potatoes grew wild. They were nutritious and had caloric values that made them trendy new crops. When the white potato was transported to Ireland, it transformed local foods and ecosystems. We'll witness in the nineteenth Century how the Irish became too dependent upon the potato. Once the potato famine in Ireland occurred, thousands of starving Irish came to our country. Yes, we sent the potato to Ireland. While Native American foods such as beans, corn, peppers, potatoes, and squash traveled to Europe, non-edible plants also made the trip. America sent our version of tobacco and cotton and they will both play a huge role in the making of America very soon.

The result was that new world diets improved that of Europeans. Eventually, the European population grew, and people abandoned the overcrowded, filthy, and overburdened European cities and came to the new world. We did send ragweed overseas along with many foods!

Trade was a very important part of the Columbian Exchange. This European contact produced a complete change in the daily lives of Native Americans. Native Americans did trade with one another before the Europeans and they were not self-sufficient. Any surplus was used only in ceremonial trades and were never shipped away. Now, beaver pelts, shells or wampum, and skills to obtain items took on new meanings. When the French established themselves in North America, they quickly became very involved in the fur trade, especially in the Northeast and Canada.

There were changes in hunting techniques because of the introduction of guns that affected the ecosystem. European trade caused some warfare between tribes because now there was competition. Tribes in the areas of French and English settlement all strove to trade with French and English because now they had help to overpower their traditional enemies. Most important, gender roles changed.

Look to Mexico and Hernan Cortés (1485-1547) who destroyed the Aztec civilization. Cortés was a conquistador, or conqueror. He brought 600 men to Mexico and used every means available to achieve this conquest. He used enemies of the Aztecs, the spread of disease, namely smallpox, and most importantly the support of a woman named Malinche. Malinche, was a captive and became Cortés' interpreter, representative, and lover. By 1520, Moctezuma and the Aztecs were crushed, and the Spanish built their new capital, Mexico City, on top of the ruins of Tenochtitlán.

Jared Diamond in *Guns, Germs, and Steel,* brings forth a statement on the difference between the U.S. and European,

"The modern United States is a European-molded society, occupying lands conquered from Native Americans and incorporating the descendants of millions of sub-Saharan black Africans brought to America as slaves. Modern Europe is not a society molded by sub-Saharan black Africans who brought millions of Native Americans as slaves."[14]

Columbus didn't have the monopoly on the Americas. Other nations attempted settlement. The Spanish established the first lasting settlement in North America in St. Augustine (which is now in Florida), and built forts all the way up the coast to the Carolinas. The French made numerous attempts to settle, abandoning the Carolinas and establishing in Florida, but there were religious wars in France between the Catholics and Protestants and new world settlement was on the back burner. When people refer to Jamestown or Plymouth as the first settlements in America, they are wrong. Again, the first permanent settlement in North America was St. Augustine, Florida. Visit it today and relive the days of the conquistadors.

Hawaii

I'm placing a paragraph about Hawaii. It didn't become a territory until 1900 and a state until 1959, but it is America. It was settled in 400 BC when Polynesians from the Marquesas Islands came to the Big Island in canoes! This was an amazing feat considering the Marquesas are 2000 miles away. The first European was in 1778, Captain James Cook. Their Columbian Exchange occurred in the 1820s when Christian missionaries arrived and brought disease.

A Word About the French

The French settled into present day Canada and Catholic missionaries, namely the Jesuits, came as early as 1608 when Quebec was established. Initially, the French and Indians kept an amicable relationship because they established a very lucrative fur trading business. This relationship helped them later during the French and Indian Wars. The bigger problem was getting French citizens to emigrate. Even if one could afford to pay his or her own passage to settle in this uncertain new-land, other factors were discouraging. Canadian weather could be extremely cold in the winter, the Indians could present a problem, society and cities were not as sophisticated as they were in France, and there were religious restrictions.

There was a great solution when an early version of 'mail order brides' was introduced. 800 French women arrived in New France between 1663 and 1673. Their ages ranged from 16 to 40 and they were known as the *les filles du roi* or King's daughters. These women were selected and screened for strict morals and any not meeting the expectation, were sent back to France. This program was introduced to build the population by offering incentives for male immigrants to settle, marry, and raise families. The women were single, orphaned, or had few resources until the king paid substantial dowries! However, there were never enough women to meet the demand and even though many men and women went back to France, enough remained and as a result, today many of their descendants are the French-Canadians.

In our day, Eastern Canada has a high population of French, especially in the Province of Quebec; and French is Canada's second language to English. For many years in the province of Quebec, there has been a movement to secede from Canada. Different values, concepts, religion, and ideals from the rest of Canada reinforce this state of mind. Quebec City, for example, where street signs are in French, allows a person to feel like he or she is in Paris on the European continent, rather than in a city in North America.

As other nations emerged as powers, each had their own distinction. The Dutch became powerful in Europe and established the Dutch East India Company competing with the Portuguese in slave trading. Henry Hudson sought a western passage to India for the company. They settled in what is now the Albany, New York area (Fort Orange), followed by New Amsterdam/Manhattan. This New Netherlands became a haven for European religious refugees. On a typical day in the settlement, one could encounter Calvinists, Lutherans, Quakers, Catholics, or even Jews, and Muslims. The Dutch also established the first treaty between Europeans and Native Americans, the Iroquois tribe.

The English tried to settle but had their own problems; once again it was the Catholics and Protestants. England's priority was Ireland. During this period, surviving British control was difficult for the Irish. The British considered the Irish to be wild and compared them to Native American Indians. There was brutal suppression and huge plantations were set up on Irish land when Protestants from England and Scotland were sent to farm it. This method excluded the native "wild Irish," robbing them of their ancestral lands.

These people from England and Scotland were the Scots-Irish and settled much of the American South. There were about 250,000 Scots-Irish who were descendants of Protestant Scots who settled in Northern Ireland. If we look to the future, we have two distinct countries: Northern Ireland and Ireland, occupying the same small island. During the sixteenth and seventeenth centuries when landlords raised rents substantially, people immigrated. Immigrants from Scotland also came. Some were sent as punishment because they were criminals. Climate, terrain, economics, and sometimes sheer fate or luck, played an important part in the settlement of

America. As a result, the country became sectionalized and great differences between the North, South, East, and West grew.

Summary

People came to this continent whether it was on the land bridge or by sea and started the process of forging new nations. Society and roles were established. The Vikings explored but there was no settlement. When Columbus came to the Americas, natives numbered over 70 million people. This was equal to the population of all of Europe. Although Columbus was not the first explorer to come to the Americas, he was the first to colonize. Not a saint, he forged the way for more exploration by other countries even though the Pope authorized the Treaty of Tordesillas, which divided territory 1000 miles east and west of the Cape Verde Islands between only Spain and Portugal.

Life was not without its consequences of conquest, and the Columbian Exchange was the most significant. Exchanges of animals, culture, disease, foods, plants, and trade impacted the whole world and affect our lives today. It was the beginning of a globalization and exchange of old and new worlds and it's hard to imagine where we would be today if individuals such as Columbus didn't possess the spirit of adventure and cross into the unknown. Was Columbus both a saint and a sinner? He exploited, abused, oppressed, imprisoned, and eradicated Natives. His men raped women and killed their men. They plundered villages. They also established and colonized America. More old world came to the new, and slowly the make-up of culture and race changed.

Slowly, other nations came to the Americas. In our continuing journey through the centuries, we will ponder the making of America, visit the first settlements, become aware of the struggles of the settlers and the ideas that drove change, and witness first-hand the quest for control by various nations. The British will soon arrive and colonialization will grow as the would-be Americans take their British roots which develop over the years to American-style or American-roots. This will lead to the subsequent rebellion in the American Revolution in a quest for freedom in this land of opportunity.

***

Our America

Ask yourself, knowing what you now have internalized, how many had choices? Examine the motives, intentions, goals, objectives, plans, and morals of everyone involved. Take a look at the monarchs, businessmen, explorers, religious, natives, enslaved, and countless men, women, and children who lived during these exciting, yet troubling times. Everyone played a part and had their own role in setting a foundation for the nation that exists today.

Chapter 2

Settlement

The time came for the world to start some serious settlement in North America. A lot of events in Europe during the post-Columbian period affected our continent of North America. These pioneering events gained momentum and continued well into the sixteenth Century when we had settlement.

This was an age of exploration. For France, Giovanni da Verrazano was sailing down the eastern seaboard (and got the Verrazano-Narrows Bridge in New York named after him). He was sponsored by King Francis I of France but never found a northern route to the Indies. Jacques Cartier was also exploring the St. Lawrence River. Cartier believed he found the mythical city of Saguenay which in folklore told of handsome-blonde-haired men having gold, silver, and rubies beyond imagination. Cartier never found gold and brought quartz crystals back to Europe to show the riches! Although, the French greedily claimed Canada, Cartier and his men almost died from starvation during an exceptionally cold Canadian winter.

One of the most-well-traveled explorers from France was René-Robert Cavelier, sieur de La Salle who befriended Native Americans and mastered a dozen dialects to gain an edge. Did I mention he also explored the Great Lakes, the entire Mississippi River, and claimed the land for New France calling it Louisiana? Often, his followers lost faith because LaSalle would wander, not knowing what lie ahead because he was intoxicated with a passion for exploration. Unfortunately, his life ended when he was fatally shot.

For England, John Cabot was sailing around the coast of Newfoundland. On his last voyage hoping to find Japan, his ships mysteriously disappeared.

The Spanish were strong in Central and South America and were moving into the Southwest as Juan Ponce de Léon was searching for gold and not the Fountain of Youth that the history books attribute to him. Let's not forget Hernando de Soto from Spain who was cruising the Mississippi and given the distinction of being over-the-top with his cruelty towards Natives. Not only did he enslave them; he mutilated and executed them. De Soto had no regard for the king's order to convert them to Christianity nor to the Pope's condemnation of enslavement. When he died, he was secretly buried on the banks of the Mississippi by his men because they didn't want the Natives to know he was not immortal.

Francisco Vázquez de Coronado explored the Southwest seeking "the Seven Cities of Gold." He and his men covered thousands of miles both on horseback and walking, through the heat and cold, wearing their thirty pounds of armor. They did, however, find the south rim of the Grand Canyon.

It was not until 1565 that the Spanish sent settlers and created the first permanent settlement in the U.S. at St. Augustine, Florida. It remains the oldest-continually occupied settlement in the United States. Larger Spanish settlements were established in California or along the Santa Fe River in New Mexico (San Diego, Albuquerque, Santa Fe).

What was going on in in Great Britain and the rest of Europe? They had their own mess with wars, religion, disease, poverty, and were competing with one another. Britain's continuing problem would not go away, once again, the Wild Irish. Before we experience some more events, let me make a distinction. There are the words "English" and "British." I often use them interchangeably but let me mention the difference, so I am not chastised for an error!

There is the island of Great Britain which today is this land composed of England, Scotland, and Wales. Northern Ireland which is part of the UK is on the island of Ireland. The UK is all the above, except Ireland, and the full name is the United Kingdom of Great Britain and Northern Ireland. Ireland is its own independent country and Northern Ireland is British even though it is on the Island of Ireland. They are separate and distinct and do not ever confuse them. I cannot stress this enough. Ireland was under British rule and it was and still is a long and rocky relationship, but in 1922 Southern Ireland became its own Irish free state. There are both Catholics and Protestants residing in both Ireland and Northern Ireland.

British citizens, or those born in Great Britain, identify themselves as English, Scottish, or Welsh as far as their identity. While people born in England can be called English or British, they can identify themselves as such, stating they live in either England, Britain, or the UK.

Looking back into the times we are experiencing, the colonists considered themselves British citizens. The French were still France, and Spanish were still Spain. Confusing? At any rate, I use the terms England and Great Britain and think everyone during our journey understands the meaning to draw the distinctions between the old and the new world!

The Protestant Reformation was taking place in Germany in 1517. This was followed by the Protestant Church separating from the Catholic in 1534 in England when the Catholic Church refused to give Henry VIII a divorce from his first wife, Catherine of Aragon. They were married for twenty-four years and the marriage was far from anything that could be called 'marital bliss.' Henry was fickle, had six wives, and was hardly a good husband. When he needed to move-on to a new wife, he had the old one charged with adultery and beheaded or got the marriage annulled. Marriage to his fourth wife lasted only six months. Not having his way, Henry established his own church, the Church of England or Anglican Church. In America, the Episcopalian Church is a member of the worldwide Anglican Communion which grew from the Church of England.

Then there was the Irish Problem. When the famous Henry VIII proclaimed himself King of Ireland, he tried to introduce the English Reformation. He wanted to conquer and assimilate all the Irish lordships. Henry cared little about tradition, families, their Catholicism, and didn't understand the strong ties in Gaelic Ireland. The crown's policy of plantation took Irish land and gave it to settlers from England, Wales, and Scotland. Thousands of English and Scotch Protestants came to Ireland and displaced Catholic landholders who were long established before the new policy. These huge British Protestant communities replaced the Catholics who were the elite or ruling class.

Henry's policies forever changed the Irish identity and heritage and caused an on-going "civil war" between the British Protestants and Irish Catholics. Gone were the clans and dynasties, replaced with new revolutionary political attitudes, ideas, and actions. Some things change, and some don't. Centuries from now we'll look at Ireland and British Northern Ireland and the forthcoming bigotry, discrimination, and hatred.

The British became more of the pirate class and continued looting Spanish ships that were loaded with gold. It was a lucrative way to wealth and power, although dangerous. However, weather was one factor which affected everyone.

There was the Little Ice Age which affected the entire world. It was a period from around 1300 to 1850, depending upon where you lived, where temperatures were well-below normal. It was the opposite of global warming and could be called "global cooling." Some areas had long periods of drought, while others had extreme rains which caused flooding, but nonetheless, summers were short or nonexistent. Unlike our present Global warming, sea ice expanded rather than melting. The impact was catastrophic and affected the world from agriculture, trees, and wildlife. A short or no growing season caused food shortages. It was survival of the fittest. Gone were animals to be hunted or fish to be caught. Since people needed timber to keep warm, trees were cut down and deforestation occurred. Seventy-five 75 percent of Europeans were peasants. Nevertheless, people did not become celibate but continued to procreate. The populations grew steadily. It also affected America. In England, there was death, disease, filth, starvation, and inhospitable conditions. In the meantime, other nations were establishing themselves in the Americas.

The Spanish conquered Latin America, moved into the Southwest overcoming Native Americans, and sent missionaries. At the same time, the French were settling Canada in areas which are now the Northeastern United States in the Lake Champlain area. In New France, they were trading with the Native Americans. Beaver hides were exchanged for axes, knives, metals, pots, tools, and ornaments. The French continued to do one thing better than the English, they established trade with many Indian tribes.

Let's not forget the Treaty of Tordesillas? The Treaty of Tordesillas was authorized by the Pope and divided discovery to 1000 miles from the Cape Verde Islands by a line – giving the West to Spain and the East to the Portuguese. Spain was blessed with the Americas and Portugal received

Brazil and most of Africa. England ignored it, and from day one didn't play by the rules. There were the aforementioned British exploratory voyages, but England never followed up with land claims.

Over ninety years passed when Sir Walter Raleigh, hero and Irish War Veteran, along with his half-brother Sir Humphrey Gilbert convinced Queen Elizabeth I, daughter of Henry VIII and Ann Boleyn, to allow them an expedition. The year was 1584. Elizabeth I or "Good Queen Bess," only allowed a small group to test them. Raleigh was a sight to behold! He was tall, dark, handsome, and a favorite of the Queen. As a favorite, she refused to allow him to go off sailing. Although called the Virgin Queen because she never married, there was wide speculation about that term.

Even though monarchs approved expeditions, they didn't control them. Raleigh had three voyages under Elizabeth. Raleigh outfitted and planned the trips, but he never accompanied them – he wasn't there.

The first expedition reaching North Carolina was in 1584 when it reached the North Carolina shore but they didn't settle, because the men were unprepared for settlement, and couldn't deal with the Native Americans. It was a failure. Keep in mind, these were men and there were no women or children. The men Raleigh commissioned were lazy, didn't grow food, and stole from and desired to control the Native Americans. They never concentrated on agriculture and instead decided to exploit the natural resources of metals, pearls, and pelts. Obviously, the colonists were often hungry!

At first, the Secotans or Roanokes, helped them with obtaining food, taught them hunting and fishing techniques, and offered friendship and mentoring. The Englishmen had other ideas and forced them into slavery and hard labor, turning relations from bad to intolerable. In 1585, there was another attempt to permanently settle, and it was also a failure. This time the English enslaved the Indians (which is used interchangeably with Native Americans), killing their chief, Wingina. Wingina had been their only hope and could have used to their advantage (1586).

Raleigh never gave up and made a third attempt. The men went back to England and tried again when Elizabeth authorized another trip the following year. He then obtained financing from London merchants and reached the Outer Banks of North Carolina at Roanoke Island. This was the same location as before but he founded another settlement on the island. This time he brought families.

Remember that Raleigh obtained the funding but he was not on the expeditions. This time, a colony was formed. In the meantime, the war with Spain was going on and it forced the important male leaders back to England. The men were going back to England for supplies, promising a return expedition shortly. Try to imagine being left on the island. There were men, women, and children, and two years' worth of supplies. However, those left on the island, were forced to fend for themselves. This meant getting along with the Secotans. What if you got sick? Their leader, John White, left with the group returning to England after his granddaughter, Virginia Dare, was born. Well, the years passed and three years later in 1590, a group led by White came back. Apparently, they made prior attempts but had some bad luck with pirates, storms, and the ongoing war. What happened?

The story is that when they returned in 1590, the colony was deserted. This was the Lost Colony. All that remained was a simple marking on a tree that said, Croatoan. Early in the settlement of the colony, all agreed on a code. A marking would be placed on tree(s) if the remaining colonists relocated. Only if it was a forced relocation, a Maltese Cross would be added. However, there was no cross, just Croatoan, the name of a neighboring island. What happened to over 100?

Apparently, because of bad weather, White and his party never searched in the surrounding area for the missing colonists. What would you have done if your family was missing and after three years you finally made it back? Granted, it was three years later but it was a long time to wonder and not find the answer. Years later, there were historical accounts stating there were Native American Indians with blue eyes. Tree rings indicated the weather caused extreme drought conditions. We now know that during this period there was the worst drought in 800 years. Was there intermarriage or murders? Did everyone die of starvation?

The latest is more than a theory. It states that the colonists survived and relocated 60 miles west on Hattaras Island at the confluence of Salmon Creek and Albermarle South. A thousand acres of coastal land has been acquired and eventually there will be a state natural area. It is preservation instead of the condo and marina that were previously planned. Perhaps, we will find an answer to the mystery that White never could, five centuries later.[1]

Raleigh had fallen from the Queen's graces prior because he secretly married one of her maids-of-honor. Elizabeth was livid, decided no more sanctioning, and imprisoned the once-handsome Raleigh. When Elizabeth the Virgin Queen died in 1603, England was then ruled by King James I. James decreed there would be no more adventures to the New World unless there was settlement. What did James do with Raleigh? James kept him a prisoner in the Tower of London, gave him a short reprieve to attempt more settlement in 1616, and once more put him in jail. The Tower was both a castle and a gloomy and macabre prison.

Strong-willed Raleigh never learned from his mistakes and when he disobeyed and fought the Spaniards instead of bringing back the so-called gold, he told James he had found in South America, he ended up imprisoned once again. James gave him a new accommodation in the Tower of London for the rest of his life. He was imprisoned in a room with a window - overlooking water, the Thames River. Raleigh was eventually executed for treason in 1618.

At the time, it was common practice to embalm the head after execution. It was given to Raleigh's wife who carried it around with her in a fancy bag until she died 29 years later. Although his body was buried in St. Margaret's Church, adjacent to Westminster Abbey, there is still speculation as to where his head rests, possibly in St. Mary's in a small English village. Be sure to visit Raleigh's final resting place if you ever visit Westminster Abbey/St. Margaret's.

Summary

We have already traveled into the sixteenth century when many nations were poking around the North American continent. The world was coping with the Little Ice Age. Europe was struggling with the Protestant Reformation, while the British had their wars and Irish settlement issues. Privateering became very lucrative with the Spanish galleons becoming the prime targets. Other countries were exploring our continent and the Spanish have already settled in Florida and the Southwest as well as keeping their strongholds in the islands, and Central and South America. It is the English colonies that will settle and decide that the time may be ripe for emancipation from the Mother Country, but first the English needed to establish something permanent on the continent!

Finally, in 1584 Sir Walter Raleigh tried settlement in North Carolina for the English. Unfortunately, the remaining colonists mysteriously disappeared when some of the men went back to England where wars never seemed to end. Three years later, they came back and the only clue as to what happened to the settlers was the word, Croatoan. What happened? We are slowly finding answers to the Lost Colony today. We often marvel our scientific discoveries and logic in putting together the pieces, and yet, much of the past is forever buried and we are still digging to find the truth.

Raleigh suffered the fate of execution and the English did little until the next century, the seventeenth, when colonists came to Jamestown. Better luck next time! Remember again, discovery is nothing unless there is settlement. Therefore, we have Columbus Day and not Leif Erikson Day.

With existing conditions in Europe getting worse day by day, the time was ripe for exiting the country and finding a new land ripe with opportunities. Businessmen were the first to realize opportunity and smell the financial possibilities in this foreign land, we now call America!

Chapter 3

Fort Jamestown

In 1606, King James I met with a group of London businessmen who had a proposition for him. They wanted permission to go to the new world. There was only one motive, and that was to make a huge profit. James said "yes" if there was a contract between himself and the business. Two companies were created in 1607 and they were Joint Stock Companies. The agreement created the Virginia Company of London (aka London Company) with the investors being merchants from London, and the Plymouth Company who were merchants from England.

Jamestown, Virginia was established by the Virginia/London Company and the Pilgrims established their colony through the Plymouth Company. Joint Stock Companies existed for one reason only and this was to make a profit for the investors. Money was pooled together for trade or colonization, and there was the promise to make a profit. The profit was split between investors and what remained went to the crown. The London Company had control of the South Atlantic and the Plymouth Company controlled the North.

Look at how the world was operating at-this-time. Countries made agreements, gave authorizations, collected money, and supported enterprise. They were exploring new lands which, in fact, no one owned. Herein will be the problem over territory, government, and rights.

The only agreement between the two joint stock companies was they wouldn't settle within 100 miles of one another. This was to establish mercantilism, wherein a mother country created colonies in a new world for one reason alone and the reason was profit. Raw materials would go to the mother country to process. In turn, the mother country sold the goods anywhere and everywhere in the world, taxing materials from other nations.

Mercantilism is a complete economic system. Colonies cannot trade with others. The government controls an economy for its own national well-being. The colonies exist because they possess raw materials unavailable in the motherland.

Have you ever heard the term 'soldiers of fortune'? They were adventurers, lured by potential riches. These men came to the South wherein those who initially came to the North did so for their own religious freedom. Travel to the North today and note churches in the middle of town. Not so for early Virginia. Virginia developed a new kind of life. It offered hope, adventure, and no mandatory religious participation. It was rugged individualism that carried these hopefuls through and religion didn't matter.

The Establishment of Jamestown
(The Virginia Company of London)

Three ships were dispatched, the *Godspeed, Discovery*, and *Susan Constant*, for a total of 104 men. There are replicas of the ships at the present-day Jamestown Settlement. In 1607, they landed in America after stopping in Puerto Rico for supplies, and attempted colonization. Fort Jamestown was named in honor of the King. The crew had been instructed to establish themselves in a safe area where there would be no fear from pirates.

The colonists were safe from pirates, but the location was poor. Picture yourself, newly arrived, and start looking around. Fort Jamestown was not a hospitable place. It's in a poor location, surrounded by a malarial swamp, and inhabited by the Powhatan Indians. It's cut off from the mainland, making hunting impossible. Look around at your fellow-investors. Some of the men are upper-class and never lifted a finger to do an honest day's work in their whole lives. Can these untrained wealthy survive on their own or will they attempt to establish some type of understanding with the natives to help them?

We soon realize that some are just impatient and hoping to get rich quickly and not even thinking about tomorrow. Their greed brought them across the Atlantic to this inhospitable land. It is May and there is plenty of time to plant seeds and grow some crops. Besides, the Virginia Company wants results quickly and if there is nothing in return, financial support will dry up just as quickly. They're all employees of the Virginia Company, aka London Company.

As these thoughts race through our minds, we reflect upon the beginning of the journey with prayers and a worship service based on the English Book of Common Prayer, officiated by The Rev. Robert Hunt. The service brings hope. However, now that everyone is here, all they talk about is finding gold while they continue to eat from the stored supplies. The weather is nice now but we need food for the winter, adequate shelter, and good water.

By the way, who is leading the group? There seems to be no shortage of bugs, mosquitoes carrying malaria, and awful tasting brackish water from the tidal James River. It's no wonder that the finishing is so poor. Little did these early settlers know that the river was saturated with arsenic. I wonder how long it will be before we are all overwhelmed with Dysentery, salt-water poisoning, or fever. I don't see any gold here for the taking. Let's go back and look at this objectively since we have the advantage of information that the colonists didn't know or venture to think about.

The Indians were the Powhatans. Chief Powhatan was the chief of thirty tribes and initially helped the colonists, especially through the first winter of 1607-08. Despite this, two-thirds of the 104 or 105 men died and new arrivals came. The colonists struggled until John Smith took command. He was the fourth man to attempt to establish leadership and order. He was like a cat and was saved several times. Smith was a solid leader but left in 1609 after a year and a half, when he had an injury due to a mysterious gunpowder explosion. Like Columbus, his men mutinied, and he was almost executed when the settlers first arrived. However, when the group opened the orders from the Virginia aka London Company they realized he was to be on the governing council.

Smith was hated and tried to provide iron-clad leadership by using a strict rule. There was jealousy between the men resulting in power struggles wherein people never worked as a team for a common goal. The major problem was they wanted to get rid of the Natives. Smith established a military rule and a no work, no eat policy. More settlers arrived including non-Englishmen who were skilled in crafts, as well as the first women. They tried silk making, glassmaking, lumber, sassafras, pitch and tar, and soap ashes, but failure loomed. Nevertheless, Smith established the order and discipline that the colony needed during his very brief and colorful term.

There is the Pocahontas story. Originally, she saved John Smith from execution (1607) but history must remind us that she didn't marry Smith but John Rolfe. As relations between the Powhatans and colonists deteriorated, the colonists faced starvation because they didn't cultivate and plan ahead.

The Powhatans were now at war with them and the attempts to reach the settlement with relief supplies were unsuccessful. The weather did not cooperate and resulted in numerous attempts by the English to reach them and two inadequate supply undertakings being sent. When the *Sea Venture* reached them in late summer, it brought more misery and unwelcomed guests, another 300 colonists and little food. Somehow, once again, no recent arrivals planned ahead nor had any idea about what awaited them in the new world.[1]

I don't think we want to be here during the winter of 1609-10, the first winter. It was called the Great Starving Time. At the beginning of the winter there were 500 colonists, but when spring finally came, there were about 50. George Percy, the governor wrote of searching for horses, cats, dogs, rats, and snakes and then the unthinkable, cannibalism.[2] The national historic site now formally shows evidence of it. By 1610, 38 were left when the second supply shipment arrived just in time when the colonists were about to abandon the settlement. The settlement continued.

Despite this, investors in the Virginia Company were becoming impatient and wanted a return on their money and it became difficult to recruit more settlers. Two Years before a fleet, "the Great Fleet" with nine vessels and 600 people (six times the people in Jamestown) hit a hurricane and never made it. Chief Powhatan still ruled and there was big trouble. Colonists tried to control the Natives and took their corn. Powhatan had enough and decided once and for all to be rid of the colonists and starve them. In retaliation, Pocahontas was held captive for ransom by the colonists. Love overcomes all, and in 1614 there was peace when she and John Rolfe married.

Pocahontas was renamed Rebecca when she was baptized into the Church of England. In the meantime, the Powhatans still struggled with the settlers until 1622. Rolfe took Pocahontas and their infant son to England, where she died seven months later. He left the baby in England with a guardian and returned to Virginia, where he was a principal power in the House of Burgesses. He died of unknown causes in 1622.

John Rolfe developed the first cash crop, tobacco, which was shipped to England because Europe craved it. Native Americans smoked tobacco for centuries by rolling the leaves and igniting them. However, the tobacco was something neither you nor I would readily smoke! It had to be refined.

Before Pocahontas, Rolfe had a first wife and child and both died while they were in Bermuda when a hurricane struck their flagship, the *Sea Venture*. The colonists built two smaller ships and headed for the Jamestown Colony (the *Patience* and the *Deliverance*). Rolfe developed his tobacco crop from seeds he obtained in the Caribbean. This strain was much better for English palates.

There were more investors. Thanks to Rolfe, a strong English presence was created, which grew and became permanent, and there was no stopping the growth. Now there was a possibility of a step in the right direction and the conception of the future United States.

England, at this time, was a closed society. There was no movement between moving up from your born station in life. You were always in your class and there were a lot of poor debtors. These English debtors wanted their own fortune and land, and as a result, the Headright System evolved. It was developed in 1616 by the London Company (Virginia Company). For every passage paid for, 50 acres of land were given, with an additional 50 acres for each 'head' you brought with you. The debtors worked for the rich guys while paying off their passage, and the rich guys got the acreage.

It created a class of Indentured Servants. Their passage was paid and in return, they worked. It was not your typical servant-master relationship, that you would be involved with in England. Your recruitment was usually from the captain of the ship or a merchant, who would sell your services once you arrived in the new world. The usual period of servitude was four to seven years. Imagine, while you were paying off your passage cost, you couldn't marry, were subject to your benefactor's rules, and your term could be extended if you disobeyed your sponsor's commands. Eventually the owner would come to America to claim his land.

If you were an indentured servant there were one of three scenarios. You could work as an indentured servant if you could tolerate it. If you worked through your indentured period, you could then try to build your own life and often spend your last dime. The last scenario, most often applied by the adventurous was to disappear without supplying work.

Although tough, this servitude was the quickest way to the New World. For every man who became rich, dozens died in poverty. When freed from servitude, they were given food, such as a year's supply corn, a suit of clothing, perhaps a gun, and a little money. With few resources, few could afford good land. People had hopes and dreams and knew that anything was better than living in Europe. The fact remained, most had nothing and for every one well off, there were hundreds in poverty.

Men didn't expect to find gold but they did expect to locate and exploit other resources. *They wanted to build a New England.* John Smith originally called the Jamestown Colony New England. It became a Royal Colony and moved to Williamsburg when the King dismissed their charter in 1624. These men were mercenaries and capitalists and wanted financially feasible finances.

There were principles to be honored. If there was a religion, it was inclusive instead of exclusive. It could be any form of Protestantism just if it was Christian and not Catholic.

The desire to imitate the English country gentleman prevailed. As time progresses we will see that the people of Virginia imitate English society. They did so through their furniture, homes, what they read, and how they cultivated their minds. There was an English culture coming from South and Central England. However, slow as it was, the British accent became a thing of the past, and Americans developed their own styles of regional speech.

Then there was a capitalist mentality. People wanted stuff quickly. There was a hierarchy and the have and have nots. Social responsibility didn't exist and there wasn't sharing. You took care of your own. As far as racial beliefs, it was alright to enslave Native Americans and blacks. This created a system of both free and enslaved.

The Pilgrims didn't arrive until 1620 and the Jamestown Colony was still the settlement in what would become Virginia. The preceding year 1619, however, was a very important one. Virginia had its own self-government and the Church of England was still the established religion. The Virginia Company of London wasn't doing as well as expected and its investors were not becoming wealthier. The Company decided the colonists needed more absolute and supervised rule. A Colonial Governor in England existed but most governors never visited the settlement and were clueless as to what was going on. The residents of the colony ran it.

Sir George Yeardley was an early settler and was then appointed the governor of the Virginia settlement.[3] His orders came from the Great Charter and his assignment was to implement these instructions. His duty was to reorganize the Virginia Company's activities in the Virginia colony, put a settlement plan in effect, implement land reform, found a college, and establish a legislative assembly. The task was beyond Yeardley's capabilities and he readily admitted this. The company told him to get two men from each borough and bring them to Jamestown.

It was hot and humid in late July 1619, when the General Assembly of the Virginia Colony, met for six days, adopted the instructions, and passed new laws. What else did they do? They imposed the first taxation which was ten pounds of tobacco on every male over 16 years of age. This also encouraged the lazy to work! While the men were making the laws and proposing a government, they went through hell. Not only was the heat intolerable, but most of them came down with dysentery and other health concerns. One of the men died. This was the first representative assembly in English America. There was now self-government and the House of Burgesses was created.

England should have stopped it in its tracks but it didn't. It was the biggest mistake it could make, even though the king's council needed to ratify all legislation and there were limits, e.g., they could only meet once a year. It gave power to all white men, who had a power to vote, unlike England. This forever set the precedent for self-government. Landowners elected the representatives to the House. Between 1619 and 1776, the colonists continually took power from the Brits and this power went to their self-government. This established the notion that this particular colony in Virginia was different from any other in the world and had a right to self-government. It seems that throughout history, various groups came together and received the revelation that they were different from the rest, be it a community, nation, or world, and have a right to something. It happens today.

The most important event that happened in 1619 stands alone and was one of the most important. That was the introduction of blacks. The first African slaves came on a Dutch Frigate, the *Bautista* quite by accident or fate. A frigate is a warship with only a single deck. The ship was blown off course after a battle and the captain and crew needed food and supplies. They made a trade. Twenty Africans were being transported to the Central Americas as indentured servants. This was a novelty and a rarity because they were not slaves. For the first few years, they were indentured servants and were treated fairly and equally to the whites, until slavery raised its ugly head and they lost all rights.

Then, a separate caste was created for them. A caste divides people based on inherited social status which can be race, sex, occupation, economics, lineage, or any other justification to place them in their position. There were mixed marriages and some did not claim to be African. Only a few, were able to purchase freedom. Africans were given one name, while whites had two, and a caste system based on color began in the New World.

In 1619, the Virginia/London Company transported women to the colony as wives for the men. The average marriage lasted seven years. Some women were widowed four or even five times; but Women held their own. Just as the men, they were subject to the law and often brought to court for rowdiness, swearing, or adultery. Families were few and there was no common religion.

However, all things came to an end and in 1622, there was an uprising when Powhatan died and his brother Opechancanough became chief. Murder, starvation, disease and a quarter of the English population were killed. In 1624, a Royal Colony in Virginia was organized and founded by King James I. The Royal Colony was administered by the crown and the appointed governor chose leading men in the colony to be the advisory council. James withdrew the charter from the Virginia of London Company and the company went bankrupt. This was a little too late; the colonists already had a taste of power and control.

Indentured servitude was still the norm and insured success for the wealthy and crown-appointed officials. Within a few years the Church of England was established as the state supported official religion of the colony. What evolved over the next 50 years was very different than its counterpart in the Mother Country.

Summary

It was not until the Jamestown settlement that America had its first permanent English settlement. John Smith called Jamestown New England, as a means of competing with the Spanish and French for prestige, wealth, territory, and souls. The struggle was a difficult one but because of the mercantile system, there developed a headright system and the classification of indentured servitude.

We took our first step towards self-government in 1619 when the House of Burgesses was established. The House was founded in Jamestown, and later moved to Williamsburg, Virginia in 1698, which was formerly called

Middle Plantation. Until it was built, the House met at the College of William and Mary. A complete political system was set up. Women were treated by the courts just like the men. They often got drunk and rowdy, and were in places they shouldn't customarily have been. After all, girls also just wanted to have some fun.

The first blacks came to America as indentured servants in 1619 but soon became slaves. America was loving this taste of independence and wanted more. In 1624, Virginia became a royal colony.

The Spanish were in Florida. Spanish explorer Ponce de Leon landed at St. Augustine and claimed *La Florida* for the King of Spain in 1513. According to legend, he was searching for the fountain of youth. It's not known if Ponce de Leon actually discovered the spring. In 1565, Pedro Menendez de Aviles, was sent by the Spanish to set up a colony to prevent the French from claiming the territory and he established St. Augustine, making it the oldest continuous European settlement in the United States.

The French were in Canada, exploring the St. Lawrence River. They traded with the Indians, beaver hats in Europe became the rage, and a lucrative fur trade was established. In 1608, Quebec became their first permanent New France outpost. The Jesuits were converting and founded Montreal in 1642. Still, French were reluctant to relocate because of religious restrictions, cold bitter winters, and shaky relations with Indians, so this limited the population. They instituted a program much like our indentured servants. It involved three years of work for repayment and was mostly male until they brought female orphans paid to settle in New France. The fur trade flourished, French kings created a bureaucracy, but the institution of self-government never took hold in French colonies like it did in America.

North America now had a New England and a New France. We will now visit New England and experience religion as it existed then. Religious havens will begin with the Pilgrims will form communities. Williamsburg will become the settlement since Jamestown was totally unsuitable. Remember our visit to Jamestown, the swamp, thirst for good water, mosquitoes, and other unknown bugs? The race was on. Everyone developed their own dreams and ideas. Which country will have the strongest presence in this new land?

Chapter 4

Religion comes to the colonies

We moved from Virginia up into the North in order to observe what was happening to other groups who began immigrating to this new land of ours. Meanwhile in New England, unlike the South, people came to practice their religion of choice, without a king or queen forcing them into the royal beliefs. The fact is that the United States of America has never had a mandated religion. When we look at the world today, we realize there are still many countries with official religions. Afghanistan, Egypt, Iran, Saudi Arabia are a few. There is separation of church and state and the closest we come to mentioning religion is allowing income tax exemptions for churches meeting the guidelines and "IN GOD WE TRUST," appearing on currency. Our freedom of choice is granted in our First Amendment.

Puritanism came to America in 1620. There were two groups. One was the Non-separating which did not want to separate from the Church of England but purify it, and Separating who wanted to form their own congregations. The Pilgrims were both Puritans and Separatists. The Pilgrim was one who was on a religious journey seeking the truth. The Pilgrims believed the only way to purify old-world religion was a complete separation from the Protestant Church of England. The first Pilgrims had no trained organized clergy, and it was their beliefs that held them together.

Puritanism, on the other hand was stricter and wanted to purify or reform the Church. The Puritans believed the Church had kept too much of its original Catholic beginning. They wanted to lose Catholic beliefs and become more Protestant. Both Pilgrim and Puritan, took their teachings from John Calvin. The Pilgrims came in 1620 and most Puritans with both beliefs came from 1630-1640 during the Great Migration.

Both Groups were English Protestants who believed that the Church of England didn't go far enough to reform. They insisted that the liturgy was too Catholic and the bishops still lived in luxury and regarded themselves as kings. Religious courts were still corrupt, dating back to Henry VIII who founded them. Since the King of England was the official head of both church and state, there could be no opposition without dire consequences since rebellion was considered against both religious and civil authority.

When Catholic monk, Martin Luther posted his 95 Theses to the door of the castle church in Wittenberg, Germany in 1517, the Church realized they had many weaknesses and tried to reinvent, change, and reform Catholicism. The Council of Trent met in 1545 and continued to meet for many years but the reforms still didn't go far enough for large groups of people. The Pilgrims were the first to realize they needed to separate and took action.

The Plymouth Colony was a mix of people. A group left England twelve years before their settlement in the new world and settled in the Netherlands. These Pilgrims were families living in the Dutch Republic who had obtained their own religious freedom, and never thought about relocating once again. However, there was a price. They were not accepted as equals, were trapped in low-paying jobs, and were excluded from guilds and opportunities to improve their positions in life. Just like today, when parents sometimes believe there are outside influences that are detriments to their children, many felt their children were picking up too many bad habits from the Dutch.

This group hooked up with another group which never left England and bought a ship, the *Speedwell*. They came to England with the intention of meeting with the *Mayflower* group, and the two ships would sail together. Unfortunately, they had a leaky, unsafe, and unreliable vessel. When the two groups made contact, it was a series of unfortunate events and no matter how many times they tried, the *Speedwell* could not speed well and continued to be a leaker. The Pilgrims ventured out as far as 300 miles, only to have to come back again when the *Speedwell* kept taking on water. Finally, everyone crammed together and boarded the *Mayflower* and 104 men, women, children, and strangers, who were hired to help, set forth from Plymouth, England.[1]

After a little over two months of seasickness, one drowning, four deaths, low food supplies, and terrible storms, the Pilgrims landed on North American shores and thanked the Lord who had provided deliverance from this endless journey. A few days after arrival, the first child was born on the *Mayflower*.

There were a few problems with this deliverance. The month was November and winter in New England had set in. In addition, many had stepped off the ship with pneumonia and scurvy. By Spring, half were dead. To hide the deaths from the Native Americans, the Pilgrims buried their dead at night in unmarked graves.

The Pilgrims were told to settle within 100 miles of Jamestown but bribed the captain and settled in Massachusetts. This established Freedom of Religion – for themselves only. The king never knew what was happening.

Before they even left the ship, they agreed to the Mayflower Compact. It was the first governing compact written by the 41 men on the ship and established the rules and regulations for social survival. The Pilgrims initially co-existed with the Indians (Wampanoag Nation) and eventually created divided colonies. Cold weather did have the advantage of not having to worry about mosquitoes and diseases which were prevalent in Virginia. They quickly figured out that the water was contaminated because people got sick. To solve this, they drank a lot of beer! Distilling kills both parasites and bacteria.

There was always a need to convert the natives whatever religion ruled. Things looked up for them when Squanto, aka Tisquantum, from the Pawtuxet tribe, helped them. Squanto had been captured by explorers in 1605, taken to England, and learned English. In 1614, Captain John Smith brought him back to New England and Squanto taught the Pilgrims. They knew nothing about the land, hunting areas, and planting an essential crop, corn. The pilgrims prospered, even though the colony's population never grew to more than 7,000 and was always poor. The Plymouth Colony was established thirteen years after Virginia which was founded in 1607!

þþþ

In 1630, the Puritans sailed to America. Unlike the Puritan Pilgrims who arrived ten years earlier, they didn't break their relationship with the Church of England. The Puritans believed they could reform the Church and followed the Bible which supported their belief that their immigration was like the story of Moses and the Exodus. They were the chosen people, liberated from persecution, and bound to God by His promise. Their singular role was to establish a new and pure society. John Winthrop was the first to arrive.

As the Church of England became increasingly antagonistic towards Puritan viewpoints, Winthrop realized he couldn't remain in England, and his rebellious son, Henry, added more fuel to the fire. Like the Pilgrims who feared that their children would fall from God's graces, Winthrop knew he had to immigrate and reform the world. However, Winthrop had another reason to immigrate. He was also a wealthy and astute businessman. He had a wife and seven children to support. A financial depression was widespread throughout England which affected his mills, and collecting rents on his properties became difficult. Winthrop petitioned the crown and received a charter to colonize near the Massachusetts Bay, north of Plymouth and by 1630 six towns were founded. This colony was the second settlement in New England following the Plymouth Colony which by this time had about 900 people.

While aboard the flagship *Arbella*, Winthrop, who led the group, reminded them repeatedly, that there was duty and obligation that must be kept under the covenant. Succeed and you are blessed; fail and you are doomed. If they honored their obligations to God, they would be blessed; if they failed, they would be punished. The Puritans came to what is now New England, on the Massachusetts Bay, settled, and named their town Boston.

The colony could be called an oligarchy or a theocracy but certainly it was not a democracy. Winthrop had the upper hand. They were all Calvinists, following John Calvin's reforms. Church services were very simple and the Bible was the law. There were no musical instruments but singing psalms was allowed. God was the absolute power and humans were all evil sinners. Only a few were chosen for salvation while the rest were condemned to damnation. The mystery was that no one really knew if he or she was to be saved or damned in hell forever. This brought a lot of anxiety and everyone constantly searched for signs. One sign was the experience of conversion which could determine that a person had been saved.

Salvation was a Covenant of Grace and faith alone was the key. There had to be religious conformity in the entire community and no dissent. God expected them to live and learn from the Bible and their good example would reform those in England who remained with the Anglican Church.

Winthrop became governor for over twenty years. There were rules that were mandatory. Church attendance was compulsory, everyone paid taxes to the church, and it was understood only a small number were the Visible Saints, chosen by Winthrop. There was no tolerance for dissent because it would undermine the community and the law which was the Bible. Two members of the Massachusetts Bay Colony, Roger Williams and Anne Hutchinson, challenged the Winthrop and threatened to destroy Winthrop's vision of a City upon a Hill.

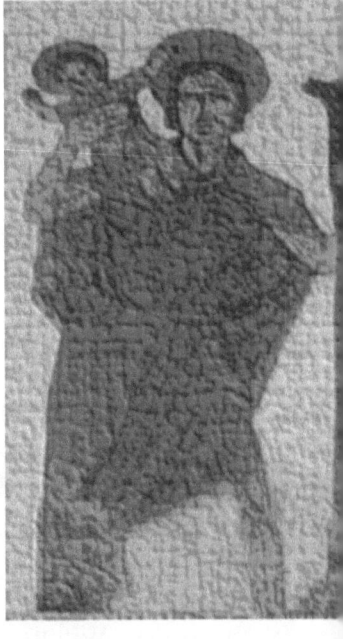

Roger Williams, one of the most famous Puritans, was banished from Salem, Massachusetts and founded his own colony in Rhode Island because he was in favor of separation of church and state and believed in religious freedom for everyone. Herein was where he and Winthrop differed. Williams also embraced some unique concepts. He believed that the Indians should be fairly paid for any land taken from them. Williams also asserted that women were equals to men and must be treated as such. His Rhode Island eventually became a haven for everyone, and included Baptists, Quakers, Jews and other religious minorities. William's unique concept of separation of church and state would be incorporated into the principal of both our United States Constitution and Bill of Rights.

Nonetheless, when Williams was banished, he was extremely ill and winter was coming, so the court allowed him to stay until spring if he kept his mouth shut. He didn't, and even challenged the king. Williams was charismatic, stubborn, and would never back away without trying to prove his point. He had many friends but speaking his opinion was a violation of his agreement. In January 1636, soldiers came to arrest him and were going to put him on a ship bound for England where he would be imprisoned or executed. Winthrop warned Williams who managed to escape and was helped by Native Americans who got him through the cold New England winter.

Williams survived and then formed his own community when families from Salem joined him. It was a long fight but in 1644 the king granted him a charter and Williams had created a free society!

By the 1630s, huge groups of Puritans arrived and began forming numerous communities. There were many dissenters, who created individual colonies in Connecticut, Maine, New Hampshire, and came to Williams' Rhode Island. You may have heard of the charismatic Ann Hutchinson. She was a mother of twelve, who spoke to the women in the Boston area in her home. She aided the sick and did good works, but was blunt and stated that she believed faith led to salvation. Hutchinson also claimed she had a Divine revelation. This led to her trial and that of her mentor John Cotton. Cotton was acquitted, but Hutchinson was excommunicated and banished from the Massachusetts Bay Colony. She started an antinomian or belief that life was guided by inner intuition and not external law. Her colony was in what is now part of Rhode Island.

History would not be complete without writing about Salem. Salem, located on the northeast coast of Massachusetts is remembered for the witchcraft hysteria that obsessed the population in the late seventeenth century.

Salem was founded in 1626 by Roger Conant and a group of immigrants/refugees from Cape Ann, upstate New York, and Canada. The name, Salem, comes from a Hebrew word meaning peace. Salem, however, never had peace and its present historical significance began in 1692.

Centuries ago, many Christians and non-Christians had a strong belief that Satan gave certain people supernatural powers to harm others in return for their loyalty. Witches were females and males were warlocks. A "witchcraft craze" entranced Europe from the 1300s to the end of the 1600s when over 40,000 supposed-witches were executed. The Salem trials exploded when the European obsession began dying out.

There was a rivalry between the wealthy in the port of Salem and those who were engaged in agriculture. The underlying causes have been debated for years. Was it this rivalry or infected rye causing hallucinations? Was it that there were overwhelming catastrophes attributed to the devil's work? Or was it jealousy, feuds, or bored teens? History changes, and there are various accounts as to how the craze began. I will give you two. The second is the commonly known epic.

The first is from a book published in 1878 which I found a reprint in a university library. The belief in witchcraft came over with the Puritans because most European countries believed in its power and punished its followers. The ministers continued the belief and they alone fueled the social influence.[2]

In 1688, John Goodwin's strong-willed and rebellious 13-year-old daughter, accused an Irish servant of stealing linen. The girl's mother who was an Irish Catholic, denied the accusation. The resentful adolescent pretended bewitchment and the Reverend Cotton Mather believed her because he witnessed for himself the barking, purring, and a convincing theatrical act. Controversy soared to epidemic proportions after the servant's execution.

This is the second and more well-known. The village had various opinions on the Reverend Samuel Parris, who became Salem's first ordained minister in 1689. Parris was accused of being strict, set in his ways, and greedy. The Puritan villagers believed all the dissention was devil's work.[3]

One freezing day in January when everyone was housebound, a strange event happened inside the Parris household. As sleet and snow showered their door, suddenly Betty Parris and her cousin Abigail began to twitch, coil their bodies into strange shapes, and shrieked and yelped words that made no sense. Betty's father, the Reverend Parris, didn't know what to make of the situation and called a doctor to examine the teens. The doctor's diagnosis was that the girls were bewitched.

As a result, 20 of the 200 accused were executed. When the hysteria died the following year, an edict was issued. It did little for those who were executed or imprisoned. It said the trials were a mistake and released all of the accused from prison. Since then, no one has been hanged for witchcraft in the United States. However, people found other charges to be brought up instead!

To this day, the truth is still unknown. Were the trials a climax of mass-hysteria? Do you think it was that the Puritans lived in an all-consuming strictly religious society that dared not question biblical teachings of the universal beliefs in the devil? Was it a single group jealousy?

The Puritan colonies survived for a while, religious passion died down, but disagreement will forever exist about the causes for these events. The Puritanical society was having difficulties and in 1679, a Puritan synod met to examine the causes of this spiritual discontentment. They decided there was increased swearing, people sleeping at sermons, sex and alcohol, taverns, immodest women, and increased lying and lawsuits.

However, life went on. There were religious colonies in the 1600s in the North and colonies where religion was a small issue. Life in New England towns used the barter system. There were families and the population grew because there weren't the diseases that existed in the South. Women were still second-class citizens and white men owned the property. Women could be midwives because men couldn't do this, and they bore, nursed, and reared children. They cooked, cleaned, and gardened. Most infants survived to adulthood and New Netherland (Dutch) now became British New York.

The Moravians converted in western Pennsylvania. The Moravians protested against Catholicism, and had a failed mission in Georgia. Catholics in the Southwest kept mestizos, people of mixed Spanish and Indian, with priests treating them like slaves. The French Jesuits tried settlement in Canada.

Back in the South which was Virginia, there were mostly young males and most were indentured servants. There were three men for every two women. Marriage was highly improbable for males and there were high death rates. One of every four infants died in their first year, and it was rare to live to age 40. Women had multiple husbands as the men died. When they remarried, which was usually the case, they still had few rights with the new husbands taking their wealth, if they had any to begin with. Nevertheless, colonists arrived and survived as epidemics killed native Indians.

A race for empire building was on: Spain vs Portugal. The French and Dutch built great ships which were small and fast and pirating and privateering were common. There was retaliation and slavery became the norm. They enslaved the indigenous people in their quest for power. Power came in many forms and was to overcome, convert, and enslave. Call it what you want, expansionism, Empire-building, Imperialism, but it all came down to domination.

Authorities and interpretations vary on what the Bible says and this will be re-interpreted throughout history, especially when we reach the Civil War. Please remember, slavery is as old as mankind itself. It goes back to the Bible – which nowhere does the Bible indicate that slavery is wrong or immoral because it never condemns it. People were sold into slavery to support their families or were the spoils of war. It is a different definition than we have today.

Every one of the original 13 colonies made slavery legal at one time or another, but only the Southern Colonies believed it was economically important. The last colony to legalize was Georgia. Established by James Oglethorpe, originally it was a military buffer zone to protect raiding of the Carolina plantations by Florida. It would be a debtor's refuge. There was to be no slavery in Georgia no large land-holding (forts), and no booze. Slaves would be competition.

The main crop was labor-intensive rice and planters wanted slaves. However, it wasn't too long when people left the colony and a great deal of pressure to legalize slavery began. Georgia changed from a military establishment to more of a Southern Colony. By 1750, slavery was accepted, and within another 20 years the enslaved were half of the Georgia population.

What needs to be remembered that if you didn't like your colony, it was difficult to impossible to move from it. Your colony was your country. There was no cooperation between the thirteen and each had its own government and currency. However, everyone accepted gold and silver. The colonies had already forgotten about England. The House of Burgesses was wealthy and the colonies altogether were the second wealthiest country in the world before the American Revolution. The first wealthiest was England. Foremost, the colonies didn't trust one another and each was concerned about his own. There was no unity. It was nothing like a United States of America and each was its own separate entity.

Another source of labor in the North was convict labor which was a form of slavery. Three-quarters came to the Chesapeake region and a tenant farmer system arose. Tenants were one step above indentured servants in New England. People continued to come to the new world for opportunity and freedom. There were the Scots, Irish, Germans, and Huguenots who were French Protestants. The gap between rich and poor widened but as wide as it was, even the poor in America fared far better than those who remained in Britain.

Maryland became a refuge for Catholics. Lord Baltimore, aka George Calvert was the head, but he died before the colony began, and his son Cecilius took charge. It was a Proprietary Colony meaning that it was the sole possession of Calvert and his heirs. A Proprietary Colony is when the English Monarch grants land to one person or a group who are the "lords proprietor." Calvert set up his own government, owned all the land, set up all of the laws. Tobacco was the main crop, requiring intensive labor. There were huge Catholic estates, and even the Jesuit priests owned slaves. The colony changed once a headright system was established here also. There was a lot of controversy about religions that allowed slave ownership.[4]

There were other Proprietary Colonies. Examples are Carolina, Maryland, and New York after it was taken from the Dutch. Charles II, now in power in 1663, granted his supporters tracts of land from northern Florida to Southern Virginia. One of these was granted to Anthony Ashley Cooper and John Locke, who were given land from Southern Virginia to Florida. This was not a religious colony; we are in the South.

Another was, William Penn and the Quakers in Pennsylvania, 1681. Penn was granted a huge region north of Maryland for a religious colony. The settlement was the Society of Friends, or the Quakers, a sect that was persecuted. Unlike the Puritans, they rejected predestination and believed everyone had grace, making salvation possible for all who heeded the 'Inner Light.' The Quakers held meetings in silence until any member of the congregation felt the need to speak and stood-up. Like Roger Williams, they paid Natives for land and in 1688, they were to first group to stand-up against slavery. This was known as the Holy Experiment and became a successful colony.

Let's watch the Penn Colony, as they will be a sore point for colonists in the next century. People continued to come to the new world for opportunity and freedom – Scots, Irish, Germans, Huguenots. During the seventeenth century, more and more colonies were formed. They include Connecticut, New Haven, San Marcos (Spanish/Florida), New Stockholm (Swedish/New Jersey), Montreal Quebec (French), and Pensacola, Florida (Spanish).

Even though Spain claimed the Caribbean, (Treaty of Tordesillas), the English, French, and Dutch went to the West Indies. The labor-intensive sugar crop, relied on slaves and it ensured British economic prosperity. Indentured servants weren't used to the hot and muggy tropical climate. Hence, African slaves purchased from the Dutch and Portuguese were the solution to the labor shortage. By 1700, the West Indies was a biracial society.

***

Let's talk a little about slavery...

The majority of slaves came to the Americas and arrived in Brazil and the West Indies. Only one in twenty came directly to the American colonies. Slavery had died out in Northern Europe but not in Southern Europe and the Middle-East. Both Christians and Muslims did not enslave their own faith so they went to the sub-Saharan dessert of Africa and black skin became the norm for slaves.

Remember, Columbus, who became the first American slave trader? He and the colonists enslaved the Indians but the Natives were tough and had advantages over them. Natives didn't make good slaves. They knew the terrain and topography, they lived close to Mother Earth, and there was camaraderie amongst them, so they could easily escape. They believed farm work was women's work and this gave them more reason to escape. Earlier, we looked at the concept that gender roles were established amongst the Native Americans, but women were not thought of as inferiors. The bottom line, is that Native Americans rebelled, refused to be enslaved, and by the eighteenth century African slaves were the norm. However, if Natives could foresee the treatment and troubles that lie ahead in the centuries to come, their plight was equal to or worse than slavery.

When slaves were brought to America, they didn't have the advantages of the Natives who knew the land. Natives were from various tribes, spoke distinct languages, and were already in bondage in a new and frightening land, if they survived the journey at all.

Indentured servitude was more profitable until the late seventeenth century when these servants were hard to find because immigration slowed as temporarily conditions in Europe improved. The North offered more economic opportunities in employment and acquiring land. When England's Royal African Company formed, it was a monopoly selling slaves to the English colonies and only the rich Chesapeake planters could afford them. This continued through 1698 when they lost rights and free competition for slaves became the norm.

Slaves, were a long-term secure investment because the enslaved had children, could not band together as a group for support, and when they escaped, they were easy to find. Once a slave, always a slave until death. It was very difficult to believe in a Jubilee or emancipation. Yet, many internalized the belief and knew some day they or their children would escape the bondage and become freed men and women.

Slaves were chained and forced into cages like wild animals, until a ship could be filled, which could be a month or so. They were then taken by canoe to the ship. Many jumped overboard and drowned rather than become enslaved, which many viewed worse than death. Death would at least reunite with ancestors. Hundreds were chained below deck for six to eight weeks in confinement of 6' x 16' with vomit, blood, excrement, and dead bodies. Many people went insane, refused to eat, and died. The crew would force-feed or torture until the enslaved came around to their evil ways and decided to live under the dire circumstances. Some decks were equipped with netting to prevent the attempts to go overboard during the "exercise" periods.

The crew aboard the ships were not eager to leave their countries and go aboard a slaver because unlike the owners and captains of the ships, they were poorly paid, if at all. These were not sought-after jobs. Often, these men owed debts and this was one way to repay them. A night out on the town could result in waking up on a ship already at sea.

Crewmen were subject to harsh rules and were frequently whipped, given little medical care, poorly fed, and left at destinations without pay. The death rate of the crew was very high as many contracted diseases they had never been exposed to prior, drowned, went blind from the sun (there were no sun glasses at that time), or couldn't handle the situation and lost sanity.

Still the survival rate for the enslaved was high enough for the slave traders to make a lot of money. People were terrified, humiliated, panicked, and thought they would be eaten because they were fondled, slapped, and touched in their most private areas. The term Middle Passage was created. It was the journey in which millions of slaves were transported from Africa to the Americas and crammed into dungeons on ships.[5] Put yourself in the position. If you were chained and taken to a slave trading vessel off the African coast, what would you be thinking?

Frustration

Both England and France were dominant powers in North America and hostility continued to grow. The English took New York and New Jersey from the Dutch (wars with Holland, 1664 England takes them), and France was established in present-day Canada. Slavery was growing while relations with Native Americans continued to be in conflict. The common man was frustrated.

One hundred years before 1776, frustration led to one of the first rebellions by settlers. In 1675-76, angry colonists, freed indentured servants, and new immigrants were just fed up. The few owned everything. A group moved west into western Virginia, attacked the Susquehannock Indians, and took their land. The Indians fought back. Then Nathaniel Bacon, a wealthy new immigrant took command and led a force against ALL Indians.

The Virginia government under Sir William Berkeley demanded they stop, but nevertheless Bacon and his following of 500 paid no heed and marched on Jamestown. It became a war and both Native villages and colonial towns were put to ashes. Even the Jamestown Capital burnt to the ground. When the English navy finally arrived from England, they stopped the rebellion. Bacon had died of dysentery and the Powhatans had lost all their land. This first rebellion demonstrated the hatred for Natives. It grew and many believed that enslavement of other races showed superiority, and power, and there was a goal to achieve this.

Summary

Various religious groups have settled and are continuing to grow in numbers across the colonies. Our country consists of Pilgrims, Puritans, Quakers, Calvinists, Roman Catholics, Non-Denominational Christians, and others who never considered religion as a number one priority. Most sects have gained their own religious freedom and desire to force it upon nonbelievers. We were a somewhat-segregated country when it came to religious beliefs, in addition to the other factors which divided us.

Nations continued to compete for a foothold in this new land: Dutch, English, French, Spanish, and Swedish. Native Americans were not considered people and gradually they lost power. Blacks were property and labor-intensive crops like tobacco, rice, and cotton, made slavery very lucrative.

People were living in their own separate and unique colonies just like the Indians had for thousands of years. The masses were poor because they came on their own or as indentured servants. They were always indebted to someone, and never free. The rich got richer and the poor just got more frustrated. Bacon showed this frustration which was the first mass-rebellion.

Sandi Ludwa

I may have painted a dark picture of life on this continent, but it was still a sought-after location and place of destiny. Conditions in the old world went from bad to worse and this new land offered opportunity. The choice was yours. Was it better to stay in Europe or advantageous to come to a new land?

The colonists had one great advantage in the Bay and Virginia Colonies in that they spoke English, and this united them. They were all first or second-generation immigrants coming to this land with hope. However, the enslaved had no such power and forcibly were brought to this new land. America had a lot going on but slowly we were on the road to freedom and revolution.

Chapter 5

Shedding Our Roots

The House of Burgesses in 1619 was the first democratically-elected legislative body in the British American colonies. It set the precedent for self-government. As the years passed, year by year colonists became more unique. They became more American. The Mayflower Compact followed in 1620, setting the English up in the North.

The House of Burgesses continually took increased power from the British and within a short period, the colonists set-up the meetings, agendas, and standards for membership. They decided who could be excluded from the meetings, namely, representatives of the crown. They made the laws and collected the taxes. Even though Virginia was supposed to regulate religion, if a person showed some form of allegiance to the Church of England which was still being supported by tax money, the distinction between religious and civil authority was gone. Most colonists, religious or not, had no tolerance for non-Christian religions and women were still responsible for the family's religious life.

Every year colonists took on more-and-more of the budget. When the House started, the Royal Governor was given a budget and from it, he took his salary and living expenses. Whatever was left over was the colony's. Once colonists took power, however, whatever revenue they got was the budget of the colony and at the year-end, whatever was leftover became their salaries. This happened nowhere else in the colonial world – only in our America.

Before 1650, England made little attempt for central control. Each colony governed itself, politics were at the town level, and most colonists weren't even interested. English control still dominated most of the Colonies. The next part gets a bit complicated so please bear with me.

Charles II had been attempting to reorganize New England and he started in the North. The Massachusetts Bay Colony Charter had been revoked after its leaders refused to act on his demands for reforms in the colony. Charles wanted to be more controlling and was constantly pushed by his brother James II to do so.

It was a sad occasion when Charles expired. He was charismatic, popular, and a lady's man. He and the queen, Catherine of Braganza, had no children together, but Charles sired at least a dozen. On his deathbed, it is reported that he told his brother to take care of his mistresses! Like every other death, there were always rumors of plots involving poisons but in Charles' case, modern science believes it was strictly one of many natural medical conditions.[1]

When James became King in 1685, again he began in the North and created the Dominion of New England. James was a devout Catholic and the common fear was that James would establish Catholicism once again in England. In 1686, the Governor of Massachusetts, Sir Edmund Andros (formerly New York governor) became dominion governor and made an English super-colony to stop any ideas about colonial independence. He was despised and hated because it was his way or no way. Like present day America, many colonists were not only discouraged but angry and felt they had nowhere to turn.

Andros declared that local representation existed but it didn't. He ignored existing land titles when it suited his intentions, ruled town meetings with an iron hand, and forced participation in the Anglican Church in Puritan areas. He also enforced a series of Navigation Acts. Royal troops were not respected by their officers, who were supporters of the governor and either Anglican or Roman Catholic. The dominion consisted of the territories of the Massachusetts Bay Colony, Plymouth and Connecticut Colonies, the Rhode Island and Providence Colonies (1688), and its control was extended to include New York, and East and West Jersey.

English Protestants worried about James's governing and his Catholicism. However, the Glorious Revolution, also called the *Revolution of 1688*, was the overthrow of King James II of England who was also James VII of

Scotland. The throne went to William III, Prince of Orange, who was a Protestant, and James's Protestant daughter, Mary. Together, William and Mary became co-rulers. The political parties, both Whigs and Tories, had also united and conspired to replace James. This Revolution strengthened English authority but provided a representative government. It ensured religious freedom for Protestants, got rid of the Dominion of New England, and set a foundation for voluntary loyalty and not forced submission.

When William and Mary were crowned at Westminster Abbey, the Archbishop of Canterbury refused to officiate since he was still a fan of James. This was a big deal since the Archbishop was the top dog in the Church of England. Nevertheless, the colonies were happy with their ties to England. However, not all was well in Boston. A few days after the coronation, there was rebellion and Governor Andros quickly attempted to escape from the city disguised in women's clothes when the Boston Militia did arrest him.

It was good news, a lot changed, voters didn't have to belong to the church, and there was religious toleration for **all** Protestants, ending Puritan control. Remember, it was still Protestants only. Catholics still were not tolerated, even in Maryland where Lord Baltimore had established a haven, they lost many freedoms.

In 1698, the House of Burgesses moved to Williamsburg and colonists were interested in the Age of Enlightenment. It was a movement in Europe during the late seventeenth and early eighteenth centuries that stated natural laws operated our universe and humans would discover and understand these laws. They could and would, in fact, improve human conditions. People began to question and think.

Meanwhile back in England, the English were still engaged in a series of wars: King William's War against the French and Indians, Queen Anne's War (vs France and Spain), and the government wasn't paying a lot of attention to the colonies other than starting to pass a series of Acts to collect revenue. England was also busy trying to protect their "New England" from any foreign threat on the new continent. It was all part of a bigger picture. An example was the French and Indian Wars designed to secure and protect the Mississippi River Valley. England was footing bill for this, protecting the colonists, and England was successful. However, it needed money and men because the colonists did little and let England handle it. "Let England fight and protect us," they said.

The final straw was the French and Indian war known as the Seven years War, (1754) which removed enemies from the Mississippi River Valley. During the war, the colonists traded with England's enemies while England was doing all of the fighting. This gave the English a lot of territory to administer especially with the debt hanging over their heads. There were colonists such as George Washington who did back the British system of mercantilism. It was lucrative and did allow some to climb up the ladder of success.

The colonies were the second richest nation in world but they were not a nation, yet. The colonies produced commodities that England wanted but it was the Southern Colonies that produced what they really needed. The world was changing. Remember the Mercantile System? What developed over the past 50-60 years was no longer valid. America now said what was equivalent to "too bad, so sad, we'll ship to anyone we want. Go stuff it." This was illegal under the mercantile system. Major trade routes were created with nations outside of England and as a result, England didn't make the money it felt it should be generating. England reacted and passed a series of acts over the next 30 years under name of Navigation Acts. What were their options or alternatives?

First, they said that colonists could only trade on ships that flew the British flag. Being as creative as they were, a whole new industry in our North was born. It was ship building. Colonists knew they were considered British citizens so they flew the British flag. Then another new Navigation Act passed and everything shipped had to go to London first where it was taxed and then sent out to the rest of the world. No problem, another whole new industry developed and it was fast ship building, which meant "We dare you, catch us if you can."

That didn't work so the English said no trading in contraband. Creative as the would-be Americans were, once again, they came up with yet another new industry, smuggling. The Navigation Acts failed. England wanted profit in the British Empire and colonists wanted their own money. There were a series of small acts, wool act, hat act, etc. Colonists didn't care. Still, up until the very beginning of the American Revolution, many colonists took great pride in their ties with the mother country. These strings were cultural, economic, and political.

Meanwhile, Religion in New England

So, what happened to the Puritans; any guesses? This was the society that gave us some of our great colleges: Harvard, Dartmouth, Yale, and Brown. Well, every church, eventually, has a crisis when they realize the younger generation has their own ideas. Does this sound familiar in today's world?

The Puritan church was the strictest of any religions that came to America. It started experiencing a crisis so severe that they had to do something immediately because the younger generation didn't care about religion. John Calvin firmly believed that a certain number of people were predestined by God to go to heaven. The Half-Way Covenant was introduced and made it much easier to become a visible saint. It relaxed religion in America and religion became less English and more American, or less old world and more new world.

The Covenant was a plan dealing with declining church membership, adopted in 1662 by the Congregational churches of colonial New England. It allowed adults who had been baptized because their parents were church members but had not yet experienced conversion, to have their own children baptized. Without the Covenant, this third-generation stayed unbaptized until their parents experienced conversion. It seemed, however, many parents were not receiving conversion. The covenant was a type of part-time church membership and was promoted by the Reverend Solomon Stoddard. Stoddard believed that the colonists were souls who had lost their pathway and somehow forgotten their original map leading them to their religious purpose.

The result was that the Covenant temporarily saved the church. Still, the younger generation persisted in their uninterest, and by 1700 religion was unimportant. This new generation was busy making money, engaging in commerce, enjoying a healthy social life, and as a result, the colonies moved away from God and created an emptiness or void. There still existed a great need for something more.

In the 1730's – 1740's there occurred the Great Awakening. It was an extraordinary renewal or revival in colonial America. This was a time before radio and television and the attendance figures were amazing for the time. Twentieth Century preachers such as Oral Roberts, Jim and Tammy Faye

Bakker, or Billy Graham would have been envious of the crowds. Come with me and witness one of the events.

Men set up tents and spoke to whoever showed up, black, white, and both sexes; it made no difference. Let's experience an old fashioned "awakening" or "revival."

Look around, and there are thousands standing in the tent and pouring out into the countryside. We're in an open field with a few trees for shelter. It's very hot, probably around 95°F and we are all eagerly awaiting the speaker. It's finally time and a trumpet blares to quiet everyone down. The trumpeter sends a few more non-melodious blasts until it is deadly silent. Sweat is pouring down on us and many are using make-shift fans to survive the heat. The preacher is stepping up to the front of the tent in a heavy suit.

The missionary begins preaching. It is all hellfire, brimstone, damnation, threatening, and is scaring the American audience. The preacher is trembling and shouting out the powerful words. There are multiple reactions from the crowd, all moved by the passion of his words. He displays rage at mankind's sins and we are all feeling like we'll be condemned to hell within the next few minutes. The holy man displays his dedication with morality and intense emotion as he continually wipes his brow.

Some in the crowd begin to shake, cry, wail, and experience moral conversions. Others appear agitated and have fainted or are being supported by those around them. Some disciples are shouting "amen" while the preacher shouts all the louder to overcome the noise in the tent and from the believers in the field who are overcome with spirit, ecstasy, and heat. We are overwhelmed with the realization that everyone is coming together and there is no segregation. We are all one. This was very different from traditional American religion that has a long history of being discriminatory. Now, no one is asking questions about our background, financial situation, job, and we're all coming back to God. At the height of the presentation, a collection box is passed and the proceeds are carefully guarded so that no unscrupulous person gets any ideas about helping only himself. Amen.

One of most well-known and popular men of God was Jonathan Edwards and one of his most famous sermons was "Sinners in the hands of an angry God." Edwards had a monotone, boring voice but it was the words. He did not shout but spoke softly, unlike the others. The words scared people and sermons were extremely emotional experiences. This was very unique to America. The only persons opposing these public displays were those who wanted segregated congregations, and they were a distinct minority. Edwards did not travel most of the time, but preached to his local parish.

Another was George Whitefield who came from Great Britain. His sermons, presentations, and performances lasted for hours. Words to describe his sermons were heart-wrenching, theatrical, spectacular, and by today's terms, awesome. People cried, wailed, begged for forgiveness, and the word Revival was born. In towns with few people, often over 20,000 would attend. In one year, he journeyed over 5,000 miles and preached around 350 sermons.

"There is no want of power in God to cast wicked men into hell at any moment. Men's hands cannot be strong when God rises up: the strongest have no power to resist him, nor can any deliver out of his hands. He is not only able to cast wicked men into hell, but he can most easily do it."[2]
—George Whitefield

Even Benjamin Franklin who was extremely frugal, admitted in his autobiography that he gladly emptied his pockets because he was impressed with Whitefield's good deeds.[3] There was one unique idea that all shared and that was that religion shouldn't be formal and mysterious but casual, unpretentious, spontaneous, and very personal.

Whitefield may have been a charismatic preacher, but he also had his other side. Whitefield believed in the institution of slavery. When many wealthy landowners converted to the Light, he was offered slaves which he duly accepted at his Georgia plantation. He became very influential in the decision of the colony of Georgia to give up its ban, and soon slavery was the norm. There is ongoing controversy even today. Evidence speaks for itself and Whitefield undoubtedly had a profound influence on religion in America. However, his views on slavery are controversial. His view changed from youth to the time when wealth was accumulated. Was Whitefield a product of his time with no thoughts on the immorality of enslavement or did he compromise his beliefs?

The New Lights became commonplace. They were a distinct group which formed their own churches because they couldn't worship with sinful members. However, the Awakening didn't come to the South until the 1760s. It was the birth of the Baptists who wore plain clothing and criticized the wealthy and their habits of drinking, gambling, socializing, dress, and pride. The gentry, on the other hand, resented the Baptists because they preached to slaves. There arose an evangelism and a correspondence between European and American ministers with new world periodicals to read, such as "Christian History" which gave insight into true religion.

Conditions in Europe got worst and there were mass migrations. For example, the Germans who were part of small uniquely distinct city-states, saw horrific winters, and the Little Ice Age was still going on. There were crop failures, high taxes, starvation, religious persecution, and the French invasion 1730-60. Thousands immigrated from Europe and to America in the eighteenth century. Their labor was needed in the slave states but the majority avoided them. Indentured servants were gradually replaced in all the Southern English colonies with slaves. Another source was convict labor with 80% going to the Chesapeake Region. There was also a system like indenture called redemptioner bringing Germans to the colonies in the eighteenth century. In the South there was also fear.

Politics and Religion became Americanized. Now the focus shifted to education. A system of education was established and it was different than the British form which said education was the responsibility of the individual family. The American philosophy said that it was the responsibility of society which must create free public schools. However, there was a focus more so on higher education. In the North, universities were founded. The oldest, Harvard, chartered in 1636, was a training ground for ministers and other schools followed: Yale in 1701, and Ivy League Princeton in 1746.

In the South, it was the College of William and Mary, which was established in 1693 with a Charter from the King. William and Mary became the second oldest University in the U.S. The new world was now powerful, educated, and knowledge was a powerful weapon. There were chartered girls' boarding schools where the women learned French, music, dancing, and education befitting women of quality. These schools were intended to instruct the future mistresses of the great houses. England finally woke-up and decided it needed to do something; but it was too late.

Robert Walpole was advising the king on America. The king asked him for guidance and Walpole told him to let the colonists get wealthier and then they would act. This was known as period of salutary neglect. It affected Massachusetts and was the period in which the British failed to enforce laws. An example was the Navigation Acts which had poor enforcement and failed. Neglect ran from the late seventeenth century to the mid-eighteenth Century. Twenty years later, England passed a series of acts and laws designed to restrict the actions of the colonists. The Writs of Assistance were the first in1760, when King George III became King. It was a legal document giving the British officials the right to inspect homes and businesses to check if there was contraband. Americans were more than insulted that their privacy and their rights were infringed upon and got the notion in their heads that they had the rights to privacy and private property. This was search and seize without our modern-day search warrant.

The gap between wealth and poverty widened. Great houses were constructed by the wealthy in the mid-seventeen hundreds to show-off their success. They built gigantic parlors, which were unlike our living rooms where we all congregate, but were sitting-rooms meant to receive guests! They added second stories, wings, and elegant formal gardens. Well-to-do Americans were attempting to duplicate the old world and were emulating the Mother Country in architecture, furnishings, manners, dress, and lifestyle. For example, Deborah Franklin, Ben Franklin's wife, surprised her husband in the 1750s with new kitchen tools in their Philadelphia home. She told Ben that he deserved a silver spoon and china bowl so they could keep up with their neighbors. Was this, "Keeping up with the Joneses?"

However, newcomers found it impossible to secure property but they knew it was better than living back in Great Britain where one-third of the population received public assistance. Keep in mind, during this period our America was a variety of regionally distinctive new world communities.

In the mid-eighteenth century, Native Americans still dominated much of the continent but in the Southwest, the Spanish subjugated them. They used three methods to control Indians: *Repartimiento* used native labor for constructions projects such as forts and roads, while *encomienda* collected tribute, and *rescateuse* of slavery of ransomed captives seized from one another by Indian tribes. There were ongoing battles. Back in 1680 there was the Pueblo Revolt in with 20,000 Pueblo Indians revolted in New Mexico.

Then there was a black slave rebellion, the Stono Rebellion in 1739. It happened in South Carolina and was the largest revolt in colonial North America. The South Carolina population at the time was around 56,000 in total with 32,000 enslaved. Twenty slaves broke into a store and secured guns and headed towards the Stono River to go to Florida. The Spanish had offered freedom for any slaves who could make their way down to Florida. Another 100 joined them and together they attacked and executed whites, and burnt down plantations. Within a week, two dozen whites and four dozen blacks were killed. To bring the point home, their heads were placed on pikes, which was the custom at the time.[4]

As a result, South Carolina encouraged more white immigration and a harsher slave code was enacted. Whites were so frightened that the new code severely limited the privileges of slaves. They were no longer allowed to grow their own food, assemble in groups, earn their own money, or learn to read. Some of these restrictions were already in place, but they had not been strictly enforced. Their thoughts were that in a colony with more slaves than free white, if this happened once, it could happen again.

What was happening? The North and the South were involved in their own issues. At this time, we did not have a developed Northwest or Southwest by the English. Northwest referred to East of the Mississippi. The bottom line was that England needed revenue to pay for the protection they provided the colonists and their wars in Europe. However, the difference of opinion was in representation. There were two fields of thought.

There was Virtual Representation which was followed by the English in England. They viewed themselves as part of an extended family, ruled by males of course.

The kings were the fathers and protectors while the Colonies were the children who were expected to be loyal, appreciative, and submissive. Parliament was to maintain the balance between the monarchy and social classes. After all, Parliament understood the colonists.

Then there was the colonist version in the would-be America. Their elite were a now colonized, had never experienced the poverty of their fathers and grandfathers, and they wanted both economic and political independence. Not many of us experienced the Great Depression and only those who have lived in or witnessed poverty can understand the way of life. Property ownership guaranteed power and was common in the colonies compared to England. Colonists wanted actual representation giving them a physical presence in voice for the creation of these policies.

Summary

The Great Awakening did just that. It renewed or awakened religious fervor in the colonies. Wouldn't it be nice if this fervor existed today and people came together finally despite their differences, whether political, spiritual, racial, sexual?

Our America

The country was sectionalized by the individual colonies who were yet to come together to be <u>united states</u>. The North was industrializing while the South continued to be agricultural and relied on slaves. Slavery had brought an end to indentured servitude. It was becoming an issue and southerners feared there would be rebellion. However, slavery was not in the forefront now and wouldn't erupt until the Civil War in 1861. Right now, there was the British question.

The English in England viewed themselves as part of an extended male-dominated family. The kings were the protecting fathers, and the Colonies were children who were expected to be loyal and appreciative. Parliament was to maintain balance between the monarch and social classes. They believed Parliament understood the colonists.

In America, the elite were doing well and wanted economic and political independence. Property ownership guaranteed power and was common. Even yeoman farmers took pride in ownership, some working alongside their slave and sharing the same accommodations. Colonists wanted more. They desired actual representation giving them a physical presence in voice for the formulation of these policies.

These two differences of opinion would be one of the underlying causes of the American Revolution. Americans wouldn't allow England to control them....was England waking up 150 years later? Americans were restless, they didn't stay in one place and they were moving inland into land which was owned by others, not England. This created conflict. The French and Indian War was to remove everyone from Mississippi valley but colonists did nothing and traded with the enemy. England was paying the bill for protection.

The Spanish and French were also a presence but they were not directly involved in the upcoming Revolution. It was the colonists and Britain. The English needed money and so they taxed. The would-be Americans were fed-up and wanted freedom.

Chapter 6

Becoming Americanized

Americans climbed over the mountains and they were in present day Kentucky, Tennessee, and Missouri. England finally became concerned and declared the Proclamation Line of 1763. The Proclamation said that all Americans who have gone west of Appalachia had to settle back in the east. They had to come back. This would make governing easier and cheaper to defend colonists. Colonists reacted much the same as they did to the Navigation Acts and ignored England. England didn't understand the situation. Settlers wanted land. Then, several things happened and it came down to money.

Let me introduce Benjamin Franklin to you. Yes, he flew a kite and luckily lightning didn't strike and he didn't get electrocuted. Remember I mentioned the Quakers and William Penn? Well, they had a special relationship with England and the Penn family ruled. They were exempt from taxes and governed, setting much of the legislation. The Colony of Pennsylvania hired Franklin to go to England and represent them. Soon other colonies also hired him. Now Franklin was a rags-to-riches story. He taught himself to read and write, left home when he could no longer tolerate his other brother because he was in apprenticeship to him, and arrived in Philadelphia without a cent. No problem, he quickly climbed up the National ladder.

Franklin spent almost 15 years in England fighting for rights for the colonists in Parliament. His wife would not travel and there were long separations. Perhaps, this is the reason he was regarded as a "ladies man" when he was sent to negotiate the Treaty of Paris in 1783! Nevertheless, his inventions were numerous and his role in the founding of this country were huge. He was the only colonist to have been involved in the Declaration of Independence, Treaty of Alliance with Paris, Treaty of Paris, and United States Constitution.

Now you know my friend, Ben. His ideas were a major influence on the foundations which support the pillars that are America. He was a fascinating character and many books have been published which give you an insight into this pudgy near and far-sighted-gent![1]

Back to the English who had their hands full. First, there was Pontiac's Rebellion in 1763. The area involved was from the Great Lakes to Virginia and eight united Native tribes waged a war on the British colonists for three years. Then, there was the end of the French and Indian War. In America, England gained most of the French Territory (Mississippi and the Coast). They now had to pay off the war debts to British and Dutch bankers. England had a debt of some 130 million pounds and the interest alone consumed a half of Britain's expenditures.

A series of taxes were then passed to make certain colonists understood that the money would be spent only on the colonists. Colonists ignored this. In short, many believed that, as they were not directly represented in the distant British Parliament, any laws it passed affecting them were illegal under the 1689 English Bill of Rights and denied their rights as Englishmen.

We all get very upset over new taxes. At this time, however, there were series of taxes, one after another. However, there was one tax which really upset everyone. This was the Stamp Act of 1765, which required an official stamp or water mark on every piece of paper such as diplomas, cards, I.O.U.'s, and deeds. Lawyers and journalists were angry beyond belief. Colonists sent delegates to a meeting called the Stamp Act Congress where they would discuss it. Colonists concluded they would not pay and gave birth to the phrase, "No Taxation Without Representation."

Colonists didn't buy the idea that parliament was their representation. The Sons of Liberty arose. They were a secret organization that opposed taxation through demonstrations which intimidated the tax collectors. The sons were from upper and middle-class families and one of them, Christopher Gadsden called for National Unity, "There ought to be no New England men, no New Yorker, etc. known on the Continent, but all of us Americans."[2] Years later,

Thomas Jefferson forcefully proclaimed a similar statement about national unity.

The colonists then started burning and hanging well-hated people in effigy. To protest, they took pillow cases and stuffed them with feathers and placed the names of British officials on them. The effigy was either tossed into a bonfire or hung. As a result, England decided to send soldiers to the colonies to enforce laws.

This led to acts, acts, and more acts. There were three currency acts. Currency was first local product, then gold or silver, then paper in the form of bank notes or mortgage. Colonists were always in debt so it protected the English merchants from the depreciated colonial dollar.

Then there was the 1764 Sugar Act or American Revenue Act, an extension of the earlier Molasses Act. It was to discourage colonial merchants and manufacturers from smuggling non-British goods from French and Spanish Colonies to avoid Parliament imposed taxes. The Sugar Act increased the number of items that would be taxed when they were imported to the colonies, but it reduced the tax on molasses and sugar from 6 pence per gallon to 3 pence per gallon.

The British retaliated in 1765 with the Quartering Act. This one was a huge mistake. England sent soldiers to discipline and told the colonists to build their English forts and barracks, or the soldiers would stay in their homes. Colonists were outraged.

Every year there was a new tax. In 1767, the Townsend Acts were passed. Items such as glass, lead, paint, paper, and tea were taxed. Commissioners in Boston put an end to smuggling, so they thought. The Colonists boycotted. Soon, the Daughters of Liberty were formed and women decided to stop using English luxuries. It took three years, but Parliament repealed all the taxes—except for the one on tea. It was ironic that on that same day another event occurred.

The years passed and it was 1770 when a mob of Colonists put rocks in snowballs and pelted soldiers. The Brits also fired their guns. Several colonists were killed and the first one was an African American named Crispus Attucks. Tall, with a height of 6'2" he told his colleagues to be unafraid. This was The Boston Massacre. Things became extremely tense but calm, until the final straw which was the Tea Act in 1773.

The bottom line was that England wanted all American trade which meant all of American dollars. The British Parliament believed that they were the still the parent and knew best. Whereas, the colonists wanted a voice to formulate their own policies. The Colonists united and decided not to trade with England anymore. The English merchants were livid and went to Parliament and told them to leave the colonies alone. Parliament said they would repeal the Stamp, Quartering Acts, and other taxes but not because they were asked to do it but because of their own accord. Once again, England backed off but they did not repeal the Tea Act.

The Tea Act was designed to benefit the monopolistic British East India Company. Colonists had been smuggling in Dutch tea and our boycott of tea didn't work. A plan was hatched. On a cold-New England winter night, they had a tea party, the Boston Tea Party, December 16, 1773.

When a ship first came over from England, it sailed into Boston harbor. Three ships came in with a cargo of tea that came from China. Note that the would-be Americans were receiving imports via England from the Chinese in the 1700s. Nothing has changed. Ironically, these ships were built in the American colonies and owned by wealthy colonists. A group of 60 colonists who were Sons of Liberty, dressed as Mohawk Indians, went on board, chopped up the chests of tea and threw them overboard. Led by Sam Adams (yes, there is now beer bearing the name), 342 Chests of tea, 92,000 pounds, were thrown into Boston Harbor. As a result, England decided more of a presence was needed.

George III was still the King of England, and he decided to crack down. He told Parliament that the time was now and the colonies had to submit or triumph. There was incomplete solidarity because some colonists, like Ben Franklin, said the East Indian Company should be reimbursed! There was a second tea party the next year but since only 30 cases were dumped, no one paid attention to it.

A word about King George. He suffered from a hereditary disease called porphyria. He had recurring bouts of insanity and romantically sought a 50-year-old grandmother even though his wife Queen Charlotte bore him 15 children. He would talk until foam ran out of his mouth, using 400-word sentences. His servants sat on him to keep him in line when he wasn't in a strait-jacket.[3] My take is this would explain some of the actions of some of the kings and queens if it was, in fact hereditary, Mary, Queen of Scots, for example.

In 1774, colonists met at the First Continental Congress. This is where the wonderful quotes come from such as "I know not what course others may take, but as for me, give me liberty or give me death," attributed to Patrick Henry.[4] Everyone except the colony of Georgia showed up. The Continental Congress decided they didn't want to fight, but economically cut England out of the picture by no importing or exporting. They wrote a petition appealing to King George III. This was a result of the Intolerable Acts, because of the unorthodox 'tea party.' It did nothing.

This time merchants did not put pressure on Parliament and relationships deteriorated. Colonists anticipated war and they drilled and prepared for war. Colonists heard that the Port of Boston was closed, the Massachusetts legislature disbanded, and no changes would occur until all the dumped tea was paid for.

British troops came over for military rule. Colonists thought they were invincible. They were arrogant. As the British were marching to Boston, the Minutemen shot at them and soldiers shot back. The Minutemen were American militiamen who volunteered to be ready for service at a minute's notice. Everything led war. The time had come to make a stand, once and for all.

Summary

England was the post powerful in North America during the first half of the eighteenth century. This was not the case in South and Central America and the Islands where other powers ruled. Indenture servitude gave way to slavery. Britain had problems controlling the continent because it was involved in both European and North American Continental Wars. The French and Indian War involved everyone, not just the French and the Indians. The Natives were always a threat, colonists were greedy and tended to make their own rules, and King George III was still the ruler.

Colonists boycotted, became angrier and angrier. They believed it was Britain's responsibility to protect them, but the Mother Country shouldn't charge them for the cost of doing business. The Acts they were passing were beyond comprehension. There was a small massacre, and then they had a tea party, and finally they met at the First Continental Congress. Colonists became increasingly 'Americanized' but it was a divided group. Some would become Tories and some will become Patriots.

Chapter 7

The American Revolution: The Road to Americanism Continues

"When in the Course of human events it becomes necessary for one people to dissolve the political bands which have connected them with another and to assume among the powers of the earth, the separate and equal station to which the Laws of Nature and of Nature's God entitle them, a decent respect to the opinions of mankind requires that they should declare the causes which impel them to the separation."

First paragraph Declaration of Independence

The American Revolution continued from one to another war. We fought the American Revolution (1775-1783) which brought partial freedom, and then we went into another war with the British in 1812. I have always found this confusing. We initiated our Declaration of Independence, July 4, 1776 but we were still burdened by the British and struggled with the question, "Was our freedom worth it?" We were not yet "united" states yet but merely colonies.

There were the concepts of Virtual vs Actual Representation. Virtual is the English belief that parliamentary members represent the whole nation and not just one faction. Actual is the American version that elected officials in their districts are responsible for local interests. It created a lot of thought – Americans were all in separate colonies BUT they were all together. In later years, the big issue of State's Rights vs. Federal Law came in with the issue of slavery and the economic issue surrounding it, which led to war.

Once American Revolution began, a number of colonists had a difficult time really dealing with it. Colonists were troubled by the Mother Country and the finality of war with the killing and deaths. Talk fuels emotions and is one thing, while doing the deed is another. Meanwhile, the European nations such as France and Spain, wanted colonists to fight. They wanted the war because these nations believed that if America won, it would be so weak that they could take over easily as England would be out of the picture. France and Spain secretly provided financial support so colonists could buy supplies.

As the Revolution approached, America was split into two distinct groups. There were the Tories or Loyalists who were Loyal to Britain, and were twenty percent of the white population. They were the farmers, officeholders, Anglicans, and minorities such as the South's Scots. Their hope was there could be a solution to the tension before the Whigs or Patriots could get independence from Great Britain. Since both Loyalists and Patriots were all part of our nation and British citizens before the war, the Loyalists hoped it would remain that way. They wanted settlement not independence. Loyalists were just that, loyal to the king, and happy with their state of life being British citizens. Once the war began, things changed and they lost their rights to assemble, were insulted, imprisoned, and their property was easily confiscated. The one nation idea was gone.[1]

Then there were the Whigs or Patriots, aka Revolutionaries, Continentals, Rebels, or American Whigs. They felt that recent British laws on the American Colonies violated their rights as British citizens. Some Native American tribes such as the Six Nations of Iroquois were divided.

In 1775, the War began with the Colonists being counted as 2.5 million with one-third being slaves or Loyalists, and Britain with 111,000 men in the colonies and West Indies. Britain encountered massive desertions, injuries, diseases, and attacks by American pirates or privateers. It all came down to your status and how British laws affected you personally. How would you have chosen sides?

The famous battle of Lexington and Concord erupted when General Thomas Gage, the Governor of Massachusetts, received orders to control the rebels and regain some order. He marched his army towards the villages of Lexington and Concord. The plan was to confiscate ammo which the

Patriots' had accumulated and to arrest Sam Adams and John Hancock. The warnings came from the Patriots, one of whom was Paul Revere.

"Listen my children and you will hear, of the midnight ride of Paul Revere."

………Henry Wadsworth Longfellow

Eighty-five years later when the Civil War was about to officially begin (1860), Harvard professor Henry Wadsworth Longfellow wrote a poem about a long-forgotten ride by Paul Revere on April 18, 1775. The professor's purpose was to use the tale of the ride to warn America that it was in trouble and in danger of dissolving. Wadsworth knew the true story of Revere's ride but the poem changes. Revere hung the Lanterns as a warning and not vice versa and he was arrested before he finished the ride, which was completed by another Patriot.

Daybreak the next day began the Revolutionary War at Lexington and Concord and is considered the official start. Minutemen were killed at Lexington; however, on the march back to Boston at Concord, the Patriots were victorious. They hid behind trees, killed, and wounded British troops. News spread fast, and poet Ralph Waldo Emerson later wrote that the shots would be "heard around the world." The Patriots were confident and kept the war going, enduring the trials that lie ahead.[2]

There was a calling for a Second Continental Congress. The Olive Branch Petition was adopted by the Congress on July 5, 1775 as a final attempt to avoid total war between Great Britain and the colonies. Their goal was not complete separation but a recognized identity and modernization of the existing political structure. The colonists presented this "olive branch" hoping for some peace and reconciliation. A week prior, the Congress had already authorized the invasion of Canada and there were casualties. The petition asserted there was colonial loyalty to Britain and pleaded with King George III to stop the threat of this future conflict. The Declaration of the Causes and Necessity of Taking up Arms followed the next day.

In August 1775, the colonies were officially declared to be in rebellion by the Proclamation of Rebellion, which was once again rejected by Great Britain. This occurred even though King George refused to read the Olive Branch Petition before declaring the colonists traitors.

A Continental Army was quickly formed. These Minutemen were untrained, had very few experienced military, and served short terms. There were some signing bonuses, promises of land, or just promises because the army had nothing to begin with.

Enter George Washington, both ambitious and smart. He became its Commander and built a decent army from the rag-tag group. The Continental Army now had discipline but Washington had to overcome many things. Soldiers were low on the social scale and considered riff-raff. Both the British and the soon to be-Americans had desertions, starvation, low pay, and low morale. Washington established some pay.

At one point the enlistments for his men were up and they demanded hard currency, not Continentals. Washington begged and borrowed and was able to give them something, retaining about 1,400 which he desperately needed. Slaves often helped the British and later went to Canada. Martha often accompanied George during his winter encampments. However, the average daily ration for the Colonies was supposed to be:

1-1/2# flour or bread
1# beef/fish or 3/4# pork
1 gill whiskey (1/4 of a pint approximately – 4 oz)[3]

Battles ensued and a lot of unbelievable events happened, and it was similar to reading a fictional novel. First there was the Battle at Breeds Hill, which we know as Bunker Hill. The British had many losses and over the next months the British abandoned Boston and fled to Canada. Then, Lord Dunmore, the Royal Governor of Virginia fled from Williamsburg. Some slaves tried to side with England but early battles in Virginia and North Carolina predicated that England would be of no help. The colonists did have a victory in Charleston (then Charles Town).

Colonists were a nation of readers. They read Thomas Paine's *Common Sense,* pamphlet. It was an argument that America needed to break free and Americans would always be the children if they remained an English colony. King George was nothing but a bully. *Common Sense* ended with "the blood of the slain, the weeping voice of nature cries, tis time to depart, tis time to depart." It sold 125,000 copies and was a best seller of its generation. In today's market it would be 47.5 million books given relative populations as they were then. It asserted that the colonists had no choice, had made their decision, and turning back was a mistake.

This all led up to one document. It had to deal with war and explain why there was a war. The colonists created a committee to write a document and explain to the world why they were doing this. This document is the Declaration of Independence. It defines why we are what we are today and was dated July 4, 1776.

Jefferson wrote it because John Adams said Jefferson had a better handwriting. It took the principles from largely John Locke, a British seventeenth century philosopher and physician. He was the same Locke I mentioned in an earlier chapter who allied with Ashley Cooper and had land granted from Virginia to Florida. The Declaration of Independence is based on the theory that legitimate government is an agreement between people and their rulers. People are bound to obey laws only if the rulers provide protection. It is a called a Contract Theory of Government. Locke had two views of slavery.

The first was legitimate slavery which was captivity with forced labor imposed by the winning side in a war. Think about ancient civilizations and how the Trojans conquered the Romans or the Ottoman Empire. Once you conquered, you had a captive audience, and slaves.

The second was illegitimate slavery which was a dictatorial deprivation of natural rights. Locke didn't try to justify or explain either black slavery or the oppression of American Indians. It was his theory that caught everyone's attention.

He published Treatises that were printed in 1773 Boston. His thoughts on liberty and the social contract that existed were major influences in the American Revolution on the writings of Alexander Hamilton, Thomas Jefferson and James Madison. In fact, the Declaration of Independence quotes one passage from the Second Treatise.

Here are its parts:

Part I: Is the Propaganda piece. It states that King George is guilty of everything and there are exaggerations and lies. It explains why colonies are revolting, listing taxes, the standing army, harassment of citizens, and no trial by jury.

Part II: Jefferson explains what America is about. Power is in the people and it is not in the divine rights of kings. Just being born into kinghood in America won't cut it.

There are certain unalienable rights, (incapable of being denied or transferred), and these rights are: life, liberty and the pursuit of happiness.

Individuals have dignity and all men are created equal. This does not refer to females, natives, and blacks. It is only all white men. In his first draft, Jefferson did call for freedom for slaves but because of Southern opposition, he didn't do it.

When a government ceases to be responsible to a people, it is the right and responsible for people to overthrow. Revolution should be resorted to lightly, but it is then the people's right to throw off the government. (Herein Locke's "contract theory of government.)

The Declaration now needed something to create the form of government. This created a form of national government called the "Articles of Confederation," 1777. On one hand, this document was inevitable. On the other, it was an absolute disaster because it refused to have any central government. All of the power was given to colonies who would eventually become 13 states. We were not all Americans but members of our various colonies first. We had a long way to go until we became one.

The Articles had three major failures:

They created only one branch of government, the Legislature. Each state had one vote.

To amend the articles of confederation, required 13 votes, which was impossible.

The power to declare war was left up to states as was taxation, negotiating with Native Americans, and creating a military. This was understandable because they were rebelling against one central power. For example, North Carolina doesn't and didn't tell South Carolina what to do. It was a form of government that couldn't last.

During the Revolutionary War, England never allocated more than one-third of its military strength because it was impractical. England was 6,000 miles away, they were fighting with other European countries, and were much more concerned about keeping England secure. The Revolutionary War was unpopular in England and was the 1700s equivalent of the Viet Nam War. This was not a short war. It was fought fairly, got expensive, and dragged on and on. As it continued, people at home in England were getting annoyed.

We live in present-day America and have not witnessed wars on our soil in our own lifetimes. The Civil War was the last war fought here, and obviously no one is alive who witnessed it. We have only written, photo witness, and stories passed from generation to generation. This is what fighting was about during the Revolutionary War. I use the scene of many battles and my own back yard in North and South Carolina.

Battles ranging from Kings Mountain, now Kings Mountain National Park, North Carolina, Cowpens, and Camden were a few American victories. However, everything was at a cost. The costliest was Camden, South Carolina with a loss of 1,050 Colonists and 314 British. In Cowpens and Kings Mountain, 90 percent of the Brits were taken prisoners or died. The Brits didn't dedicate the power and you can't win with one-third of necessary military power. There were many, Loyalists or Tories, especially in the South, who did not want to fight, and remained loyal to the crown throughout the war. This was about 20 percent of the free population.

Just like future wars, you had a choice. You could fight for England, sit it out, or leave and go to Canada. What didn't occur in America was any kind of social revolution. The have nots didn't become the haves, slaves were not freed, and there was nothing different for those who weren't white men. The same people stayed in power. There was absolutely no change in class, or the economy. The War went on from 1775-1783. It was neighbor against neighbor. (Viet Nam lasted 25 years). It helped separate us into two countries: U.S. and British Canada.

There has never been accuracy as to the losses in the war. The counts are underestimated but the high count is: 25,000 Colonists and 24,000 British. (17,000 due to disease on the American side). Diseases were Malaria, Yellow Fever, Dysentery, and the worst, smallpox. Smallpox epidemics were commonplace. Smallpox is caused by a virus and spreads only from person to person. It can take up to fourteen days before a person exposed to the virus will show symptoms such as fever, headaches, body pains, and eventually the dreaded rash. The suffering is horrible and in the 1700s, people prayed for death, which usually occurred within two weeks. If someone survived, it could take up to a month to recover fully but they were left with scars, and lifetime immunity.

Remember the Columbian Exchange? European colonization introduced smallpox to the Americas in the late fifteenth and sixteenth centuries. Then, in a little more than three centuries, outbreaks only came sporadically in colonial America. In Europe, smallpox became endemic and by the early eighteenth century there was usually childhood exposure, and virtually the entire adult population became immune.

The American colonists, however, went for years without any exposure to smallpox. No exact figures were compiled as to the number of smallpox deaths during the Revolutionary War, but there is some indication that Washington's army lost more troops to it than in combat. Some scholars suggested that for every soldier who died in battle, ten or more died from some type of disease. Washington also survived smallpox. When traveling to Barbados in 1751, he contracted a mild case but he never keep a record, only retaining a scar on his nose.

To give you an idea of what fighting was like in your own back yard, follow me into the everyday war. Many soldiers were taken prisoner and one in every twenty able-bodied white man fought. Most figures show this was three percent of the population. Estimates disagree, since most fought in their own makeshift units and didn't belong to the Continental Army. People lived in small-isolated and remote communities and the British could be everywhere, even on your property.

This is a small example. Men were away for months and the women took care of things at home. In rural Chester County South Carolina, Jane White lived with her husband William and they had nine children. John was away during the fighting for long periods of time, because it was common to be gone months or even years at a time.

Battles were fought on private property, not huge battlefields. It was backcountry and the fighting was with unpaid volunteers. These were mountain men eager to fight for their cause. Cannon fire and muskets, were heard outside of homes. Boys 16 and younger joined while children as young as seven or eight became buglers, message carriers, or drummers while women became the head-of-household.

When Cornwallis' troops marched from Charlotte to Winnsboro, South Carolina, they took household goods, food, and Jane's clothes. Most women had one or two outfits at the time. Jane, feisty and furious as she was, went to headquarters and demanded her belongings, telling the soldiers that the day of payback was close. This work is from a book written in 1850 – *Women of the Revolution,* E. F. Ellet.

Women helped the war effort. Camp followers cooked and looked after the men but Washington considered them a burden because they had to be fed. Abigail Adams spoke out and told her husband to "remember the ladies" as they wanted rights also. Abigail was one of the first to advocate for women's rights! She also opposed slavery. When we move on to the number of slaves presidents owned, you will see that the Adams family owned none. Colonists were beginning to see how wrongful slavery had become as they were witnessing first hand that they were slaves subject to Britain and its whims.

Leaders called themselves Republicans (not Democrats). Republicanism came from Renaissance Europe and held that self-government by citizens or representatives provided a more stable foundation for the good of society and individual freedom than that of kings. It derived power from the people and the citizens were expected to sacrifice self-interest for the greater good.

The turning point of the war was the Battle of Saratoga in New York in 1777. France was convinced we could win and supported the colonies with treaties and support with trade and finally sending troops four months later. As a result, Spain and the Dutch Republic warred on Britain. Britain had a lot to deal with in Europe. The war became an International War.

In October 1781, the British surrendered at Yorktown. British General Charles Cornwallis brought 8,000 troops. They expected help from British ships coming from New York but the ships never arrived. The Treaty of Paris was finally signed nearly two years after the Battle at Yorktown. What took so long?

After the Battle of Yorktown, Britain's King George III did not think he could win the war anymore, but he still didn't want to give the American colonists independence from Great Britain. Please remember King George III and his disease of porphyria and his 400-word sentences. Well, America sent three men to Great Britain to work out the terms of the peace treaty. They were John Adams, John Jay, and Benjamin Franklin. It took them a great deal of time and effort to finally convince King George III that America wouldn't sign a peace treaty ending the Revolutionary War until that treaty included American independence from Great Britain. The details had to be accepted by the other parties involved who helped the American colonists, the French, the Spanish, and the Dutch, and they had their own agendas.

We did do a few things, before Paris. We finalized our national emblem. Ben Franklin wanted an American turkey because the turkey went back into ancient times when it was used as a symbol. A committee was set up with Franklin, Jefferson, Adams to accomplish our Great Seal and the only items that were kept from their suggestions were the E Pluribus Unum and the Eye of God. Franklin wanted a crowned pharaoh on a chariot, holding a sword dividing the waters of Red Sea after the Israelites passed. He envisioned a pillar of fire in a cloud which symbolized Divine presence, while Moses stood on the shore looking jubilant. Then there would be the statement, "Rebellion to tyrants is obedience to God." Fortunately, a compromise was reached.[4] Until 1956, E Pluribus Unum was considered our motto until we officially coined, IN GOD WE TRUST. The next time you look at a dollar bill, note the "eye" the "E Pluribus Unum" which means "out of many, one," think about frugal Franklin and our forefathers' dilemma!

In Paris, a peace treaty was signed on September 3, 1783. John Adams (who became our second president), Ben Franklin, and John Jay (first chief justice U.S. Supreme Court) negotiated it. An aside on wise-ole grandfatherly Ben Franklin was that he was not your typical grandpa. Remember what I told you about Ben previously? Contrary to what history books tell us, Ben was quite the ladies' man and would probably be called an adulterer in today's world. Reading his autobiography, I got no indication of this but after researching found that this is now public knowledge. Review the sources footnoted prior for further information if you would like to read a bit more. Ben was quite a hit in Paris and spent much of the last years of his life on the Seine River.

The Treaty of Paris did a couple of things. First, it involved how England would now treat America. It recognized American independence to the Mississippi River. England said it would leave the already built forts and stop constructing new forts. It said it would treat America as a trade partner the same way they treated everyone else and would allow America to sail off the coast of Canada and England to trade and American ships on high seas would not be stopped unless they posed a threat.

The Americans in turn decided they would pay their debt and pay back all they owed, going back years. We agreed to return confiscated property to the

Loyalists. We also agreed to restore rights to Loyalists if they had stayed or returned and would treat them with equality.

On September 3, 1783, the treaty was signed, and it was ratified in 1784. In a short period of time, people saw the devastation and asked if that was what they fought and died for. Independence was not all it was cracked up to be. There were 900,000 square miles and the population was three million, and to top it off, there was a weak form of government. The question was, "Did Americans really gain independence?"

Summary

There were many issues but the two which will linger and cause problems for centuries follow. There was Virtual vs. Actual Representation and State's Rights vs. Federal Laws. We still argue about them today. Once the would-be Americans got into the war, the country was divided between those who remained loyal to the British, known as the Tories or Loyalists, and those who wanted freedom known as the Whigs or Patriots.

Other nations urged the colonists to fight. They hoped the colonists would win and as a result the new nation would be so poor and unorganized, that they could step in and take over. However, that was not the case despite the fact that after they declared the Declaration of Independence, a weak form of government was formed under the Articles of Confederation. Finally, there was the Treaty of Paris.

What did the new Americans gain? 900,000 square miles of land, 3 million people to be governed, and a totally weak government. Was America truly independent, or would we have to revamp, find a new form of government, and fight another war?

Chapter 8

Building Our Own Nation

We now had the Treaty of Paris in 1783. The form of government in the 13 states was the Articles of Confederation. Why did our forefathers create a government with so many limitations? The articles reflected very clearly what they wanted...a weak central government. The Government was conventional but it didn't work. Absolute power existed within the states themselves. This had long been a conflict of state's rights vs federal rights and we see it today increasingly in our twenty-first century.

Was the American Revolution truly over? Americans were excited that the Mississippi River was now the border of this new country. There were barges on the mighty Mississippi which could bring goods down the river to New Orleans rather than overland to the east coast. Although its origin was in what is now northern Minnesota, and it flowed down to New Orleans for over 2,300 miles, there was one problem.

The Spanish owned the Port of New Orleans and no European country would give America a break. Farmers were angry, to say the least, and went to the Confederation Congress on the Articles of Confederation but they had no power to do anything about it. From very beginning, the Port of New Orleans was closed. If you're involved in trade across the Atlantic, it's worse.

Our America

The British stopped our trading with others and the other Europeans did the same because they too were not getting along with others, e.g., Spain, France.

It's one thing being stopped by British and maybe France, Spain, and the Dutch, but bandit pirates were overpowering American ships. Pirates have existed for centuries, collecting their toll and tribute and they were ruthless. One thing though, because the British were still the most powerful nation on the globe, pirates didn't mess with these British ships. The Americans, however, were a different story because no one was afraid of America. All of the nations wanted her to fail and then they could step in and take over.

Congress fled Philadelphia in fear because they were told an enemy army was coming to conquer them. The army was "The Americans," veterans of the American Revolution who were marching because they were never paid. They weren't paid because Congress had no power to pay them. Congress could only give states quotas which were useless because the federal government was powerless. States gave them nothing. As a result, there was no budget. Reality was sinking in and Americans asked once again, "Is this what we fought and died for?" America was weak, everyone wanted her to fail, and things were bad.

Remember what I stated earlier, that history repeats itself. When we witness the twentieth century, you'll see how the veterans from World War I marched on Washington in 1932 demanding their pensions. This was called the Bonus March and they wanted cold cash to redeem their certificates that called for payment in 1945. They wanted to put food on their tables. The war had-ended in 1919 with the Treaty of Versailles and to wait another 25 years was insane especially since America was in the midst of the Great Depression.

The American Revolution did not accomplish a social revolution and the greatest fear was that one might occur soon. People were angry: farmers, vets, merchants, businessmen, and even George Washington. Thirty to forty percent of those fighting were casualties. In 1786-87, one Massachusetts farmer had enough. Daniel Shays, was finding out that he and friends were about to lose their farms under repossession. Most farmers were heavily in debt and were infuriated because of unfair taxes which discriminated against them. Shays organized a small militia, which was like an army.

They decided to march to Boston. On the way, word spread and the Massachusetts militia marched towards them. Both sides fled after guns were fired, but the media called it Shay's Rebellion. It amounted to nothing but it was just the belief that went into symbolism or an image. Does this sound familiar? Its importance is that if Shay could organize, so could someone else. It was symbolic of the discontent of our growing nation and shouted, "Wake up America." For the most part, the Articles of Confederation were a failure, but it was a start and we needed to try again. What would America do?

Two important things came from the articles. The first was the Land Ordinance of 1785, aka the Northwest Ordinances. There were three of them. If you were fearless enough to leave one of the 13 colonies and went to undeveloped territory, you had no idea of what you were in store for. Everyone was a squatter or speculator and Native Americans still possessed their lands. This Ordinance, however, was the first systematic survey of all the land in the West. For clarity, the West was really what we call today, the Midwest. The West Coast, which we consider West, was still unknown territory.

The Land Ordinance established reasonable and organized procedures for surveying land north of the Ohio River on a Grid System. It created six-mile by six-mile blocks of land, divided into smaller blocks of 36 sections. The cost for a grid of 640 Acres was $1 an acre in hard currency. Each had a specific purpose, e.g., some reserved for vets, highest bidder, several for current military to protect, small block for public education, others for whatever. It was designed on the New England system to keep the shiftless and "undesirables" out and settle this land with "enterprising" individuals and families who could afford it. Although Native Americans still occupied the area, squatters came by the thousands.

This created a survey system that eventually covered three-quarters of the area of the continental United States. It stayed in effect until 1782 when the Homestead Act was passed.

The Northwest Ordinance of 1787 put forth criteria so people knew their rights. United States territory created by Congress in 1787 was the region lying west of Pennsylvania, north of the Ohio River, east of the Mississippi River, and south of the Great Lakes. Virginia, New York, Connecticut, and Massachusetts had claims to this area, which they ceded to the central government between 1780 and 1800. It defined the steps for the creation of new territories and eventually states. It also forbade slavery while the area was still a territory, leaving it wide open for slavery when and if statehood was established. Most people had no idea of the perimeters and looked to settle in uninhabited land.

Our America

It went like this. When area met 5,000 people it was regarded as a territory and the government would give that territory a territorial governor, secretary of state, and a territorial judge. When the territory reached 60,000, they could write a constitution and apply for admission into the union as an equal to the 13 states. This would be the same level as the 13 colonies. This guaranteed that the territory could eventually come into the union and be equal to the original colonies, while it also guaranteed Northwest expansion. The important thing was since there was to be no slavery, it set the precedent for dividing lines.

Americans needed some direction. The call went out for a conference and 55 delegates from 13 states traveled to Independence Hall in Philadelphia. All of the states attended except Rhode Island. The assembly started in May 1787 and secrecy was mandatory. This was not a typical meeting, because its intention was to revise the Articles of Confederation. Very quickly the men learned that the articles were beyond repair.

One of the greatest things about America is that we all have our own opinions and it's or right to differ, peacefully! There were three schools of thought. The first was that everything was wonderful and nothing needed to be changed. The second opinion was that the articles needed some minor improvement. The third was to throw everything out and start all over.

The delegates were off to a star-crossed start. First, weather conditions were unbelievable. It was a long and hot summer. Windows were nailed shut, and for five long months, in the heat, they argued, fought, and compromised. Delegates from both the North and South, free and slave states, farmers, and commercial businesses, all had their own ideas but made a couple decisions quickly.

George Washington was chosen to lead it. Have you ever looked at portraits of Washington? He had that cold and threatening stare. Washington banged on the table, stood up to his full height of 6'2" and would stare people down by intimidating them. The second decision was to elect James Madison who had a nickname of bird legs, or "Bird" for short.

Madison had formulated the Virginia Plan eleven years earlier and this was a bias. The plan was presented by Edmund Randolph to the Constitutional Convention on in 1787. The Virginia Plan proposed a strong central government with some uniqueness. There would be three branches: legislative, executive, and judicial. Madison is often referred to as "The Father of the Constitution." There was also a New Jersey Plan which wanted a strong central government but called for equal power among states, whether they were large or small. Think about it – what would happen today if there was equal power between all states and population didn't count?[1]

Connecticut Representative, Roger Sherman, suggested a compromise. The Senate would treat all states equally but the House would reflect population differences. The Great Compromise also hammered out a solution of how to count slaves for both tax and representation purposes. It brought about some important points but first and foremost was taxes and representation. Since the South had 3 million slaves, the question was, "Are they property?"

The answer was yes, since the most important assets for southern gentlemen were land and slaves. How do you tax property and if they are property, should they count as representation? Hence, the Three-Fifths Compromise was agreed upon. The Three-Fifths Compromise made slaves three-fifths of a person, but Native Americans didn't count. Now, three-fifths of the slave population were considered for taxes and representation. Keep in mind the diversification of the men at the meeting and understand points of view. Once again, it was the federal government wanting its due and yet the whole idea put forth was that people were property!

The delegates agreed trade legislation would require only a simple majority of Congress and Congress gained fiscal powers. Southerners received a 20-year protection for further slave importation. Slave importation, not slavery, was not outlawed until 1807, taking effect in 1808 which was the earliest date permitted to forbid Importation.

In the final compromise, the delegates, with Washington in mind, set up an executive branch allowing the president "discretionary" powers. A Supreme Court would be approved, but its powers were yet to come.

The document that emerged was the United States Constitution. It was a creation that consisted of negotiation, cooperation, and concession. It was the Great Compromise which was ratified 1788 and effective in 1789. When the delegates left Philadelphia, the whole country debated the issue.

The struggle over ratification of the Constitution was dramatic and passionate. There were the Federalists who supported the document, against the Anti-federalists who opposed it because they were suspicious of any type of strong government. Some of the Anti-federalists such as Patrick Henry, Elbridge Gerry, and George Mason had been Patriots. Ultimately, the Federalists succeeded because of their political knowhow and they quickly got their point across. There was the power of the written word. James Madison, Alexander Hamilton, and John Jay banded together and published a series of essays, the *Federalist Papers,* to convince the masses. They all feared that failure would doom the nation and to a position worse than being English subjects.

The Anti-Federalists believed the states had given up too much power to the central government under the constitution and they pushed for and received protections under the Bill of Rights.

Summary

Finally, the Constitution of the United States of America as a result of the Great Compromise was created. America had a good plan for its government. Will the three branches of government solve everything: Executive, Legislative, and Judicial? It's a start and the Bill of Rights added to the Constitution's strength.

Not everything was perfect, however, and there was the beginning of an idea of parties. There were the Federalists and the Anti-Federalists. It went back to the question of which had more power, the feds or the states?

The issue of slavery was always the hot topic in government and in the South. How would the government tax slaves who were considered property? A short-term solution was the Three-Fifths Compromise. How about new states, slave or free? By the way, the Brits still maintained their presence here in America.

Sandi Ludwa

Chapter 9

The Constitution and Bill of Rights

We the People of the United States, in Order to form a more perfect Union, establish Justice, insure domestic Tranquility, provide for the common defense, promote the general Welfare, and secure the Blessings of Liberty to ourselves and our Posterity, do ordain and establish this Constitution for the United States of America.

Preamble to the United States Constitution

The product of compromise was the United States Constitution. Thirty-nine delegates signed the basis of our nation in one document. Getting back to slavery, a major issue that was worked out and compromised, and the diversification of the group, brings us to which presidents owned slaves.

Our first president, George Washington, owned somewhere between 250-350 slaves, which is more than any of the presidents. In his will, he affirmed that when Martha died his 123 slaves were to be freed. Keep in mind, there were additional slaves who would also go to the Custis heirs. There was one problem and it was fear. Martha was terrified that she would be murdered because she dwelled upon the idea that there would be a slave rebellion. Why would she fear?

Well, she was all alone. All of her children from her first marriage to Daniel Parke Custis had already died. Martha was so grieved when George died, that she didn't attend his funeral ceremony at Mount Vernon, until four days after he died. George insisted he be laid out for three days after his death just in case he really wasn't dead. He had Taphophobia, a fear of being buried alive. I would imagine being with him for that four days could take its toll.

Then, there was this huge mysterious fire that erupted at Mount Vernon. Martha was constantly afraid of a slave rebellion, so a little more than a year after George's death, she freed them. She did, however, die in the following year, 1802.[2]

Back to the presidents....Both Thomas Jefferson and Andrew Jackson had 200 enslaved, followed by James Madison, James Monroe, Zachary Taylor, and John Tyler who owned up to 100. The remaining presidents had few but remember one thing, out of the first twelve presidents, only the Adams family (John Adams and John Quincy Adams), owned none.

The second issue with the new Constitution was the system of checks and balances so that one branch didn't dominate another. Does this sound familiar today? Could the Judicial Branch overturn a law put forth by the Legislature?

The third was that the government could tax, regulate trade, conduct foreign relations, and create an army and navy. Taxes were necessary, as was trade internally and externally, but countries always needed protection in the form of armies and navies which must be government supported. The Constitution gave the small states power equal to the large states with two votes each in the Senate or upper house. Now, the House of Representatives went according to population.

The huge difference between the Articles of Confederation and the new form of government, was that the Constitution represented citizens directly, whereas the Articles of Confederation acted upon the states. Our new government was extremely powerful. In September 1787, the representatives needed at least 9 of 13 states to approve it. Three states, Delaware, New Jersey, and Pennsylvania, ratified right away with Connecticut and Georgia following.

Massachusetts dilly-dallied and Virginia said no because it didn't represent the people. The delegates went back to the drawing board and out of this came the Bill of Rights which is the first ten amendments to the Constitution. It was enacted in 1789 but not ratified until 1791. The Anti-Federalists, those against a strong Federal Government, pushed it. They believed it didn't represent the normal, rural, everyday Joe. These were men such as Patrick Henry and Edmund Randolph. There are presently 27 Amendments.

Let's get back to what the Constitution and Bill of Rights mean. Grab a chair, and let's analyze the meanings and really think about how controversial they are today.

Look at the words, "We the people," and remember that's you and me. This is Our America.

Amendment 1:

The First Amendment protects the rights of every American and defines our freedoms of religion, speech, and press. It guarantees our rights of freedom of press, religion, assembly and addresses grievances. Everyone argued as to interpretation. We can say, write, and publicize our opinions and beliefs but what about falsified information? There are liable suits, bitter arguments, and questions as to how far this goes. We can assemble, but what about the violence? What our forefathers meant about religion was there would be no national religion. There was a separation of church and state. What does the word "freedom" imply?

Amendment 2:

The Second Amendment guarantees Americans the right to bear arms, or own guns. This is a hot topic today with gun control. Every state has its own gun laws and when this was originally written it represented national laws without consideration of what states would ultimately do.

Amendment 3:

The Third Amendment prevents the government from forcing citizens to shelter soldiers in their homes. Remember the Quartering Act?

Amendment 4:

The Fourth Amendment protects privacy and prohibits unnecessary or unreasonable searches of a person's property. Remember search warrants?

Amendment 5:

In the Fifth Amendment, all Americans are guaranteed the right to a fair and legal trial. It also protects someone from testifying against him or herself under oath. Controversial?

Amendment 6:

A right to a speedy trial is guaranteed in the Sixth Amendment. What is considered speedy today?

Amendment 7:

The Seventh Amendment guarantees the right to a trial by jury in civil, or private, legal cases where damages are more than $20. Civil cases solve disputes between citizens.

Amendment 8:

Unreasonable bail or fines and cruel and unusual punishment are prohibited in the Eighth Amendment. Is the death penalty cruel and unusual?

Amendment 9:

The Ninth Amendment recognizes that Americans have rights that are not listed in the Constitution. This one is broad. Unwritten, court cases, state laws, confusing?

Amendment 10:

The Tenth Amendment says that the powers not given to the United States government by the Constitution belong to the states or to the people. Now this one is very controversial and states' rights became the issue prior to the Civil War.

    The bottom line was that the Federalists supported it and the Anti-Federalists were leery of a strong central government. However, it did ratify with 11 colonies while Rhode Island and North Carolina said no. Once government started getting created, these two states ratified it. To explain it to the people of the United States, as I mentioned earlier, several of our founding fathers, Hamilton, Madison, and Jay, wrote the *Federalist Papers* which explained the Constitution. Our first government was created and George Washington was our first President He chose an all-star cabinet and we had the first Congress and Supreme Court.

We now had a document binding 13 states together that the Articles of Confederation could not have done. **We are the United States of America**. We are Americans and not colonists. Our Constitution has only been amended 27 times in all of these years. Ten of 26 happened right then and there. Over 200 plus years have passed and it only changed 17 times although over 11,000 amendments have been proposed. The last time was in 1992 and it was the Twenty-seventh Amendment about pay raises for Congress.

The most important amendments after the first ten are the thirteenth, fourteenth, and fifteenth. These deal with the rights of freedmen and the abolition of slavery.

The State of the Nation

We were still at odds with the British but in 1790 we conducted our first census. There were 4,000,000 Americans and one quarter of them lived in New England. The Puritans didn't assimilate and few new settlers came to the area. Diversity was extremely limited because of poor soil and the cold and harsh New England winters. Blacks and Indians were a tiny percent of the population, and slavery was unacceptable. Women outnumbered men, but their rights were extremely limited. Freedom and equality was for all white males. A female's duty was to bear good Republican sons and serve the male-dominated society. After all, this was "New England."

In the American South, it was a different story. The climate was ideal for tobacco, rice, and cotton. Thomas Jefferson, guardian of liberty, was genuine in this beliefs when he said, "In a warm climate no man will work for himself, who can make another labor for him."

Blacks outnumbered the deep South's whites five to one but were less in the foothills where they were not a necessity. Political differences of opinion between gentry and backcountry small farmers were an everyday occurrence.

According to the Constitution, "all men were created equal" and backcountry folk, all white men, took this to heart.

The American West which was now the area between the Appalachian Mountains and the Mississippi, was the fastest growing part of the country. There were clashes between whites and Indians with frequent attacks. Some tribes such as the Ohio Miami's and Alabama Creek's blocked settlement of whites. We'll visit the cowboy towns in the Old West in one of our journeys, but now we are building our nation and hoping to solidify our growing differences.

Sons of planters bought slaves while poor immigrants came alone to the region. Both grasped the idea of unclaimed land. Squatters occupied the land with no legal title, hoping someday to get a clear title.

Summary

The Constitution should be read. Everything in it relates to many of our disagreements today. Times were different then, but the Constitution still holds true and we realize the commitment made by those who went before us. George Washington became the first president. Americans were happy, or were they still rebellious? There were still hostilities with the Natives as Americans wanted more and more land. Americans were moving West. The nation became sectionalized. The South remained agricultural and the North became further industrialized and the South's bookkeepers.

Everyone had a role. Women had their duties. Slavery reigned in the South where new immigrants rarely came. Why would they? Some clarification on slavery is needed. There were slaves in the North but it was different than the South. Since agriculture was not primary, people were put to work in other capacities because of the area's technology. Slaves were owned by the elites, the doctors, ministers, and merchants and were often household workers or skilled in jobs. Often having a slave was a status symbol. It wasn't until 1804 when most northern states outlawed the practice.

Chapter 10

Politics and the Election of 1800

In 1788-1789 from December to January Electors voted. Each state had Electors equal to their representation in Congress with two votes each. They would cast them for President but one vote had to be for a candidate not of their state. There were no political parties, just those with the differences of opinions, Federalists and Anti-Federalists.

The Constitution established an Electoral College wherein each elector would cast two votes, with no distinction made between electoral votes for president and electoral votes for vice president. This was modified in 1804 through the ratification of the Twelfth Amendment. The different states had various ways for choosing presidential electors. Many states held a popular vote, but in other states, the state legislature appointed the electors.

Our first president, George Washington, was of no party. There was no formal nomination process, and it was assumed that Washington would be the first president. Opposition was nil since Washington was considered essential in operating the new government. The first vice president was John Adams and the secretary of state was Thomas Jefferson. This is the order of the first three presidents. Hamilton was also in the cabinet but since he was not born in the United States, he could not become president. However, he was given the post of the secretary of treasury.

In 1789, Washington was sworn in. America's white population was 200,000 plus and Native Americans were only 150,000. Remember, I told you there were 7 million Native Americans in the U.S. and Canada when Columbus came?

Who was this man Washington who was called his highness until the cabinet settled upon Mr. President during Jefferson's term? He never shook hands with the public but bowed instead and yet, the people loved Washington the war hero, charismatic and yet stern. His 6'2" height and his bold stare certainly demanded attention. He held the spotlight in difficult times but unlike his stern expression, he could be a fun-loving guy. He didn't like to be touched, but after-all, he did love his dogs, petted them, and what's so bad about someone who loves animals? Although he has been criticized as having only a normal IQ, he used common "horse sense" and was down to earth in any situation that demanded it.[3]

Many said he was not the genius they expected him to be. He was not your typical life of the party but was reserved and painstakingly did his work. He never commanded a real national army that was well-organized, had plenty of money, and had decent equipment, so he was not your typical commander. When he looked at our troops who were bare-footed, hungry, and never in the best of moods, Washington became frustrated and knew he wasn't the best qualified for the position. He thought very carefully about any decisions he made and studied every situation before he gave a final decision. Herein lies his success. Humbled at his position, forced him to make the best decisions he could put forth for the good of the country and the men.[4]

His poor teeth affected him during his life but they were not wooden, contrary to belief. They were horse or cow teeth, or possibly elephant ivory, lead-tin alloy, copper alloy which could have been brass, or silver alloy. However, he did have a good head of hair and didn't wear wigs. No, he did not chop down a cherry tree and Martha did not spend her life baking cherry pies. Washington grew up poor, became a land-surveyor, inherited Mount Vernon when his brother died, and increased its acreage.

Washington was self-educated, fought in the French and Indian War, unanimously chosen president, served two terms, and married Martha Dandridge Custis, a widow, who was only a few months older Washington. Twenty-six-year-old, 5'2" tall Martha was an ideal matrimonial candidate and brought a great deal of wealth to the marriage. She had an 18,000-acre estate, from which George personally received 6,000 acres and 300 slaves. With this huge acreage and land that he was granted for his military service, Washington became one of the wealthier landowners in Virginia. Before Martha, George had another woman in mind but she wasn't interested.

Martha's two young children, John (Jacky) and Martha (Patsy), ages six and four, came from her first marriage at 19. Patsy died just before the Revolution and Jacky died during the Revolution, so George adopted two of his children. George was sterile and he and Martha had none together. They did have a bunch of dogs: Truelove, Sweetlips, Mopsy, Drunkard, Tipler, Madam Moose, Scentwell, Dabster and Droner. They were Foxhounds, Coonhounds, Greyhounds, Spaniels and a few more breeds.[5]

Washington became the president but Jefferson and Hamilton made his life a living-hell. Does this sound familiar today? They had opposite views of what America was to be. Jefferson believed America's future was the farmers, and agriculture should continue to be the major occupation in our country, slavery accepted. Even though he was secretary of state, he was a southerner and was suspicious of a strong central government. Jefferson believed that power should always be with people in the states and that America would continue to be common people. We will talk more about Jefferson. He led a most-interesting life.

I'll reiterate on the condition of the country at this time. In the South there were slaves, tobacco, cotton, rice, and the slaves outnumbered whites 5-1. The Scots-Irish came and settled the South and the culture was far different than that of the North. In the West, which was from the Appalachians to the Mississippi River, this had become the fastest growing area in the nation. There was a great deal of conflict between the whites and the Native Americans. The planters brought slaves while the immigrants came alone. Everyone was a squatter with no legal title. The North, however, had developed industry, banking, trade, and large cities. Hamilton saw the larger picture and that America was no longer just a group of colonies in the East. It was rapidly expanding every day and money was at the top of the list.

Hamilton was from New York. He was born illegitimately in the West Indies and came to America with "a little help from his friends." He was a hard worker and tried to make up for fact he had no family connections to brag about and help him along. But, when he married into a wealthy New York family, became educated in New York, and became friends with George Washington, it helped his rise in politics. When the Revolutionary War erupted, he enlisted in the Continental Army and became Washington's closest aid and friend.

He was a "rags to riches" story. Hamilton impressed many but believed the future was in industry, commerce, technology, and in urban areas with the growth of cities. Hamilton believed the role model that United States should follow was England, which meant a powerful army and navy, command of high seas, and most wealthy nation in world.

There were two opposite polar approaches. The first thing they did was to pass a series of laws to correct what the Articles of Confederation didn't do. The first was money. America started making people pay for the right and privilege of trading in the U.S. through taxes and tariffs. A tariff is a tax on imported goods and it is supposed to protect American business. Yes, consumers pay more for foreign goods, but Americans don't have to reduce prices to remain competitive and sell their products. They are deemed "protective." The government, in effect, makes more money.

The United States was in a great position, much improved over the Articles of Confederation. Hamilton distrusted his fellow citizens and believed people needed to be instructed to take the right path. He was street-smart, intelligent, and ambitious but at this time he couldn't become president because he was not born in the U.S. In his "Hamiltonian financial plan" he advocated several things.

Hamilton said the Federal Government would assume all the debts the states owed from the war. He thought this would create financial stability and not 13 separate economies. A National Bank could do all of that. It would not be symbolic but a physical bank. Of course, Hamilton would be the head of it. The bank would grant subsidies and give loans.

Hamilton was extremely powerful and believed the feds also must be the iron-hand that ruled. Jefferson, however, disagreed with all of Hamilton's beliefs and thought that government shouldn't be that powerful.

Meanwhile, Washington was in the middle as Jefferson and Hamilton argued. Jefferson said that Hamilton needed to show him in the Constitution where his government beliefs were stated. Jefferson was a literalist because he interpreted everything literally. Jefferson concluded Hamilton's plan was poor. Hamilton said things were "implied" and did not have to be said. It was Literal vs. Implied.

Hamilton's program caused a congressional debate and an insurrection called the Whiskey Rebellion, a.k.a., the Whiskey Insurrection. It was a protest against the Whiskey Tax during Washington's presidency. The colonists were never a nation of teetotalers and this one hit a sour note. It was the first tax imposed by the new government placed on a domestic good. Washington was livid and hated this dissent. He asserted this would be resolved only through the new constitutional government. This was the first challenge to the new federal authority.

It was Hamilton who created the Doctrine of Implied Powers. Every president up to the present day seems to get in trouble with this one. In the case of the United States government, implied powers are the powers exercised by Congress which are not plainly stated by the Constitution itself but deemed necessary and appropriate to execute the powers.

Then we had a huge compromise that came about in 1790. Likewise, it was called the Compromise of 1790 and was the only one between Jefferson and Hamilton. Hamilton wanted the national government to take over and pay state debts but Jefferson did not. Then there was the issue of the capital of the United States which had been New York and Philadelphia, both in the North. Jefferson said if it could be moved to the south, e.g., Virginia, he would throw his support to the plan. Land was purchased to form a "District of Columbia." The compromise was successful and we now had our federal government paying debts and our capital in Washington D.C.

There were more items to be worked out. Washington believed that the United States should never meddle in European affairs, and there should never be any political parties. The problem was already in existence and political parties by this time were formed. Hamilton had the Federalist mentality which became a political party, while Jefferson became an Anti-Federalist, (Democratic Republican).

Then there was the issue of Impressment. This was the practice of forcing men who were on ships to provide their services into their own particular navy. Crew members would be "pressed" into service. The British and French were still actively pressing many into their service and the United States was in an undeclared war with both navies. In our modern age, occurrences are much the same. We do nothing in government to officially declare wars.

George Washington was fed up after two terms as president and decided to go back to Mount Vernon. He could have stayed president forever because the American public loved him. Washington established a precedent for two terms and it was not until Franklin D. Roosevelt that this changed. Roosevelt is the only president who broke with this and was elected four times (1932, 36, 40, 44).

Nevertheless, in his famous "Farewell Address" Washington warned against permanent foreign alliances and the growth of political parties. He also said disunity would come from within our country and not from foreign powers. He warned about yellow journalism, national debt, and the threat of presidents whose egos were more important than national interest. Do you think Washington could predict the future?

Let's watch the next three elections of 1796, 1800, and 1804 where things rapidly change. It's 1796, Washington was gone, and John Adams, a Federalist, was selected. Electors still selected a president. This was the only election in which there was a president and vice president from two different parties. Jefferson became the vice president, as a Democratic Republican. Adams won by three votes and Jefferson was the second highest vote getter.

The Electoral College was not as we know it today. We still had electors or representatives from every state who cast the votes. Some states still appointed electors while others allowed voting. When the electors cast their ballot, the man with most votes became president and the one with second highest became vice president, regardless of political party. Now, we had two opposites and a very close election of 71-68 votes. This was prior to the Twelfth Amendment's adoption in 1804. Once again, the office of vice president was awarded to the presidential candidate who won the second-largest number of votes, regardless of which political party he represented.

In the presidential election of 1796, for example, voters chose John Adams, who was a Federalist, to be president. Thomas Jefferson, who was a Democratic-Republican, was the runner-up in the vote count and became vice president to Adams.

The fighting between powerful men and presidents and vice presidents continued. Adams and Jefferson fought about everything and nothing changed until 1804. There were no distinct parties and it was not until 1824 that popular vote was considered and each state nominated by candidate.

While Adams was president, he and Jefferson grew to hate each other; but once they left office, they began a 25-year correspondence. The irony was that on July 4, 1826, the last words Adams said was "Thomas Jefferson still survives," although Jefferson had died earlier in day. Both died on the fiftieth anniversary of the Declaration of Independence, July 4, 1826.

John Adams then emerged (1735-1826). He had a problem that many future presidents would also encounter. Besides the fact that he was snooty, he was nothing like his predecessor. Americans didn't like him because he wasn't George Washington. Adams talked down to people and was destined for failure – France vs England. He committed political suicide by the Alien and Sedition Acts. This made it illegal to criticize the United States government or the president and it also severely restricted immigration. Alien and Sedition violated the Constitution and its freedom of speech and press. Can you imagine such a law today? At one time or another, we would all be put in a locked cell.

Nevertheless, he had a wife named Abigail who was a women's rights advocate, and was the first presidential wife to live in the White House. They had six children and had married even though Abigail's mother thought John was beneath her! The Adams's did oppose slavery and owned no slaves![6]

We now had the emergence of parties, each with their own supporting groups. Hamilton's Federalists supported business, speculators, and the large commercial farmers. There were the Republicans, Jefferson and Madison, who believed in the Southern Planters and the Scots-Irish farmers. The differences between the classes was huge and by 1796 there was a lot of rivalry which was growing.[7]

In 1798, because of the dissent and the Alien and Sedition Act, the federal government was at an all-time danger and there were talks of nullification. In 1799, Patrick Henry delivered his last speech. He was 63 years old and in poor health. Throughout his life he was renown as being a great orator, but this speech was his most difficult. George Washington had begged him to run for the state legislature and he had become a Federalist. Let us go to the scene.

It is March 4, 1799 and Henry is struggling to complete his mission and deliver his heart-felt speech to the Virginia Legislature. Henry thinks to himself that he is remembered for his statements 25 years ago, but now, it is an effort to attend while traveling over 20 miles from his home in Red Hill. He knows he will soon pass on from what we now know as stomach cancer. The 63-year old struggles to get up to the podium as he has been seated during John Randolph's speech. Randolph was also running for the legislature.

There are throngs of people, citizens, university students, and congressmen. Everyone knows that this is their last chance to hear the famous patriot and orator. He looks worn and there is a sort-of grayish cast in his face. His voice is cracking but he gains momentum and becomes involved in the words. They are from his heart. There is an almost "supernatural" light in his eyes. In his speech, he addresses the issues but is appealing for unity to preserve the union. We are mesmerized and cannot remember most of the words, but I jot down some that will remain with me. He asserts:

"Let us trust God and our better judgment to set us right hereafter. United we stand, divided we fall. Let us not split into factions which must destroy that union upon which our existence hangs. Let us preserve our strength for the French, the English, the Germans, or whoever else shall dare invade our territory, and not exhaust it in civil commotions and intestine wars."

He steps down from the podium and the crowd embraces him. He is so fatigued that they are carrying him to a nearby tavern to "rest." Two months later, he died. He did win the election but could never serve the term.[8]

Let's fast forward to 1800. The Election of 1800 was called "The Revolution of 1800." There was the Federalist and the Democratic-Republic Party formed by Jefferson and Madison. From 1792 through 1824 this period was considered the First Party System, which was sectionalized and often based on a candidate's popularity and social status. It represented the two parties and represented whomever was in control. The Federalists were in control until 1800 and beyond that it was the Democratic-Republicans. During this time, they were both competing for the Presidency.

As the Republicans went towards the Planters and farmers, the Federalists lured the Businessmen. It was the first time that a government of a country went to the opposition without one drop of blood being shed. Jefferson became our third president and the Federalists didn't suffer at all. Jefferson said, " We are all Republicans; We are all Federalists; We are all Americans." It demonstrated the fact that government can move from one group to another without bloodshed.

When Adams was up for re-election in 1800, it went to the House of Representatives and Jefferson won by 36 votes. It was a disaster. Thomas Jefferson and Aaron Burr both ran as Democratic-Republicans. Each legislator cast their two votes. Adams received 63 electoral votes, while Jefferson and Burr tied with 73. The Constitution stated if an election was not resolved it was to be thrown into the House of Representatives for the final decision.

The situation was that most of the House hated Jefferson but they loathed Burr. Burr's reputation was that he was power-hungry and would do whatever necessary, ethical or not, to achieve his goals. They claimed Jefferson was a drunkard, an enemy of religion who advocated separation of church and state, and the father of numerous mulatto children. The House was concerned that there could be a reign of terror to eliminate opposition, just how it was run in Europe. It was suggested there was a "back-room-deal" but after the thirty-sixth ballot, Jefferson got the position. The Constitution was soon amended so this would not happen again. Burr was livid.

Summary

George Washington, our first president, had his work cut out for him. He had his views but it was a constant battle between his Secretary of State, Thomas Jefferson, and Secretary of Treasury, Alexander Hamilton. John Adams, who became the second president stood in the limelight while Jefferson and Hamilton battled it out. It was a case of Federalist vs. Anti-Federalist and they agreed on nothing. Is this like our Democratic and Republican Parties of today?

At any rate, after two terms Washington had it and he went home to Mount Vernon, attempting to get some peace and quiet. He had never expected Washington DC to be such a political hell. In his farewell address he warned the country about events that could shatter it in the future. Was Washington a brilliant man or could he foresee the future?

Washington was a tough act to follow and John Adams was never popular with the American people. He further infuriated them with the Alien and Sedition Acts. No one could speak up against the government. It was a violation of the basic freedoms of speech and press, wasn't it? He didn't own slaves, however, and this was one bright point about him. By the turn of the century, there was political turmoil. Patrick Henry delivered his final speech which attempted to instill patriotism and solidarity into Americans.

When the election of 1800 was underway, it turned into another feud. When Jefferson and Burr were tied, the election was thrown into the House and Jefferson was picked. Burr was livid. This would set-off some dark events in American History as a result of the election because of Burr's rage at the decision.

Chapter 11

Politics, Discontent, and Another War?

"The government that governs least, governs best."
...Thomas Jefferson

In 1799, George Washington died. Adams was out of office and Thomas Jefferson took command. The century turned to 1800. Thomas Jefferson was president and he was different than his predecessors. He and Burr had the same number of votes but Jefferson applied and got the position because he was better suited. Jefferson started the title of Mr. President. He brought the position down to the average Joe. He was amazing and interested in everything. Gone were the days when seating was designated by importance because Jefferson believed in round tables and the first to arrive earned the best seats, regardless of who you were.

He was president for eight years and at Monticello where he is buried, he designed his own tombstone and wrote his own epitaph. Jefferson never even mentioned the presidency because in life at all times he regarded himself as a public servant. It states,

"Author of the Declaration of Independence [and] of the Statute of Virginia for religious freedom & Father of the University of Virginia."

He was what today we would call a Renaissance Man. Jefferson was an architect, food lover, reader, writer, astronomer, and wine connoisseur. He was also a slave owner. His life-long affair with Sally Hemings is what most people remember about him. Before I go onto his accomplishments as president, let's talk about Sally Hemings.

Sally Hemings was of mixed race, beautiful, owned by Jefferson, and they had six children together. The word was that she was the illegitimate child of Jefferson's deceased wife's father. This would have made Martha Jefferson and Sally Hemings half-sisters. Although Jefferson talked about black inferiority and didn't believe a biracial relationship could peacefully coexistence in eighteenth century society, the union continued although Jefferson was married.

The issue has been romanticized. A 37-year relationship, love, caring, or the fact she was still a slave existed. She could have left Jefferson when they were in Paris because slavery was illegal, but she chose to stay with him in exchange for privileges for herself and future children. In Paris, Hemings was reunited with her brother who Jefferson had sent to France two years prior to study French. She didn't ask for freedom in Virginia. Sally was 16 years old at the time. Was she treated better; what was the draw? Was she afraid to face freedom on her own because of her young age and inexperience? Was she astute enough to understand it was a pathway to freedom for her children, or was there love? I leave that to your imagination.

What kind of president was he? "The government that governs least, governs best" was one of his statements reflecting his belief in no strong central government but forever states' rights. He was a southerner and his unwavering faith was in American farmers. He inherited problems when the United States still didn't command a lot of respect. England and France wanted America to take sides in their war the same way they did with prior presidents. Impressment continued while many Americans believed these countries were inciting the American Indians. Everyone was pointing fingers and both England and France were accused of building new forts in America east of the Mississippi River and violating America's neutrality.

Then there was the Louisiana Purchase of 1803. Our problem still existed ever since we obtained our freedom from England. We could travel down the Mississippi but once we got to the Port of New Orleans, it was a different story. Spain was losing power and transferred the Louisiana territory to the French in 1800, but not control of the Port of New Orleans. Economic sanction was Jefferson's approach but England and France didn't care. Jefferson wanted and needed the Port of New Orleans owned by Spain. It may have been given to France, but they had yet to do anything with it. The Spanish were still there.

Napoleon became the strongest conqueror in Europe because he had a strong French military. Jefferson knew Napoleon was a megalomaniac, a person obsessed with their own power. Napoleon anticipated he would establish a new empire in the Americas because he was running into trouble in the Southern Americas. Saint Dominque which is now Haiti and the Dominican Republic, were French territories but there was a slave revolt far too powerful for Napoleon to overcome. The outbreak of Yellow Fever and the strong independent spirit of the people were difficult to contend with. The end result was a government take-over by a former slave, Toussaint L'Ouverture.

New Orleans was the only port accessible to transport produce down the Mississippi. We had the temporary right to transport and keep our produce at the dock awaiting export, but Spain revoked it. Americans assumed the order came from Napoleon who did own Louisiana but hadn't taken possession of it. Jefferson knew the threat that faced him. Once Napoleon took possession, America would have a serious problem. Jefferson knew he had to obtain Louisiana.

Napoleon, however, had one huge problem. He needed money to fight his wars to conquer Europe. He also realized that ruling Saint Domingue and ending American rights in New Orleans, weren't worth it.

Jefferson sent an American delegation led by James Monroe to Paris to negotiate a deal. He did give them some guidelines. We made an initial 7.5 million offer for a small part of it, which was authorized by the Federalists. Napoleon said, "No." He asserted he would sell to the British, but then turned around and offered the whole dog and pony show for $15 million. Jefferson had not even conceived of obtaining the whole carrot.

Jefferson didn't waiver and authorized it again. Remember, implied powers? The Constitution said nothing about acquiring land and Jefferson knew this massive region would double American territory. He knew he had to act quickly.

He went over Congress' head and bought it without their approval. We got the land before it officially became ratified by the Senate and he doubled our country in size! Some talked about impeaching him but nothing became of it. (In 1812, it was renamed the Missouri Territory). To keep things in perspective, the Louisiana Purchase came before the Missouri Compromise, the 1819 financial panic, and the Indian removal act 1830 which we will witness first-hand. The cost was fifteen million dollars. Broken down, this is .13 and one half-cent per acre – what a bargain! The U.S. doubled in size but what do we do with all of it? 827,000 Miles consisted of Spanish, English, French, and Americans. There were never any boundaries so no one knew where borders were; people just knew of this purchase.

Back in the 1800s, the government didn't give out expense accounts. James Monroe who would become our fifth president (1817-1825) was almost bankrupt when Jefferson sent him to France. Jefferson appointed him and counted on him to get the job done. To raise money for the passage to France, Monroe sold off his silver flatware, porcelain plates, and a white-and-gold china tea set. Monroe struggled with debt for the rest of his life, even after receiving a $30,000 congressional appropriation for losses and sacrifices.

In 1803, Lewis & Clark were chosen to map the Louisiana Purchase area. The entire nation became involved and wondered what lurked in this unknown territory. This mass of land had never been surveyed before and the territory went up into Canada. The expedition was a tremendous success and Jefferson realized the mining, forestry, and agricultural potential. Lewis and Clark had accomplished what would have been considered a miracle just a few years prior. They mapped and learned about Indian languages, customs, climate, plants, animals, insects, and reptiles. There was mystery, intrigue, and fantasy because no one knew what was out there and now the public was anxious to find out for themselves.

Jefferson hoped they would find a water route across the continent to the Pacific. This was his main ambition. He told Lewis and Clark to be scientific and trace the Missouri River to its source and follow the best water route to the Pacific. They had done their job well.

Meanwhile, Jefferson had a laundry list of additional problems. The first was Aaron Burr, his vice president. Burr's ambition, power, and greed had cost him the presidency and now he decided one way or another he would rule a country. Burr assembled a large group of national and international supporters and together they worked to create a new country. Burr would be its king. Rumor or gossip are as-old-as-time and they moved quickly in this nineteenth century America.

Then there was the national debt incurred by the Federalists. Just paying the interest required more taxes and taking money from farmers, whom

Jefferson considered the backbone of the Republic. Jefferson and his secretary of the treasury, Albert Gallatin, put their heads together and repealed a great many taxes, cut down on foreign expenditures, and reduced the size of the army.

The Judiciary Act of 1801 made him furious. It was passed during the last hurrah of the Adams' presidency to keep Federalists in power. It reduced the size of the Supreme Court from six judges to five and eliminated the judges' circuit duties. To replace the justices on circuit, the act created sixteen judgeships for six judicial circuits. Jefferson knew this would strip him of any chance to appoint a justice. It was repealed in 1802.

However, a court case developed, *Marbury v. Madison* which established a precedent for judicial review and it continues to this very day. In 1803, the Supreme Court announced that a court had the power to declare an act of Congress void whenever it was inconsistent with the Constitution. Once again, in the last hours of the Adams administration, Adams appointed William Marbury as a justice of the peace for the District of Columbia. When James Madison, a Federalist refused to deliver the commission and didn't deliver it before the midnight deadline, Marbury, and three other appointees petitioned for a writ of mandamus which would compel delivery.

When Marbury petitioned the Supreme Court, Chief Justice John Marshall ruled former President Madison should have done it, but legally. He didn't have to because of the Judiciary Act of 1789 that stated the Court Authority was unconstitutional. For the first time in American history, the court asserted its authority to void an act of Congress on the grounds it was "repugnant" to the Constitution. Jefferson was more than upset that the court only lectured Madison on his morality instead of his legal obligation. The bottom Line was that it ruled the judicial department could state the law and interpret what it was meant to be.

So, it goes with history repeating itself. In recent times, remember the Obama administration attempting to appoint a Supreme Court justice before the end of the term and the Republican push-back? How about the struggle for the Trump administration to get an appointee approved?

Another four years passed and we're at the election of 1804. Now Jefferson was shaky on some federal policies. Charles Coatsworth Pinckney was running with Jefferson. Congress changed the law and ratified the Twelfth Amendment in which said people must run as a ticket because of this two-party controversy. Two separate beliefs were developing between the president and vice president. Hence, since the 1804 election, candidates for president and vice president came together like a team on the same ticket. It prevents our nation's two highest elected officials from being from opposing political parties. The amendment made it trickier, but not impossible, for voters to elect members from two different political parties.

The Vice President has one job which is to be President Pro-tempore of the senate. He only gets to vote if there is a tie. He can do nothing unless the president dies. Rumors were getting to Jefferson about Burr's plot to form an independent country somewhere in the Southwest and Jefferson took quick action. In 1804, Jefferson got a new running mate, Alexander Hamilton. Burr returned to New York and ran for governor. It wasn't over yet because Burr wanted power.

As to Hamilton's citizenship, the delegates wanted to make a clear distinction between two sets of persons who might seek the American presidency. They welcomed persons 35 or older, who had been residents of the United States for at least 14 years, and who had either been born in America or were American citizens when the Constitution was adopted. Any others, need not apply.

The problem was Alexander Hamilton, who also lived in New York, and despised Burr. Hamilton had made numerous statements slurring Burr and Burr demanded an apology. Hamilton refused. Burr was desperate and challenged Hamilton to a duel. The following continues to be controversial. During this day and age, you had no choice but to accept the challenge of a duel. Picture these gentlemen in their fancy dress. They are back to back, need to go ten paces, point their guns into air and it's done and over, no disgrace. This was all that was required and usually no one died. Since Hamilton's nineteen-year-old son had been fatally shot in a duel, Hamilton had no intention of even wounding Burr. Hamilton shot into the air, and some said his gun jammed. Nevertheless, Burr killed Hamilton. Even though dueling was legal but starting to vanish from popularity, it resulted in Hamilton's death.

Contrary to public belief, Burr was placed on trial for treason because of his attempt to establish a new and independent country within the United States, not because of the legal duel. Although there were charges brought forth because of Hamilton's death resulting from the duel, they were dropped. Burr was acquitted of treason in 1807 and fled to England. He later returned to our country and died in New York.

1807 Was another year in which two very important things occurred. Congress passed a law which forbade importation of slaves into America. It is imperative to understand that not all southerners believed in slavery and even as late as 1820, there were more antislavery groups existing in the South than in the North. Many did believe, however, that blacks were an inferior race. The idea of slavery was always identified with the South, never the North.

Remember the Three-Fifths Compromise wherein slaves became 3-5ths of a person and Indians didn't count? This was part of the Great Compromise which led to the United States Constitution. Southerners had received a 20-year protection allowing for further slave importation. Twenty years have now passed and it is March 2, 1807 when Congress passed an act stating that it prohibits "the importation of slaves into any port or place within the jurisdiction of the United States...from any foreign kingdom, place, or country." This took effect January 1808, the earliest date permitted to outlaw importation. Let me give a little more clarity.

In his 1806 State of the Union Address, Thomas Jefferson called for its enactment. He endorsed the idea since the 1770s the general publics' trend was toward abolishing the international slave trade. Virginia was first and was followed by all of the other states except South Carolina. South Carolina reopened its slave trade and Congress first regulated against in the Slave Trade Act of 1794, which limited involvement only. The 1807 Act ended the legality of trade with the United States. However, it was not well enforced and slaves continued to be smuggled into this country.

All the Northern states had ended slavery by 1804, but ownership remained legal in all the Southern states. The 1807 law did not change that, but just made importation from abroad a crime. The domestic slave trade within our country was unaffected by the law. Britain, who was the major power involved in the Atlantic slave trade to the Indies, passed the comparable Abolition of Slave Trade Act that same month.

Second, for the next four years, both England and France blockaded American and European ports so we couldn't trade with either. This is how it came about. Both Britain and France were involved in a long war. Jefferson adopted the Embargo Act of 1807 because he was trying to gain some respect from foreign powers and the anticipated effect was supposed to be economic hardship for both. This would force Great Britain and France to end this, and to end their attack on American shipping, respect our neutrality, and stop their policies of impressment.

Impressment had been the issue since the Revolutionary War. The British continued kidnapping American seamen, even in American waters. England needed soldiers because they were fighting Napoleon along with both the Spanish and Portuguese. Although they had the largest army in the world, desertion was common. Brits hired onto American ships, because they were paid as much as five times more, and overall they were treated more fairly.

The embargo, however, turned out to be highly impractical, and failed both diplomatically and economically. The legislation placed tremendous burdens upon the American economy and its people. It was supposed to be only on exports but it affected imports also. American ships couldn't go to foreign ports while ships coming into American ports left empty, without return cargoes. We boycotted but it backfired. The British had other customers in South America and the natives were rebelling against the Spanish.

Remember our friend Napoleon, who sold us Louisiana? Napoleon also seized American ships. It caused sky-rocketing unemployment because seamen were out of work, and the result was debt. Farmers were absolutely devastated and unable to export or sell produce at a reasonable and profitable price. There were foreclosures and all of those speculators were hurt. Especially hard hit was New England which formerly was the largest shipping area.

It did, however, push money into manufacturing and textile mills flourished. We will soon visit the northern mills and get an idea about manufacturing and America's uncontrollable young people. To get off the subject a bit to summarize, nothing was different in the 1800s. In the North, children questioned authority and faced the age-old question of staying with their parents or leaving the nest. Young unmarried women often went to the textile mills, such as Lowell Massachusetts. Children as young as seven were forced to work as doffers removing bobbins from machines, and the work was dangerous. Many women didn't marry and became independent, voicing their views.

Jefferson was deemed a philosopher and a dreamer. He never solved all of the problems and maybe that's why he didn't want the word president on tombstone. He was followed by James Madison. The same stuff was going on and Madison believed economic sanctions were the answer.

Madison faced new youngsters and they were the "War Hawks." They were the young, overconfident, and very self-assured. They told Madison to declare war on England. Two famous War Hawks were John C. Calhoun of South Carolina and Henry Clay of Kentucky. They forced him to declare war because of the issues with impressment, trade restrictions, etc. They wanted to acquire Spanish Florida and Canada. We attacked Canada. In the Spring of 1812, the War of 1812 aka, the "Second War for American Independence" began.

   James Madison served two terms and from 1808 to 1812 it became Mr. Madison's War. New England, the Federalists, voted against the war and sat it out. At the Hartford Convention in the middle of the war, they mentioned secession and wanted to take all of New England with them. It was only talk at this time and we entered the War of 1812 which was another repeat of the American Revolution. Does this sound familiar? Viet Nam became Mr. Nixon's War.

Madison had one asset and that was Dolley Madison. Dolley had acted as First Lady for Jefferson, who at the time was widowed. A recap of the War of 1812 follows for all of you fans of this war.

The Chronology follows:

First, in 1809 Governor William Henry Harrison of Indiana (future president) stole Indian lands for two cents an acre to open it for white settlement. Tecumseh, the Shawnee chief and his brother were livid. This led to the Battle of Tippecanoe ("Tippecanoe and Tyler too" was the future presidential slogan), and made Tyler a hero. By summer 1812, the United States tried to attack Canada unsuccessfully but Tecumseh had British help.

Tecumseh setup an alliance with the British but in 1813 they were defeated, Tecumseh was killed, and the remaining Natives withdrew from the alliance. There were battles in Ohio and New York such as Put-in-Bay with Commander Perry and the Battle of Plattsburgh, New York, also known as the Battle of Lake Champlain.

Perhaps the most significant engagement was the Battle of Bladensburg and Burning of Washington in 1814. The British troops entered Washington, D.C. and burnt the White House to retaliate for the American attack on the city of York in Ontario, Canada, in June 1812. Let me draw a distinction. Although I refer to the White House as such, during this period it could be referred to as the President's House, or the Executive Mansion, or even the President's Palace. It was not until Theodore Roosevelt became our president, that it was given the White House name. It requires close to 600 gallons of paint to cover it and make it white![1]

When the British arrived at the White House, they found that President Madison and Dolley had already fled to safety in Maryland. Soldiers sat down, ate a meal made of leftover food, using White House dishes and silver, before ransacking the presidential mansion and burning it.

President Madison had left the White House on August 22 to meet with his generals on the battlefield, just as British troops threatened to enter the capitol. Before leaving, he asked Dolley if she would wait for his return the next day. Dolley persevered, collected important papers, and prepared to abandon the White House at any moment.

The next day, Dolley used a spyglass waiting for either Madison or the British army to show up. As British troops approached, Dolley decided to abandon the couple's personal belongings and instead saved a full-length portrait of former president George Washington from desecration. Dolley was pretty smart.

Since the portrait was screwed to the wall, she had the frame broken, pulled out the canvas, and rolled it up. Two unidentified men from New York took it away for safe-keeping. Dolley didn't know the portrait was actually a copy of Gilbert Stuart's original. The first lady left the White House and was reunited with her husband at their meeting place in the middle of a thunderstorm. Although they returned to Washington three days later, when British troops had moved on, they never again lived in the White House. Madison served the rest of his term living at the city's Octagon House. In 1817, President James Monroe moved back into the reconstructed building. The war continued and it seemed endless.

In 1814, at Fort McHenry we withheld Brits for 25 hours of bombardment by the British Navy. This is when, Frances Scott Key drafted a poem on the back of an old letter, which was to become our nation's anthem, the Star-Spangled Banner. Key was a lawyer who was initially against the war but became involved in the cause after the capitol was burnt, prisoners of war taken, and he became witness to the brutality. Throughout the night of September 13, he recalled the red glare of the rockets and the sounds of the bombs bursting, and the sight of deliverance when the American flag still flew.[2]

The Battle of New Orleans in January 1815 was the final major battle where we stopped the Brits from taking New Orleans and land acquired during the Louisiana Purchase. General Andy Jackson became a hero and because news of the Treaty of Ghent reached America shortly after the battle, many Americans believed the Battle of New Orleans won the war.

The White House burnt but in 1814 England decided to write a treaty which was the Treaty of Ghent, Ghent Belgium, 1815. It did nothing to spell out the terms. It was mute on impressment, Indians, blockades, and concluded with "Status quo antebellum." So, we're back to way things were before the war. However, a wave of nationalism and ardent patriotism swept the country and impressment ended. The treaty was a poor one but it got rid of the problems. "We are now invincible," Madison said, and the United States was reborn.

Summary

The Jefferson presidency was a difficult one. Jefferson was a Renaissance Man. He was interested in everything around him. People either loved or hated him. He had a relationship with his slave, Sally Hemings for over close to 37 years and together they shared children. His greatest accomplishment was the Louisiana Purchase. The United States gained 828,000,000 square miles which was purchased from France. We now have 15 states taken from it. It was a brilliant move to secure this territory from Napoleon.

The mapping of America by Lewis and Clark could be considered Jefferson's second greatest accomplishment. A lot of events did occur during his presidency. There was the Alexander Hamilton and Aaron Burr duel. Then there was the Slave Trade Act of 1807 abandoning the importation of slaves to America. Since Jefferson never accomplished all that he set out to do, maybe this is the reason he did not designate the word 'president' on his tombstone.

Yet, the fact that Sally Hemings had a relationship for decades and yet was never freed, has many entering into discussions of morality and a tendency to overlook the great accomplishments. Further reading will allow you to make that decision.[3]

The Madison presidency inherited the ongoing discussions. Madison had the asset of his wife, Dolley who was the First Hostess. The War Hawks constantly pushed and pushed for war and true freedom from Great Britain. We entered the War of 1812 and were finally free of English rule. Our national anthem, The Star-Spangled Banner, was written when our flag still flew over Fort McHenry. We were victorious at the Battle of New Orleans and Andy Jackson came forward as the hero of New Orleans. Finally, in 1815 the Treaty of Ghent was signed. Madison became president and National patriotism swept the country.

Chapter 12

America is changing once again

After both Jefferson and Madison served eight years, another Virginian, James Monroe came along. They were all accomplished gentry and slave owners but Madison was a bit different than the others because he was in political office longer and was older than the others. The Presidency was the end of his career and it coincided with War if 1812. Problems disappeared with the rebirth of Nationalism. It was the end of Mr. Madison's war. Federalists committed political suicide and were gone. The death of the party was at the Hartford Convention. It was a series of meetings from December 15, 1814 through January 5, 1815, in Hartford, Connecticut.

The New England Federalist Party met to discuss their grievances concerning the ongoing War of 1812 and the political problems arising from the federal government's increasing power. The end of the **Federalist** Party also came about because of the War of 1812. The Federalists opposed this war for two main reasons. First, they approved of the British form of government and the fact it was set up to reduce the power wielded by ordinary people.[1]

Monroe was elected without any competition and the Era of good feelings per newspapers was ushered in. Monroe went on a goodwill tour down the east coast from Virginia to New England. In New England he was treated like a hero. The newspapers said that all factions of country would embrace each other. There was still no official two-party system in America. Right now – we are all Americans.

A couple of things changed. Prior presidents took the secretary of state as the next vice president but Monroe didn't do it. He appointed John Quincy Adams. An immediate conflict was the Missouri Territory which applied for admission into the Union as a slave state. This was a big deal because before this moment states came in pairs to keep Congress equal but now there was just one state. What would we do? This was issue number one.

Issue two, was the Louisiana Purchase territory, 1803, which gave us 828,000,000 square miles purchased from France. We know this was one of the most important, if not the most important, achievement of Jefferson's reign. To simplify and not confuse you, there were re-naming's and the Missouri Territory part of the Louisiana purchase applied to the Union. Louisiana was admitted as a state in 1812 and then there was the balance of the territory to contend with.

Missouri was the first area of this purchase applying to Union and the question was, "would it be free or slave?" Congress fought its location because it was a gateway to the Louisiana Purchase. Already the compromise was a contradiction. Missouri was located north of the line and because of the line, the North got better end of deal. Southerners thought they got the better end because Jefferson had sent a mapmaker prior, and instead of "unorganized territory" the map said "Great American Dessert" so they were convinced it was all dessert and an uninhabitable wasteland. This was not why they were angry. They were angry because they woke up one morning, and realized they had given the federal government the right to draw a line. This set a precedent. The government was now making a decision affecting their state without their approval.

It settled nothing on issue of slavery or territories. Jefferson wrote to a friend, back home in Monticello, 41 years before the Civil War. He said that this would be the death-knell of the Union.

Our America was changing very rapidly but instead of joining together as one nation, the North and South continued to grow as two separate nations. In the North, there was mass immigration. For example, the Irish in the nineteenth century had endured starvation, the potato famine, absentee English landlords, and Irish Catholics immigrated to the North. 1.5 Million Irish immigrated, mostly to America. There were other groups, Germans,

Scandinavians, and the Know-Nothing Party arose. Their mission was to oppose immigration.

In 1822 South Carolina, Denmark Vesey began organizing a revolt. He started in December 1821 and planned his attack for the summer, when the largest number of white people would be out of Charleston on vacation. He was an ex-slave who had purchased his freedom after winning a lottery, but was a very bitter man. He moved the date to May after two conspirators were arrested. Unfortunately, Vesey was unable to communicate the change and the attack never happened. 130 Blacks were arrested, some pardoned, and Vesey was hanged with many blacks and a few whites who participated. As a result, there were stricter black codes. Vesey's Rebellion was a revolt that never happened but cost lives.

Next, there were huge problems in the Florida territory because people from Florida were stealing from southern states and slaves were fleeing to the territory. Monroe dispatched Andrew Jackson and the army to guard border. Jackson took orders from no one so he decided to invade Florida. He did so and took the Spanish Governor as a prisoner. Monroe shifted responsibility and said talk to John Quincy Adams. We wanted to buy Florida but the Spanish said no, so Monroe said he would leave Jackson there. The Spanish rethought their stance, and sold it. What this did was convince Monroe that something had to be done.

The Adams–Onís Treaty of 1819, also known as the Transcontinental Treaty, the Florida Purchase Treaty, or the Florida Treaty, was a treaty between the United States and Spain in 1819 that ceded Florida to the United States and defined the boundary between the United States and New Spain. There were also problems in Alaska with Russians and New Spain (Mexico, Central America, much of the Southwest and Central United States, Spanish Florida, and Philippines, Mariana & Caroline Islands).

Monroe came up with American Foreign Policy which led us to the Monroe Doctrine which still holds ground, serving today, and explains some of our foreign policy.

Four points were announced in 1824:

No part of the American Continents – Western Hemisphere (North, South, and Central America), would be open to any future colonization by any foreign nations.

Independent nations in the Americas must remain independent. Any attempt to change would be considered a threat to the security of the United States of America.

The U.S. would respect all European colonies already in existence and not interfere with their concerns.

The U.S. would oppose the transfer of any colony from one European nation to another.

America's population was barely 10 million. The Doctrine went back to the story of wars, anything that was a threat to the security of the United States was off limits. After two terms Monroe decided he had enough.

Summary

Was it an Era of Good Feelings? For a while it was and some problems seemed to get resolved while others intensified. Vesey's Rebellion brought up concerns about slave insurrections.

Andrew Jackson went to Florida and decided to fight his own war. The Adams–Onís Treaty of 1819, was between the United States and Spain and ceded Florida to the United States, defining the boundary between the us and New Spain. There were also problems in Alaska with the Russians.

Four important things were happening: the debate of states against federal rule, the Louisiana Purchase, the Missouri Compromise, and the Monroe Doctrine. The Monroe Doctrine was the biggest take-away and it set our standards to the present day.

Chapter 13

Corruption and the Presidential Election of 1824

John Quincy Adams stated to Posterity (or future generations):

> *"Posterity — you will never know how much it has cost my generation to preserve your freedom. I hope you will make good use of it."*

As the Presidential election of 1820 came and went, increasing numbers of white males believed they had no voice in the election process. The sentiment was akin to the impressions of our early colonists who believed they too could not be heard, before we obtained freedom from England. Change was in the air and some states started removing voting requirements. First, property requirements were removed, so in 1824 at least a portion of the male population over the age of 21, got to vote. John Quincy Adams was in the running and he was unpopular. He was just like his dad, Harvard educated, an aristocrat, not an accomplished hero, but a former secretary of state. The stage was sent for the likable, Andy Jackson.

What kind of man was Andy Jackson?[1] He was wealthy, a plantation and slave owner, a macho man from humble beginnings, and an extremely popular figure. He was born in South Carolina in the Waxhaw Territory and never knew his father because he died a month before his birth. He was the third son of Elizabeth, and they were extremely poor. His mother prayed he would become a minister but it was not to be. Hot-headed Andy swore, argued, fought, was a terrible student, and just wanted to have a good time.

At about the age of 12 he and his brother were fighting the British who were pillaging his Carolina territory. Both were thrown into jail and Jackson earned the scar of his forehead when struck by a British commander. Nevertheless, he did receive a basic education, taught school, and became an attorney. Jackson did try to conform and reform, but was involved in numerous scandals. The worst was when he married Rachel Donelson Robards, who was already married. It seems, her prior husband never got a divorce.

He had two sides to him, nice or ruthless. He invaded Florida with no authority, murdered Indians, and took their land, but Southerners and mountain folk loved him. He distrusted Easterners, bankers, and the British; but the common man believed he would protect their rights. Jackson fought with the Tennessee Southern troops and removed Indians from the borders of Tennessee, Georgia, and Florida, and ran a tight ship while he was in command of the Seventh Military District.

When he ran in the 1824 election, there were four candidates running as Democratic-Republicans or simply Democrats. The Federalist Party had already collapsed and the stage was set for the Republicans. Jackson ran against, John Quincy Adams, William Crawford from Georgia, and Henry Clay. Although Jackson received more popular votes (99 electoral) than John Quincy Adams (with 84), neither had the required 131 electoral votes, so the election was thrown into House of Representatives to determine next president.

Conveniently, the Speaker of House was Henry Clay. Clay made a deal with Adams throwing his political power to Adams. The Secretary of State position was a springboard to the Presidency, so Adams appointed Henry Clay. Clay got his position and Adams got the presidency. Now you see why it was called the Corrupt Bargain. The Spoils System which awarded political office based on political party loyalty was born. Sound familiar? Clay said to his dying day there was no corrupt bargain.[2]

For four long years Adams got nothing accomplished because many Jackson supporters were in office. In many ways, he proposed an American plan that was like the New Deal which would be introduced a century later by Franklin D. Roosevelt – a National university system funded by the government was one. However, nothing passed.

This brings to light the fact that adversity has always existed and each and every president has had his share of it. Nevertheless, Jackson was furious, resigned his Senate seat, and went home to plan for the election of 1824. He was not a man to have as an enemy. It wasn't long before 1828 rolled around and there was a rematch. This time, however, Jackson won significantly and put to rest this "corrupt bargain." The difference from prior elections was more men could vote as states relaxed election laws. This was still, white men only need apply. The campaign was called one of the foulest and dirtiest in American history. Do you think it stood up to elections today?

The 1828 election was a mud-slinging campaign. The fact that Rachael Jackson was still married when she and Jackson wed was the main case in point. She died before Christmas so when he took office in 1829, he was bitter because he believed the campaign hastened her demise. Although Jackson accumulated slaves and a fortune, he came from nothing, fought with the mountain men, and was one of them. He was common and not elite and overwhelmingly won the election. After the loss, Adams became the only president in history to get elected to the House of Representatives and the only ex-president to drop dead at his desk while in the House.

Jackson and Adams hated each other and it was evident on inauguration day. The long-held tradition was that the new president elect would pick-up the outgoing president to go to the inauguration. Adams was the only one who didn't do it until Truman, because Truman didn't like Ike. Until the early twentieth century, the departing president usually accompanied the newly elected president on the carriage-ride from the Capitol to the White House following the inauguration. In the early years, the procession would deliver the former president to his residence. The former president usually quietly and discretely vacated the White House a day or so before the inauguration. This was the time before the new tradition that developed in the twentieth century wherein the outgoing president quickly left the Capitol immediately following the inaugural ceremony. For example, Obama wrote Trump a letter.

Let's go to the inauguration and get a first-hand account of it. Jackson was to be sworn in as president and John C. Calhoun as vice president.[3] All prior inaugurations were boring but not this one. Many mountain men from Tennessee turned it into a party as tens of thousands went to DC to see their man. All of the rooming houses were filled so people slept in the streets from the night before, awaiting their hero. Jackson walked, hatless, the six blocks from the National Hotel, aka, Gadsby's Tavern where he was staying, to the capitol. There was a mix of rich and poor. The ladies wore lots of purple and scarlet and wore their hair in a frizzled look, which was the "in look" for the season.

Jackson gave his speech, took the oath of office, and bowed to the crowd. This was not enough because Americans wanted to see their president and shake his hand. They crowd broke through the cables which were erected to keep them at distance. As they advanced towards Jackson, the president mounted a horse, fled, and made it safely to the White House. He didn't really escape because everyone followed. There were men, women, children, both humble and elite, mounted or walking.

Once they got to the White House, the mob climbed through windows. The scene were riotous, rowdy, and wild. Women fainted, people were crushed together, and many were left bleeding. Everyone wanted to experience the celebration. To leave, Jackson's cabinet passed him from the House out the window to a hotel. However, it wasn't over yet because the house was destroyed.

The crowd wanted souvenirs and cut squares of carpet, wallpaper, furniture, china, and pieces of paintings. Mud covered the expensive carpets. The only way to get rid of the crowd was to place liquor in bowls on the White House lawn. Was this the rise of the common man or mob rule? I might add, public receptions were the norm during this era and nothing like we experience today. Imagine being able to access the White House without a controlled tour. Two years before his last public reception, Jackson was given a gift of a 1,400-pound cheese-wheel, which he couldn't possibly devour. In 1837, it was not put out in the East Room for the public to eat. Within two hours, it was devoured.

Inaugural evening 1829, there was a ball which cost five dollars to attend. Jackson didn't go but the Calhoun's attended and everyone snubbed Peggy Eaton. This was only the beginning. More gossip about Peggy shortly but let's get acquainted with Jackson's vice president.

Who was John C. Calhoun?

Who was John C. Calhoun? He was a strong-willed states' rights advocate from South Carolina, Jackson's vice president, and he often defied the president. Calhoun had also been vice president under Adams. As time went on, Calhoun became more vocal, despising tariffs, and becoming a state's rights sectionalist. Calhoun became increasingly focused to get views across and hoped to eventually become president, a job that so-far had eluded him. He believed the only way to preserve the nation was to allow greater states' rights, limit government, allow free trade, and nullify if necessary. He now opposed John Quincy Adams who ran once again against Jackson in 1832 and lost.

Like Jackson, Calhoun was a lawyer and born in South Carolina. His family believed that states should have the power to regulate themselves and not allow the federal government to interfere. After all, the federal government was run by outsiders. Calhoun married his first cousin which improved his social status, and he entered politics. He graduated from Yale with honors and had a residential college named after him but in 2018 his name was removed and it is now the Grace Murray Hopper College. While at Yale, Calhoun was told by the President of Yale that one day he would be a president. When the War of 1812 began, Calhoun was one of the most influential men in Congress, became Secretary of War, reorganized the department, managed Indian affairs, and owned 80 slaves.[4]

The Peggy Eaton Affair

There was the Peggy Eaton Affair. Secretary of War, John Eaton and Peggy O'Neale Timberlake were involved. Peggy was still married at the time when her husband was off with the Navy. I know what you're thinking, how could one affair with a member of the cabinet be so serious? Well, it almost dissolved Jackson's cabinet. Calhoun and his wife, Floride, instigated public scandal to discredit Jackson and help Calhoun's ambition to become president. Peggy was snubbed by all of the society women and the entire cabinet, except Van Buren, resigned. Strike one against his vice president from the 1828 election, John C. Calhoun, and more to come.

Jackson empathized with the now married Eaton's. He knew what he went through with his wife Rachel who was not divorced when they married. There was also speculation that Peggy's husband committed suicide.

In 1828 and again in 1832 South Carolina was fed up with tariff policies. There was a protective tariff in 1816, rates continually went up in 1824 and by 1828 they went up 50 percent. This was called the "tariff of abominations." South Carolina was an old cotton state and prices remained low after a national panic in 1819 because people were moving West. The effect on the antebellum Southern economy was devastating. It set a 38 percent tax on 92 percent of all imported goods and its purpose was to protect Northern Industry.

By 1832, there was a big problem. Calhoun, loyal first and foremost to South Carolina, asserted that a state had the sovereign power to declare an act of the national government null and inoperative. Calhoun said, "If we don't protect our own rights, the Federal Government will trample them." Henry Clay stepped in once again with a compromise and it was the Compromise Tariff which gradually lowered tariffs. It was fall 1832 when South Carolina called a special convention to resist the Tariff of Abominations and adopted the Ordinance of Nullification. It said the tariff was null and void in South Carolina and if the federal government attempted to collect, South Carolina would secede from the Union.

Jackson called this treason and was prepared for war unless South Carolina rescinded their decree. South Carolina was waging states' rights v. federal and was confident other southern states would follow their lead.

Jackson passed the Force Bill putting down nullification by military force and sent seven war ships to Charleston. The rates lowered slightly and nullifiers temporarily backed off. This was a dire warning almost thirty years before the Civil War and was truly a Nullification Crisis. The state stood alone in 1832-33 but twenty-nine years later, South Carolina was the first state to secede from the Union when shots were fired at Fort Sumter. This time, South Carolina did not stand alone.

Jackson was livid, Calhoun resigned the vice presidency, and became a South Carolina senator. It was controversial whether he was forced to resign or chose it. Calhoun became a symbol of the South and slavery and given the title of the Great Nullifier. It was business as usual until 1833 when a compromise tariff was passed.

Jackson and Native Americans

One of the bleakest chapters in our nation's history, was about to unfold. There was no question, Jackson hated Native Americans. In 1830, the Indian Removal Act was passed by Congress. It was approved at Jackson's insistence for one sole purpose, to take Native land and give it to white settlers. It removed and resettled Indians to the West and allowed the president to use force, if necessary. Some tribes moved peacefully while others fought the move in various ways. When Georgia wanted the Cherokees removed, the Cherokees took legal action. They were a very smart tribe, spoke several languages, and even their chiefs owned slaves and lived in Plantations. The Cherokees sued Georgia twice, *Cherokee Nation v. Georgia* and our Supreme Court ruled that Georgia could not take their land.

Here again, we have one branch of government fighting with another, executive vs. judicial. Jackson sent the Federal Army to remove them from Georgia because Georgia also refused to uphold the decision. The Treaty at New Echota, the Cherokee Nation capital located in Georgia, agreed to sell the United States Government all of the Eastern tribal lands in exchange for $5 million and new land in the West. As part of the agreement, the government was supposed help cover the Cherokees' moving costs and pay to support them during their first year when Indian territory was signed.

John Ross, part Scottish and part Cherokee, was the Chief and he believed the tribe must preserve their ancestral land. While in Washington in 1835, a minority of the tribe signed the Echota Treaty. When Ross found out about the treaty, he was furious and argued it was illegal. Nevertheless, in 1836 it was ratified by a single vote in the U.S. Senate and signed by President Jackson. The treaty gave the Cherokees two years to vacate their lands.[5]

The Cherokees were forced to evacuate in 1838, after Jackson left office and Martin Van Buren was president. The Trail of Tears stretched from Georgia to Oklahoma. There wasn't just one trail. Native Americans were divided into 13 groups, but the largest group of 12,000 that went a Northern route through Tennessee, Kentucky, Illinois, Missouri, and Arkansas, were sent to detention camps for assembly before being forced to make the long journey on foot. Of the over 16,000 total, one of every three died along the way, from exposure, disease, malnutrition.

In June 1839, after the Cherokees were forced to relocate to Indian Territory, several leaders of the so-called Treaty Party, who'd pushed for the New Echota agreement, were assassinated by tribe members who had opposed it. When the Civil War broke out they were politically divided. Those who escaped or came back, established the Eastern Branch of the Cherokees in the area around Cherokee North Carolina in the Smoky Mountains.

Ironically, Jackson had one adopted Indian son, Lyncoya. When Jackson's men murdered most of men, women, and children in a village, the remaining women would not take the infant and they begged Jackson to kill him. Instead, Jackson adopted the child and treated Lyncoya as he did his other adopted white children. Jackson had plans that when he matured the boy would go to West Point. However, he died at age 17 from tuberculosis. He and Rachel had no natural children.

Nat Turner's Rebellion

In August 1831, the most successful, largest, and deadliest slave revolt in American History occurred in Virginia.[6] Nat Turner was a slave who was intelligent, could read and write, and had visions from God. He prayed, fasted, and watched for signs to lead his life. In February 1831, he observed a solar eclipse and believed it was a sign from God to lead his people out of bondage.

He led slaves on his plantation, killed his master, and as a result, 66 people were killed. Turner and his group were apprehended and executed. Turner delayed the rebellion for nine days because he was ill and a new date was set to August 22 but word didn't get around. If the revolt had gone according to schedule, the mass-killing may have radically increased.

The reason this revolt was a big deal is that it scared Southerners and added to the strain which brought about the Civil War. There were very few slave rebellions, but this one was important. The last rebellion that really frightened the South was 100 years prior, the Stono Rebellion in 1739. As a result of Turner's Rebellion, there were more slave trials, and the following year the Virginia legislature passed a law making it illegal for slaves to read or write. Southern states started passing harsher slave codes and being watchful for any signs of insurrection. By the time Tyler was president, Southerners had determined that even though we were all the United States of America, we really existed as two separate nations.

Jackson's Second Term

Jackson was re-elected in 1832 and his troubles were just beginning. Once again, Jackson declared his own wars on the Supreme Court, banks, and states.

Banks – A little about banking. It does get complicated. Have you ever thought about the economy without paper money? The Constitution only authorized the federal government to issue coins, not paper money. Prior to the Civil War, the banks printed the paper money. For America's first 70 years, private entities, and not the federal government, issued the paper money. Notes were printed by state-chartered banks, and could be exchanged for gold and silver. They were the most common form of paper currency in circulation. From the founding of the United States to the passage of the National Banking Act, some 8,000 different entities issued currency, which created a crazy and confusing money supply and caused a lot of counterfeiting.

Before our gold and silver discoveries in western America in the mid-1800s, we lacked an ample source of metals for minting. We did accept foreign coins as legal tender because of their metal content. When the first national bank of the United States was established, our nation was very rural and agriculture was of primary importance.

This first Bank of the United States was given a twenty-year charter, expiring in 1811, just before the War of 1812 with Britain. Our problem was that without a bank, the feds had no financial resources to wage a war. Even those opposing this central bank, approved the charter of a second national Bank. Madison signed it into law in April 1816 and it opened in Philadelphia the following year. It was similar to the first Bank. During this interim period, we had no bank and were heavily in debt.

Here comes the corruption, greed, and politics. It gets messy. In 1816, the Second Bank of the U.S. received a 20-year charter. It was a creditor to state banks, issued bank notes, and could demand repayment in specie, which is gold or silver coinage. It regulated state banks from printing and lending excessively. It was a financial agent that held federal deposits, issued debt, and issued and redeemed bank notes that were deposited in state-chartered banks. It was also a commercial bank, that accepted retail deposits and made loans to people and businesses in its twenty-five-bank network.

Our federal government controlled little and gave the exclusive rights to the Bank of the United States and its stockholders who made it easy or difficult for businesses to borrow. It was the richest corporation in the world.

Early-on, the bank's record was murky, but that changed in 1823, as Nicholas Biddle took the lead. His management brought economic growth. However, since Jackson viewed the government similarly as former President

Jefferson, Biddle and Jackson fought a personal war. Jackson viewed the bank as corrupt because it had power without oversight by the government. It failed to help individual states which needed its support to make changes in their local economies. The bottom line was that he didn't trust the banks nor the people running them. Senator Henry Clay of Kentucky, however, was with Biddle, thought the bank was working well, and believed he could gain support for the Bank and then pave his way to eventually become president.

We now had many ambitious men who desire the presidency: John C. Calhoun, Henry Clay, and Martin Van Buren. Clay pushed for an early renewal of the second bank ahead of the 1836 schedule which passed in Congress but was vetoed by Jackson. It culminated after Jackson's victory in the 1832 election, when he declared war on Bank of the United States, with the intention of dismantling it before the re-charter came up in 1836. The bottom line was he thought it was too powerful because of wealthy and important people on the board who controlled our country.

When Jackson decided to break the bank seven "pet banks" arose. They were state banks that received deposits of federal money in October, 1833. As the U.S. bank called in loans and Jackson took out federal deposits, he placed them in state banks. The term using Pet Banks was used as an insult because they were selected by the U.S. Department of Treasury to receive surplus treasury funds by their loyalty to the Democratic Party.

This scheme backfired and there was a national financial panic in 1833-34. Jackson tried the pet banks and thought it would work to break the U.S. Bank, but it didn't work. State banks did the same thing: printed money, offered easy credit, and Americans tried "get rich quick schemes." As a result, Jackson issued the Specie Circular, to correct it. All government land must be paid for in specie. This prevented normal middle-class Americans from buying land.

In 1836, the Second Bank became a private corporation in Pennsylvania and was liquidated in 1841. Federal deposits remained in State Banks and even though the individual states could not issue currency, they did have the right to charter private banks who could then issue notes. As a result, there was a great deal of paper money and it is still debated whether this helped or hindered commerce in pre-Civil War America.

In addition to private banks, municipalities, transport companies, insurance companies, and stores, all issued scrip, which is a certificate of money given to a bank or company, entitling the holder to a formal certificate and dividends. Notes were payable on demand and were only as strong as the bank or company itself.

The problem was, if too many notes were presented at once, a bank could close its doors and default. Think of it as the "Bank Holiday" of the twentieth century. To make things more difficult to cash in bills, offices were made in inaccessible places in the middle of nowhere. From this we get the term, "wildcat" bank since the animal could be the only customer who could complete the journey to the bank.

The Civil War brought the return of governmentally issued paper money to this country. On July 17, 1861 Congress authorized the printing and circulation of Legal Tender paper worth 60 million dollars. They were Demand Notes and were not backed by gold or silver. On February 25, 1863, President Abraham Lincoln signed the National Banking Act, originally known as the National Currency Act. This was the first time in American history that the federal dollar was established as the only currency of the United States.

Now that banking was taken care of, a whole new political party was born, the Whigs, modeled after the England Whigs who opposed "King Andrew I. Now for first time since 1812, there was a two-party system. Jackson went through three secretaries of the treasury, the Bank of the United States was gone to pet banks, and nothing happened.

After eight years, Jackson hand-picked Martin Van Buren as his successor. Van Buren from New York was nothing like Jackson and another president destined for failure because of the powerful president before him. The economic faltered, because of Jackson who went back to Tennessee, and Van Buren was blamed.

Summary

The Jackson presidency came off to a rough start following an election called one of the most corrupt in American History. The mud-slinging was largely about Jackson's possibly bigamy, when Rachael was still married to her prior husband when she and Andy tied the knot. There were problems with Vice President Calhoun. The Peggy Eaton Affair caused most of the cabinet to resign, except for Martin Van Buren, who became Jackson's next vice president and future President of the United States.

Sandi Ludwa

The Indian removal Act was passed in 1830, which led to the Trail of Tears in 1838, not during the Jackson administration. Then there was the Nullification Crisis in 1832 led by John C. Calhoun who resigned his vice presidency. The crisis was based on tariffs which handicapped the South and Calhoun opted for secession by the state of South Carolina. No other states followed and the crisis was concluded.

In his second term Jackson declared his war on banks and formed his pet banks. They failed and Van Buren was the scapegoat after he became president. The United States finally had a national currency. Political tempers flared during a national financial crisis. Power-hungry men stood in the forefront. There are now two strong-willed men who wanted to become president: Calhoun and Clay.

This has been a busy time with one dramatic event following another. If we were to read the news of the day, our heads would be spinning. What was truth and what was fiction? Politics aside, most Americans were concerned with their own livelihood and became involved when the issues affected them personally. Some stood apart as they battled for equality, emancipation, and pondered the best way to achieve their goals and purposes.

Chapter 14

Sectionalism – Discontent Arises from the Embers

Are We Two Separate Nations?

In 1836, one term president, Martin Van Buren picked by Jackson, became our nation's leader. He was called the "Little Magician," because of his shrewdness in politics. Van Buren was five and a half feet tall, a New York lawyer, and had been the vice president under Jackson. How many presidents have we had in the past who followed powerful and popular leaders and didn't quite fit their big shoes? Van Buren was indecisive, and his magic disappeared once he took office. Powerful abolition movements increased and families agreed and disagreed on the issue of slavery. Van Buren ignored the fact that the Nation was splitting apart and embers were becoming a massive fire that would overtake America with the entire world watching.

Van Buren was not idle and did a few things. He blocked Texas' annexation because he believed it would further slavery. He promoted free trade. Van Buren also enforced the Trail of Tears with the Cherokees with the last of this once powerful tribe removed in 1838. The Trail of Tears was in 1838, after the removal act which was passed in 1830 during the Jackson administration.

In 1837, barely three months after his inauguration, there was a banking crisis. The Bank of England tightened credit policies and raised interest rates, and reduced credit to British vendors who worked in America. The demand for American cotton fell which had a devastating effect because this crop was the main security for loans issued by United States Banks. There was a rush on the banks, high unemployment, protests, and depression which continued until 1843. This was one of the worst depressions in our history, lasting five years. Southerners lost property, both land and slaves, and many quickly relocated, escaping from their creditors.

Jackson had tried the "Specie Circular" which said large tracts of land could be purchased only with specie, which was coin or metal. Bankers were totally against it because it sent money West. Van Buren inherited this fiasco of easy credit. Didn't something similar happen repeatedly and in this century? At any rate, Van Buren tried to re-establish the Democrats' shoddy image by establishing an Independent Treasury System. The plan was that the Treasury would conduct business only in gold and silver coin and store it in regional vaults or sub-treasuries. It finally passed in 1840. It restored faith and trust in our government but a lengthy depression ensued.

Anti-slavery movements had already been in existence for a long time. In 1831, William Lloyd Garrison started his abolitionist newspaper, the *Liberator* which had a profound influence. He published it through 1865, the end of the war. Southerners truly believed that most Northerners thought this way and did all they could to defend slavery. Ultimately, this led to the Gag Rule in Congress which forbade anti-slavery petitions to be heard; there could be no discussion. Southerners said it existed in the name of security.

The Anti-Jacksonians now called themselves Whigs. The opponents of the Democrats were the National Republicans, an early version of Jefferson. The Whigs in 1840 ran William Henry Harrison and the Second Party System was truly born. It dominated politics until the Anti-slavery Republican Party in the 1850s. Divisions were formed because of the bank controversy. Harrison was another respected military hero who defeated the Shawnees at the Battle of Tippecanoe (Indiana) giving more power to the whites. He ran for president in 1840 and won.

Harrison's inauguration is one we wouldn't want to attend. Harrison was anxious to prove that he was the great one the nation needed. He wrote a speech, which was and remains the longest inaugural speech of any president. It lasted about an hour and 45 minutes. The weather in Washington that day was bitterly cold and rainy. Harrison was 68 years old, and stood, without hat, coat, or umbrella and then attended three balls while his wife remained at their new residence, ill. One month to the day, April 4, he died.

Originally it was diagnosed as Pneumonia but now it is suggested it was a bacterial infection from drinking contaminated waste. He spent his last days being treated with opium and enemas.[1] Vice President John Tyler was sworn in and our nation inherited the "Accidental President" or "His Accidency."

His Accidency

Tyler had 17 children. When his wife died, he married someone younger. Tyler had a lot falling upon him. He was the first Vice President to become president because of the death of a president and he had to convince everyone he was really the president. The Whigs had disowned him and he became a man without a party because Tyler didn't embrace the entire Whig philosophy. He was ready to compromise on the banking question, but Clay wouldn't budge. Tyler vetoed Clay's bill which would establish a National Bank with branches in several states. A similar bank bill was passed by Congress on states' rights grounds and Tyler also vetoed it.

There were now two Americas. The Southern America was one of slavery, agriculture which was the cotton crop, tobacco, rice, indigo, and the plantation system. Northern America was commercial, urban, industrial, and turned southern cotton into finished goods. Overall, many people in the North weren't against slavery because it was immoral, but because they knew it was a system preventing the United States from growing more quickly and becoming a major world power. It was strictly economic. What southerners wanted and what the rest wanted, didn't work.

The West was a mixed-bag and the issue loomed of slave or non-slave in these territories. Clearly, it's North vs. South. Two groups developed: the abolitionists who believed slavery was wrong, and the anti-slavery people. Abolitionists started out in churches but then around the 1830s the public took note, evangelized the mission, and national organizations were forged. Abolitionists knew it had to be a gradual emancipation and a solid and reliable plan had to be established to determine what to do with the enslaved once they were freed. Some believed slave owners should be compensated. On eve of the Civil War, the value of slavery in the South was 9.7 billion, or 107 billion dollars today.

The South wanted no part of either. A different form of abolitionists emerged and they were the radicals who wanted an immediate abolition. They were the most powerful, threatening, and placed fear in the hearts of southerners. It took about ten years until they reached their peak of influence. These radicals gave speeches and sermons, and published pamphlets and newspapers. The written word was and is powerful. William Lloyd Garrison was the most radical, with his publication. *The Liberator* newspaper which was extremely influential.

Summary

We've moved towards two separate nations. Slavery separated us. Congress invoked the Gag Rule to control talking about slavery. There was Nat Turner's Rebellion which scared Southerners and harsher slave codes were passed. People often ask why there weren't more rebellions, after all, slavery was cruel and harsh. Well, plantation life was remote and it would be tough to organize large groups. There were laws, repression to control them, and punishment wasn't worth the risk. Was there trust between slaves? People are human and often turn on one other for their own survival – we'll see how true this is during World War II.

It was not only slavery but the difference in economics and cultures which led to other factors. First, the North wanted a high tariff, a strong central government, and railroads, bridges and canals to transport their finished goods. The South had their own agenda and wanted none of this. They were more concerned with their own issues. Note, when the Civil War does come about, one of the biggest weaknesses of the South was their lack of laid rail track.

Remember the Articles of Confederation with its weak Federal Government? Then we replaced it with the Constitution and a strong Federal Government. Many opposed it and the issue of State's Rights vs. Federal Rights was still a strong issue, especially since the United States was such a diverse area. Let's remember nullification with John C. Calhoun in 1832. A desire to leave the union grew and the movement was getting stronger and stronger.

The country evolved through Van Buren's do-nothing presidency to Harrison's short-lived rule, and onto Tyler, Mr. Accidency. Tyler inherited Manifest Destiny which swept the country. Tyler was pro-annexation but nothing happened. He was pro-annexing Texas and for four long years he tried. When he became president, his whole cabinet resigned. The parties were equally balanced for a while. What was happening was a balance of parties.

As the United States continued to expand westward, every new state added shifted the power between the North and the South in Congress. This is happening today wherein both parties are worried about losing their majority in Congress. Southern states feared they were losing power and eventually they would lose all their rights. Each new state became a tug-of-war between the two sides for power. There evolved Sectionalism and Nationalism was gone for a while.

What was America? Rich, poor, Native American, rural, citified, ethnic, slave?

Sandi Ludwa

Chapter 15

The Many Roads that Led to War

The Mexicans

There was now Sectionalism, not nationalism. An editorial was written by John L. Sullivan wherein he stated it was America's responsibility to keep going West. The article which appeared in the New York *Democratic Review* in 1845 dealt with Texas' annexation but the term "Manifest Destiny" was created. Sullivan asserted that God gave Americans the right to continue moving and grasping new opportunities, and it should expand from sea to shining sea. Americans embraced the idea in the decade of the 1840s and Manifest Destiny convinced them that they were better than everyone else because they possessed this God given right. Expansion was inevitable and ordained. Any resistance, e.g., Native Americans, would result in God's fury because Americans were God's chosen people, just as the Jews had been in the Old World.

Manifest Destiny rationalized any bad deeds to accomplish the one sole goal to go from ocean to ocean, sea to sea, and the world could be American! As always in history, there was usually a border problem. This time it was that Mexico, Spain, and England owned land. Nevertheless, hundreds of thousands immigrated West, associated with Native Americans, settled, and believed this was God's plan. Many went above-and-beyond. They were arrogant and, could do no wrong. Americans believed they could do whatever they wanted because they were invincible.

In the Southwest, it was Napoleon's occupation of Spain that resulted in revolts all over Spanish America. In 1810, Miguel Hidalgo y Costilla, a Catholic priest, prompted the Mexican War of Independence when he issued his *Grito de Dolores,* which translated is the Cry of Delores. In it, he asserted there must be an end to the Spanish rule of Mexico. He advocated the redistribution of land and racial equality for all. There was some success but in the end, Hidalgo was defeated and executed. The movement, however, didn't die.

Hidalgo was followed by other peasant leaders, e.g., José María Morelos y Pavón, Mariano Matamoros, and Vicente Guerrero. These men assembled armies consisting of native and racially mixed insurrectionists who rebelled against those in power. The irony was that by the 1820s, Mexico was tired of being part of Spain (20 years before Tyler) but they didn't have enough people to settle North, fight the Comanche Indians, and keep their land under a Mexican rule.

General Antonio Lopez Santa Ana was one who rose from the ranks, wanted freedom from Spain, and slowly took power. There was freedom, and on September 16, 1821 Mexican Independence Day was declared. The Republic of Mexico was established, but it was a rocky road which led to the making of a republic. It was a shaky situation because no one held power for very long and from 1821 to 1836, Mexico had 13 presidents.

For the next 15 years, this territory had presidents who ranged from extremely liberal to exceptionally dictatorial and none could keep a republic together. The Northern Province of Mexico (Texas) was sparsely populated so the Mexican government invited Americans to settle. Americans saw this as a golden- opportunity wherein they had nothing to lose. Or did they? The first group came led by Stephen Austin. Then Americans came in herds and by the 1830s, there were a lot of southerners who owned slaves, grew cotton, and became very wealthy.

In 1830, the Mexican government reminded Americans who settled of several things. First, Mexico IS part of a Spanish Empire and the official religion is Catholic. American settlers were told to convert. Remember, the United States had no official religion and we don't have one to this day. The second was considered worse: they must pay taxes. The final blow was since there was no slavery in Mexico, slavery must be abolished!

What do you think Americans said? Austin tried to negotiate but was imprisoned and then war broke out. Americans in Texas said, "shove it" and the Mexican government decided that the border between Mexico and Texas should be reinforced with a Mexican army. The army left much to be desired and Mexican peasants were forced off their land and impressed into the army.

Nevertheless, the Americans drove the Mexicans out of their seat of government in this territory, San Antonio, and oversaw the old mission, the Alamo. There had been a prior battle and the Americans were the victors. However, Antonio Lopez de Santa Anna, (1834) was the dictator now in power in Mexico. He was enraged and decided to put an end to this and punish Texans. Get rid of the foreigners once and for all! During this war there were no prisoners. It was fight to the death.

The following is the story. I have read many sources and conclude that much of the information we have today is through oral history recorded many years later, speculation, or the fact that since there was murder, burning, and strife, the truth cannot be found. Many accounts surface as tales, stories, and novels woven to make an entertaining story but I'll incorporate what we do know. What follows is my take on the Battle of the Alamo. So, let's go to the Alamo and witness it first-hand.

It was a quiet mid-winter morning on February 23, 1836 in San Antonio. The Alamo was an old mission in the heart of the city which was falling apart and could have used a good wrecking crew. The Texas Territory wanted its freedom and from February 23, 1836 through March 6, 1836, the Battle of the Alamo lasting 13 days, ensued.[2]

Santa Anna had assembled an army of over 8,000 men; the number is questionable. However, as they came across Texas, the weather was cold, frigid, and both men and horses died along the route. The Americans knew they had to build up reinforcements and had been struggling to do so with Jim Bowie in charge of volunteers and William Travis controlling the regular army. There was a bit of a power struggle here.

On February 22, Santa Anna had conquered the city, but he had yet to capture the Alamo. The Americans were angry and fiercely determined, and what they lacked in numbers, they made up for in spirit. It was then that Santa Anna instructed his army to bombard the mission 24/7 to wear the Americans down. Still, there were reinforcements and the Americans had somewhere between 180 and 190 people. At 4 a.m., on March 6, Santa Anna attacked and charged the Alamo. In 90-minutes it was over.

All of the Texans died. Their numbers vary depending upon which source one reads, to anywhere from 135 to 257. Santa Anna's loss was anywhere from 600 over 1,500 men while hundreds of Mexicans were wounded. Santa Anna said this was a small victory and cared little about the deaths of his men. Most Mexicans were given Catholic rites but since there were too many, too few alive to bury them, and no room in the cemetery, they stacked the bodies in piles along with dried kindling wood and set fire to the bodies.

Gone were Davy Crockett, Jim Bowie, and William Travis with all who were not killed in the battle being murdered and the corpses burnt in the fires. Texans were enraged, to say the least, and decided to organize. On March 2, Texas formulated its own Constitution for the Republic of Texas. It was now the "Lone Star Republic." This was during the fighting at the Alamo. They had been working on the flag for some time with this end in mind and on March 2 it was flown.

In April 1836, Sam Houston organized group of about 180 Texans who caught nearly 4,000 Mexicans off-guard at San Jacinto. While the Mexicans were taking a siesta, Houston and his party took Santa Anna as a prisoner. The Tejano people, Spanish-speaking settlers of Texas, also believed in the Texas Revolution. They had been terrorized, abused, and intimidated, and wanted control over their towns and villages without federal interference. The Tejanos fought with Houston's troops against Santa Anna's soldiers. However, after the war everything changed and there was quite massive disillusionment and mistrust. The Americans, who now swarmed into Texas, didn't see any difference between Tejanos and Mexicans. In the next ten years the Tejanos were completely locked out of the new Texas government as well.

Stories abound that Davy Crockett may have escaped death at the Alamo, only to be executed later, and may have abandoned his comrades fleeing for his own safety. Another is that the ashes of Bowie, Crockett, and Bowie were retrieved and buried in an unknown location. If you want to read some true-to- life western sagas, follow the lives of our three heroes who had checkered pasts. Did William Travis draw a line in the sand with his sword, asking his men to cross the line if they were going to stay and fight?

But the facts remain, why did these men choose to die in this broken-down mission on the desolate plains of Texas, knowing they did not have enough reinforcements to defend it? My take is their commitment. They knew this was their destiny and it would make a big difference. It did. Their collective sacrifice brought about Texas independence. Now Americans could go to the Pacific and settle in a land adding more than a million square miles. This lowly mission became a shrine cherished, respected, and venerated all over the world. Remember the Alamo!

For chronology, it was in March 1836 that Texas declared independence and became the Lone Star Republic and nine years later it became a state. Texans really wanted to be annexed to become a part of the United States but again, the big issue of slavery arose. If Texas came into union it would be a slave state so the rest of America wanted no part of it. Northerners didn't know what this territory would be. How many states? They made it clear to

John Tyler. Texas was part of what? The United States and Mexico disagreed on the border. The border problem still exists today.

In April 1836, before the Battle of San Jacinto, Santa Anna fled but the Americans captured him. They never realized they had him until he was brought back to camp and the Mexican prisoners started saying "long live Santa Anna." Santa Anna thought he would be executed and his only recourse was to sign an order telling his troops to withdraw. Nonetheless, the Americans let Santa Anna go and what do you think he did? He started rebuilding his army and attacked again. The Americans were victorious and Santa Anna returned to Mexico disgraced. Santa Anna was removed but regained his dictatorship of Mexico, eleven times in total.

America did declare war on Mexico in 1846, capturing Mexico City in 1847, because Mexico never did recognize Texas' independence, despite Sana Anna signing the agreement. Finally, in 1848, Mexico signed the Treaty of Guadalupe Hidalgo. Mexico agreed to the annexation of Texas and the Rio Grande as the border between Texas and Mexico. Mexico also gave a large area of land, the Mexican Cession, to the United States.

Meanwhile, in the British territory of our present Washington and Oregon, there was a lucrative fur territory. The British were willing to compromise and suggested they would take the current state of Washington and they would give us Oregon. This didn't fly because we were Americans, and wanted it all.

Summary

The fight for Texas independence culminated with the Alamo, when the Americans lost. However, it brought about defeat at San Jacinto and eventually the Treaty of Guadalupe-Hidalgo. Americans used Manifest Destiny as a God-given religion. The Lone Star Republic was granted statehood in 1845.

Texas was just one example of sectionalism and not nationalism. There was no consensus between the Tejanos and settlers. There existed, as in the South, castes, misunderstandings, and greed for land. Many settlers already had their slaves with them in Texas.

The bottom line: President Tyler had some tough situations to consider:

- Manifest destiny

- Texas (The Lone Star Republic)
- The Northwest Territory (Washington and Oregon)

It was up to Tyler to settle these issues and he was unlike his predecessors. Tyler was southern and wanted to please the South. Likewise, Congress was at war with him, and there was ongoing dispute with the Texas territory and British with Pacific Northwest. The South wanted its slavery, while the North said absolutely not. Tyler was trying to do something to be remembered but he was so unpopular that by the end of four years no political party wanted him. He became an outcast. The Presidential election of 1844 was wide open.

What did Tyler accomplish? As far as one term presidents, he did everything he said he would do.

He annexed Texas for one. He did reorganize the U.S. Navy, and gave us a weather bureau. Strike one up for the North when in 1842 Tyler signed a tariff bill protecting northern manufacturers. The Webster-Ashburton Treaty ended a Canadian boundary dispute.

Tyler had replaced the original Whig Cabinet with southern conservatives. In 1844, Calhoun became Secretary of State. Later these men returned to the Democratic Party, committed to the preservation of states' rights, planter interests, and the institution of slavery. Whigs became more representative of northern business and farming interests.

When the first southern states seceded in 1861, Tyler led a compromise movement which failed. He then changed gears and worked to create the Southern Confederacy. Tyler was not idle. He became a member of the Confederate House of Representatives and died in 1862.

America was growing by leaps-and-bounds and there was no limit to the exploitation. Black slaves, the Mexicans and Tejanos, Native Americans, European immigrants, Chinese, and I'm sure I missed some cultures. It was all part of the building of our country and humans displayed many of their worst and best traits in their actions. We were attempting to become the most powerful country in the world. We cannot turn our backs on past events but can only look back, learn, and move on to the future.

Chapter 16

Technology, Immigration, Factory Life, and "Yes Marie, we have Leisure Time."

We need a break from wars, men with powerful ambitions, politics, and politicians. Let's move up from the Mexican border and witness the great cities and industrialization. What were women doing? How was living in the North different from the South for the average person? Was there an average American? What were Americans doing for recreation? How were they making a living and what kind of standard of living did they possess?

If we were to experience life from the 1820s to the mid-century, we would witness America experiencing an Industrial Revolution. The South remained a single-crop farming economy with few large cities, but large-scale manufacturing replaced agriculture, in the North. Slaves weren't needed because there was an abundant immigrant workforce. If you were interested in agriculture, you certainly wouldn't want to move South and endure production of labor-intensive crops, namely cotton, then rice and tobacco, if you were doing the work yourself.

There was less capital invested in southern industrial development, homesteading was discouraged, and government spending wasn't designated to railroads or canal building. This resulted in fewer factory jobs for immigrants. As a result, seven out of eight immigrants, came North, rather than settling South. Yes, there was prejudice, violence, and injustice, but they settled in the North, Midwest, or West. There were jobs, cheap land, and conditions were far better than in the old country.

Communities of like immigrants and cultures formed. Many Slavs went to Pennsylvania, while the Germans and Hungarians went to the Midwest to farm. While the Irish went to cities such as Boston and Chicago, Italians settled and flourished in New York and New England. These new immigrants often competed with native born white-Americans for low paying jobs. For the Irish, many came to flee the Great Famine (1845-52). Overall, immigration increased dramatically, especially between the 1840s and mid-1850s. There was always an underdog. Once one nationality moved upward, another replaced them.

As the American transportation system flourished, raw materials were transported to mills and factories, and finished goods were again transported, and then sold. The North had more natural resources than the South, and large cities became larger. They had factories, a strong industrial base, and lots of people. Old rutted paths that had passed as roads, were revitalized or replaced by railroads, canals, and steamboats. Everything and everyone moved more quickly and goods became cheaper.

As areas that were once remote were now growing, crafts and trades were disappearing and new jobs were created. The South remained stagnant, and most people lived in rural areas. There were few cities with large populations. Plantations were remote and never located in large populated cities. Large plantations were constructed along the coast beside rivers that flowed into the sea and labor-intensive crops such as rice, indigo, and tobacco flourished.

Railroads came from coastal cities and moved inland. The Charleston and Hamburg Railway when completed in 1833 became the world's largest railroad with 136 miles of track. However, most tracks were laid up North. In 1852 the locomotive was revolutionary and a rail line through your small town was a God-send. The railroad made and broke small settlements. The small towns that grew and prospered, secured luxuries and goods not formerly available, and business techniques quickly changed. During the 1830s, they depended upon state-funding but the depression caused changes and voting banned financing from state support. In the South, Federal funding of railroads was viewed as an invasion of state's rights and was one of the downfalls for the South by the time of the Civil War, by not creating enough track. When people looked at government to solve problems, it was with state government. Federal funding unavailable until the Civil War approached. Speculators were heavily investing, purchasing land, and receiving their funding from New York City where securities and stocks were traded on the New York Stock Exchange.

As industry and transportation expanded, there was still the prejudice for immigrants but the inequality in the North concerning color of skin far surpassed it. There were those who took action. Frederick Douglass continually pushed for equality and there was an interesting story. He continually would buy first class train tickets during the 1840s, would enter the car, only to be thrown out and pushed into the Jim Crow car. He would do this on his twenty-five-mile ride from Lynn to Newburyport, Massachusetts.

The railroad and occupants in the first-class car were embarrassed as they witnessed the abuse. The rail line countered by eliminating the stop in Lynn, much to people's disgust. Douglas gained community support and one female contacted the rail executives stating that the line allowed pets such as monkeys and dogs so why wouldn't they allow such a distinguished and reputable person such as Douglas aboard? The policy changed, the train stopped in Lynn, and there was no further issue with first class ticket holders.[1]

The Erie Canal was a miracle. It was the first waterway system that linked the east to the midwestern markets. Irish immigrants were coming in great numbers. In 1825, when the Erie Canal opened, a new age of transportation was born and it made New York City. The city became the largest trading center, far greater than Philadelphia and Baltimore. Government built the canals and roads, and private industry built the railroads.

The National Road went from Maryland to Illinois by 1850. It took 39 years to do this. Although private industrialists-built railroads, the federal government eventually gave public land grants to speed up the process. The government pushed competition and the court case of *Gibbons v. Ogden* made an impact that affects us today. In the Supreme Court Decision, it ruled that the United States Government had the exclusive right over interstate commerce. We don't get an Interstate Commerce Commission until 1887 but this case was important. The case was originally set-up in New York and was about a state-granted monopoly involving steamboats in New York and New Jersey. Back in those days, there were no cars, just steamboats, horses, mules, and feet.

From around 1820 to 1850, populations went to the cities. If you were a gateway city having a river or railroad or canal, successful trade was ensured. The great cities of Chicago, Milwaukee, and Buffalo, for example, grew rapidly. Factory cities like Lowell, Massachusetts grew as immigration of the Irish and Germans rose and filled the mills with new workers. The Irish Potato Famine went on over a period of years and the Irish were forced to do something as people were starving to death. America was an answer if one could find the means to get here. Conditions were so dire in Ireland that priests urged couples to delay marriage and families. Strong ethic pockets developed in the major cities.

Manufacturing changed and the American manufacturing system used interchangeable parts. Home made goods were replaced by machine goods and manufacturing covered the northeast. It used to be that the merchants would distribute their materials to rural people who would finish them for manufacture. Skilled artisans would open small shops, teaching apprentices or journeymen, but now they were a memory. A mechanical sewing machine revolutionized the system providing both speed and accuracy. Technology meant that science was being applied for practical usage.

Major technological advances were Eli Whitney's cotton gin which took away the tedious jobs of taking seeds out of cotton, quickly, and allowed farmers to grow more. Unfortunately, it increased the demand for slaves because more cotton was being produced. Then there was Cyrus McCormick's reaper for grain crops worked up North. The South wasn't interested.

Technology changed the way cattle were fed, and new soil techniques and fertilization increased output. Many learned the hard way about the importance of crop-rotation, something that was lost for a while and had been used by the early Native Americans.

How about medicine, germs, and disinfection? In 1842, anesthesia was developed!

Education about diet started, even though it has changed over the years. Improved printing and the "Penny Press" Newspapers were inexpensive reading in the 1830s. They didn't cater to the rich but to anyone who could read.

Americans were forward-moving and fun-loving also. Many had leisure time and were literate. What did they do when not toiling? Not only were Americans reading more newspapers, they were writing books. It is difficult to imagine that New York was once a wilderness, but James Fenimore Cooper wrote about the frontier in New York! *The Last of the Mohicans* became a classic. Ralph Waldo Emerson believed our ideas of God and freedom were inborn traits and transcendentalism was popular. This seventeen-letter word, centered on the belief of divinity of individuals and nature. Then there were Edgar Allan Poe and Walt Whitman.

Let's not forget Henry David Thoreau who advocated standing up and defending a citizen's right to disobey unjust laws in *Civil Disobedience*. As we travel into the twentieth century in later years, we'll look at Mahatma Ghandi and Dr. Martin Luther King's philosophies and make comparisons.

Art such as the Hudson River School painted scenes around the Hudson (1820-70), George Catlin painted Native Americans, and Frederick Law Olmsted, the father of landscape architecture, designed Central Park.

We could go to a stage play, or the theatre or the Minstrel Show. This was the era when Minstrel Shows became popular. Whites would dress as blacks and dance, sing, and tell jokes, and it was meant to be imitating and mocking. Much later we got the term "Jim Crow" when these Jim Crow laws passed. It depicted a black man dancing to a white man's melody. Entertainment was transformed.

Formerly people created their own activities but now everything changed and people were given a variety of choices. Entertainment became diversified, exciting, and both rich and poor mingled. Newspapers were inexpensive and everyone could afford them. It was a joy when the circus came to town. Entrepreneurs such as P.T. Barnum presented the circus which became complete family entertainment. Music was written and songs for patriots such as "My country tis of thee," were presented. If you were refined, there was the ballet.

Technology was great, but it had and has its downside. Women and children worked in "sweatshops." Although this additional income allowed some young children to stay in school longer, there was a gloomy side.

Technology thrived as early as the 1790s when Samuel Slater founded the first American Cotton Mills in Rhode Island. Females were the predominant workforce. The work was difficult but offered some freedom and women willingly chose to enter it. Cities and Textile mills were the up and the down side of the North. There have been comparisons between factory work and slave labor. You are the judge.

Chaos reigned in the early 1800s. Factory cities grew as immigrants and rural young adults moved to the cities. There were tenements, the wild Irish, and free blacks. Hogs roamed the muddy streets as manure provided a distinct odor, and people didn't bathe. Bathrooms were outdoor outhouses or privies, and there were epidemics. Earlier, we witnessed the Columbian Exchange, and now cities were bringing out some of the same conditions existing in the large European cities centuries ago. It was in this era, however, the vast transportation system helped it along.

Poverty, lack of education, and disease brought forth public institutions such as schools, hospitals, orphanages, almshouses, and prisons, which were expected to meet these problems. The real problem was they were overwhelmed. Money was status and it opened the doors to opportunity.

Factory Life in New England[2]

Take a walk with me and we'll look at Lowell, Massachusetts in 1842. It's daytime and not a soul appears to be on the street, but look, through the closed windows I see clouds of lint flying in the air. How could the windows be closed, it's almost 90°F today? The noise sounds like buildings are falling. I think I need my earplugs. Over there! It's 7 p.m. and women are suddenly bolting out into the common. Let's find out about this town.

The Lowell Mill was an experiment in society. Our fictional person, we'll call her Molly, will enlighten us. We asked Molly why she worked in the mills. She stated she was 16 years old and came for the money. She was hopeful and possessed her dream. Molly said she prayed she would find a rich man and marry within the next few years. Others came to escape from parents, a possible forced marriage, or just freedom to do their own thing. Molly stated some were really old, maybe 35, and sometimes helped her. Life in the country was lonely and the only people to rely on were family. Molly appreciated talking to an older woman at the mill after hours because loneliness and missing her mother often came in spells of melancholia. Most of the women were never married and single.

"What hours do you work, Molly?"

She said she works about 70+ hours a week. It is 5 a.m. to 7 p.m. and Sundays are a day off. The town provided a gym, church, and library. We noted that the mills were filled with rural women and Molly told us they were called "mill girls."

"Where do you live, Molly?"

She said she lived in a boarding house and paid rent which was a large percentage of her wages. She shared one tiny bed with two other women. "The money is really good. I earn about three times as much as I would if I became a servant in someone's household," blurted Molly.

"How much do you earn, Molly?" I asked.

"Two dollars a week," she bragged.

"I've heard there was a turn out (strike) eight years ago when they cut wages, but it didn't work and everyone went back to work for the cut wages. We might as well accept it. This is a good job, and I know I'll be able to leave once I find my true man," whispered the girl.

"What do you do for fun?"

"We have curfews at 10 p.m., but after working 12 hours, I'm too tired to do anything other than eat and fall into bed," she retorted. "The matrons at the house really watch us and keep us on the up-and-up, and I've seen girls have to leave because they were considered too wild for the likes of this town."

"Well, how did you find this job," I asked?

The men are called "Slavers" or recruiters and they come to farms as well as posting signs in the nearby town.

Molly further stated that once she got acclimated to the mill, she quickly learned the procedures and where she ranked in society. She knew that mill girls were at the bottom of the list of jobs available to women.

Molly said that recently, 1830ish, new technology and competition expanded capacity and prices fell. Changes had to be made so they made the workers work faster and production was doubling. The women worked under unbearable conditions. There was lint in the air. I asked why windows were closed. Even in 100°F weather where it was up to 115°F inside, humidity was necessary to keep the cotton flowing and machines to working properly. Even one single snapped thread could shut down a machine.

She further stated that if you fainted, were ill, or couldn't keep up, you could be fired. Molly was troubled by persistent sinus infections, headaches, and some serious breathing problems. She asserted that she heard the more serious byssinosis or brown lung (fatal) were commonplace and that was why many of the older ladies were fired.

I asked if we could go somewhere to talk privately. She said she was afraid and had to go back to the boarding house for dinner. She pleaded that we wouldn't say anything about our "talk" and that I had caught her at a bad moment.

Reports from other past and present employees revealed lost limbs, especially fingers, head bruises, scalps, broken arms, and punishments were common. The men over-seers who were in-charge, much like Southern overseers, were often brutal and abused the women. They were accountable to the owner and needed to get the job done. In Rhode Island there was evidence of a "whipping room." Some cases went to court, but usually the parents were awarded a small sum, if any. The alleged abuses were choking, being forced to stand on a hot stove, or sexual in nature.

Some states, e.g., Massachusetts, required the younger children to attend school three months a year but even children of seven worked in the mills. They worked long hours on family farms so working in the mills for longer hours was no exception. They had no childhood. This was just an exchange of type of work.

When in 1845 the Irish Potato Famine began, (remember potatoes came from America), immigrants replaced American women who were disgusted with the continual wage cuts and horrible working conditions. American factories became likened to the sweatshops of Europe. It was not the equivalent of southern slavery but near enough in many women's minds. Women organized "turnouts" or strikes but were fired or blacklisted, never to work in a cotton factory again. The 12-14-hour work day still existed. By the Civil War, factories closed because there was no raw material, the southern cotton.

There was a growing middle-class in the North and old jobs became the new jobs of African-Americans and immigrants. Women practiced a "cult of domesticity" and practiced etiquette and temperance to protect morality. There was a term used called Separate Spheres that defined the gender roles. Nothing had changed because men worked and were involved in politics while women took care of family and stayed close to home.

Since the male was the public sphere, he supported the family and was determined to succeed. Since the female managed the private sphere, she maintained her inborn traits of purity, humbleness, and submission. It was concluded that together there was harmony and she would have her husband's protection, security, and social status. She was a reflection of "his" accomplishments." Understanding Victorian thinking, helps us to understand why mill girls may have been looked upon as the bottom of the caste.

When attempts were made to form unions, the nativists, people who wanted only native-borns, no immigrants, attempted to shut immigrants out because they were competition. Prejudice began and this was one of the ways it grew by leaps and bounds. People were concerned about their own well-being. Such was the South after the Civil War when whites were increasingly concerned about the quickly growing power of the emancipated and the threat they presented.

Two important people I haven't introduced to you are Angelina and Sarah Grimke (the Grimke sisters). They are usually associated with the anti-slavery movement but they were strongly speaking for women's rights.

In 1848, there was a convention in Seneca Falls, New York. It put together a women's Declaration of Independence but it failed to pass. Women's suffrage was not a huge issue until after the Civil War but trailblazing women such as Elizabeth Cady Stanton and Lucretia Mott took the forefront and pushed for rights.

Education

Public education in the North was attempting to change. Rural parents didn't do a lot, and basic literacy was all that was required; but reformers wanted change. One reformer was Horace Mann, who shifted financial support from parents to the state of Massachusetts. Mann believed school was the most important thing parents could do for their children. Catharine Beecher, who was Harriet Beecher Stowe's older sister by 11 years, opened the career to women and promoted *McGuffey Readers*. She didn't write them.

Education was important to native-born Americans who didn't like the immigrants coming in. Few blacks attended school in the north. Nevertheless, changes were made and gone were the one-room school houses. Classes were now divided into grades and free tax-supported schools came about.

Summary

Technology brought progress and profit and America was moving into a period of tremendous growth. Transportation excelled. There were railroads, roads, and canals and having one in your town or city determined if your locality would live or die. New inventions such as the cotton gin, reaper, and sewing machine changed lives. People had some leisure time and went to the circus, mistral shows, read newspapers, magazines, and books. Life was different for all Americans depending upon your geographic location, sex, nationality, family history, finances, and color of your skin.

Technology, however, brought some negativity. Gone were the home businesses, trades, artisans, and apprenticeships, as young women came to the cities to work in mills. Cities were filthy and diseases were common. Standards of living were low. Was factory life like slavery? Women did have the power to leave, or did they? It was still a Victorian society and women had few rights. The mill girls were at the bottom of the ladder.

Although the mill owners provided facilities for gyms, libraries, and recreation, the long hours made it difficult to enjoy these amenities. Single women hoped to marry and leave the mills and most considered the life temporary. Some sought more lucrative positions and became prostitutes, because it paid much better.

Some women, such as Elizabeth Cady Stanton, went to Seneca Falls, New York in 1848 and started the ball rolling for women's rights. A little progress was made in education, and America grew by leaps and bounds, while forming a larger gap between the sexes, rich and poor, and where you lived.

Chapter 17

The Rumble of Thunder Continues as Lightning Approaches

Despite his resume, Henry Clay, aka the Great Compromiser, ran for president as a Whig in 1844 but he had no powerful supporters on either side, even though he was a southern slave owner. He thought there should be a compromise for Texas but the South would not budge. As a result, he sacrificed southern support. Here is the changeover.

How about Democrats? They had to settle for James K. Polk, a southerner and a slave owner. His mentor was Andy Jackson who taught him the art of politics and being pushy. The issue was Manifest Destiny which obsessed the nation during the mid-1840s. While campaigning in true Jacksonian fashion, Polk called for a re-annexation of Texas and the re-occupation of the Oregon Territory. He asserted that it was America's in the first place. If you were an expansionist that was great, but if you weren't, you would vote for a compromise and elect Clay. Polk's campaign slogan was, "54-40 or fight." The 54th parallel which is in Canada, would be ours. This is how it came about.

In 1818, the United States and the United Kingdom, which controlled British Canada, established a joint claim over the Oregon Territory. This region was west of the Rocky Mountains and between 42° north and 54° 40' north, the southern boundary of Russia's Alaska territory. The northern boundary of Oregon was the latitude line of 54° 40'. The territory included what is today Oregon, Washington, and Idaho, as well as land up the western coast of Canada.

Joint control of the area had worked for over 15 years, but the time had come when both agreed that Oregon had to be divided. Americans keep moving West, outnumbered the British in the northwest 1830s, and by the 1840s, Americans were coming in droves on the Oregon Trail.

Then there was the Texas territory. Polk won the election and in the last hours of Tyler's administration, Tyler signed an executive order annexing Texas and making it part of the United States. No one really knew where the border of Texas really was when Tyler signed the bill. When Polk became president, Polk asked Texans, "Where's the border?" They said it was the Rio Grande River.

More land and possible war, so Polk immediately began to negotiate with the British because last thing he wanted in the Northwest was a war in addition to a Mexican war. Mexico had never recognized our independence so Polk knew war was inevitable with Mexico. He negotiated a treaty with the British which is the 49th parallel, the current border with Canada. There were some minor quirks but they were resolved and Polk is credited for his negotiation. However, these were not normal times. We were in a period of rapid expansion, lust for land, and feeling invincible and entitled. Population was growing rapidly through natural procreation and immigration.

Polk called for expansion that included Texas, California, and the entire Oregon territory. People took it that he wanted no slavery in the North, but he was willing to go to war in the South in order to get his slave state. It stood to reason, that since Polk was a slave owner and sectionalist, he obviously wanted the institution of slavery to continue. The big problem was with Mexico.

James K. Polk was president for one term (1845-1849) and told voters from the very beginning that he would only serve for four years. He served his term and died three months later of Cholera. What did he do during his presidency? Territorial expansion was the big one. He accepted the Rio Grande as the border but Mexico said it was the Nueces River which runs parallel to the Rio Grande. The mistake that Mexico made was they allowed this land to become part of the United States. Mexico should have said no; all of that land was theirs and not America's to begin with. By acknowledging, they agreed to a border instead of staying firm and claiming that it's all Mexican and there was no Texas. Between the two rivers in question, it was a no-mans-land and the United States Army was sent by Polk under General Zachary Taylor to guard the Rio Grande border.

Mexico called this an invasion. Congress now united against Polk, especially Northerners. To make matters worse, there had been another revolution in Mexico and there was a new government.

Then, something strange happened. A first term House Representative stood up and offered eight resolutions, called the Spot Resolutions. He wanted to know the exact spot where American blood was first shed on American soil. This man was Abraham Lincoln. People laughed at him and called him "Spotty." Lincoln was defeated when up for re-election and was convinced his career was over, and that he had committed political suicide.

In the meantime, our army and navy were being built up and we had our first professional army. Our army hadn't been used since 1812. There were West Point trained soldiers who knew military tactics, maps, and strategy, and Polk knew we would win the war. He went before Congress and asked for a declaration of war and said the same thing Lincoln said, "American blood on American soil." There were enough Congressmen who passed it. Polk achieved an across-the-board victory in the Mexican–American War, which resulted in the cession by Mexico of most of the American Southwest.

He did a couple more things. 1846 Was a good year for him. He secured a huge reduction of tariff rates with the Walker Tariff and also achieved his other major goal, re-establishment of the Independent Treasury System.

The Wilmot Proviso affected the next election in 1848 which involved land from the New Mexico and Utah Territories. Lewis Cass, a Democratic Senator from Michigan, suggested this territory be organized based on the concept of popular sovereignty. Should the people who reside in a territory decide if there slavery would exist or whether it should be outlawed?

Why should anyone but the people in the area living there decide if they wanted slavery? Cass got no credit for the idea, it but it was placed into the minds of Congressmen, and the idea didn't die. Cass ran against a Whig, Zachary Taylor who served in Mexico during the Mexican War. Remember, under Polk he went down to Texas to guard the border? We are guarding the border today, isn't that interesting.

A group of Democrats split their party, voting in the 1848 election and allowed Taylor to win. They were called "Barnburners" and their opposites were the "Hunkers." The name came from the fabled Dutchman who burned down his barn to get rid of rats; by implication, the *Barnburners* could and would destroy corporations, public works, and anything that stood in their way to do away with abuses, such as slavery.

It was difficult for Cass to run against a military hero. Keep in mind that Taylor was a general, and some generals have a hard time transitioning to the presidency. We saw how, at this time our military heroes were becoming presidents. It began with Washington, and continued with Jackson, Harrison, and Tyler.

The problem was that the New Mexico-Utah area became heavily populated because of the gold rush. People came by the thousands. Over 300,000 came to Sutter's Mill, Coloma, California when gold was discovered by James Marshall. The last thing they wanted to be was a territory and martial law. Just as a point of miscellaneous information, California was not the first gold-strike. It was in Cabarrus County, North Carolina which is just east of our current city of Charlotte. It was in 1799 and today exists as Reed's Gold Mine.

People came by land and sea and the population of California went from 15,000 in 1848 to 250,000 in the 1850s. There were ethnic clashes between the Americans and Hispanics, Chinese (who in the next decades would build the Transcontinental Railroad), as well as all other ethnic groups from Italian, French, Spanish, and even Hawaiian backgrounds.

There were Irish convicts who came via Australia in exile. People were well-armed. Vigilante committees were formed to protect the peace. There was unrest between those who had land protected by the Treaty of Guadalupe Hidalgo, the *Californios,* and the breed of gold crazies.

People were afraid that California would authorize an independent government and decide to become just like the Texas Republic in 1836. It wasn't until 1845 when Texas became a state. Once again, Mexico should have given the treaty more thought before surrendering "Alta or Upper California" vs. "Baja" or Lower California. to the United States. The largest gold rush in American history was soon to occur, in Upper California when the Treaty of Guadalupe Hidalgo was signed in 1848. Small towns became huge cities. For example, our present-day San Francisco was barely a town of 150 called Yerba Buena and suddenly there were 50,000 people consisting of many cultures.

The next 12-year period was one of many acts and compromises. The first were the Organic Acts. They established a territory and specified how a territory was to be governed. The first was the Northwest Ordinance. Remember, there were Northwest Ordinances such as the 1784, which said land west of Appalachians would be separate states. Then there was 1785 which established grids, and 1787 set-forth how many people (60,000) were required when the area could become a territory. Ladies, remember, this was free, adult, white-men. Women, minorities, and non-whites didn't count.

In 1850, there was the issue of the new territories established from the Mexico acquisition. We had the Territory of New Mexico (which eventually became Nevada, Colorado, New Mexico, and Arizona) and the Utah Territory (Utah) which will become part of the Compromise of 1850.

Zachary Taylor told California to go ahead and write a constitution. The people determined they wanted to be a free state and Taylor had no problem with their decision. It didn't work, and congress was livid. We had been admitting states in pairs and this would disrupt the balance of power. Northerners were enraged as well as the Southerners and didn't want California admitted at any cost.

What could we do? We had big problems with North vs. South and huge struggles with Taylor vs. Congress. This was serious because Southerners were beginning to assert, more strongly, that they wanted out of the Union. A convention met in Nashville in 1850 and secession was discussed. This issue came back to our Great Compromiser, Henry Clay who put together a program, an Omnibus Bill, which had five parts.

An Omnibus Bill is an all-encompassing one that puts together a lot of issues for one single congressional vote. A current example is the bill passed in 2018:

Mar 23, 2018 - Just hours after threatening a *veto*, President *Trump* said Friday afternoon that he *had* signed a "ridiculous" $1.3 trillion spending *bill* passed by Congress early Friday, averting a government shutdown. (*Washington Post*).

It was Clay's compromise to keep the South in our Union and the Northerners happy. Keep in mind, Henry Clay from Kentucky, John C. Calhoun from South Carolina, and Daniel Webster from Massachusetts were growing old and had been major political figures for decades. Calhoun died the same year, and Clay and Webster two years later. The Bill failed because Southerners, like Calhoun, saw it as the North's attempt to stop slavery. Even though it was debated for 18 months, it died, but resulted in the Compromise of 1850.

In "Senate Stories," there is an interesting account about Henry Clay and the Omnibus Bill. The Great Compromiser was scheduled to deliver his last compromise. Over four decades had gone by since he first appeared in the chamber. Now, he was challenged with one of the most important tests in his career. He agonized over the challenge of keeping our nation together and avoiding a long and bitter war.[1]

I can only imagine the courage it took Clay to muster his speech. He was now 73 years old and suffering from tuberculosis. It was apparent that Clay stood at death's door. The thin and frail Clay stood exhausted and tired, gasping for breath, in great pain, and coughing up blood. He was accompanied up to the stage by the chaplain of the Senate who helped him up the few stairs. Nonetheless, he offered eight resolutions. Once and for all, the dispute over former Mexican territories had to be settled. Foremost, was the issue that was drawing our nation apart – slavery.

The story goes that Clay used some showmanship. Clay had asked the feds to buy Mount Vernon from the Washington Estate and a grateful supporter had given him a small piece of wood from Washington's coffin. Clay played up the questions and asked why he was being given this token and asked if it was a sign that Washington's nation was now dying? He then answered himself.

"No, sir, no," thundered Clay, holding up the relic. "It was a warning voice, coming from the grave to the Congress ... to beware, to pause, to reflect before they lend themselves to any purposes which shall destroy the Union." Clay talked and talked and the speech went on for two days and tears came down his checks. The audience was taken back and emotions flooded the Senate Chamber. Upon the conclusion, on both days, women came up to kiss him as men came to clutch his hands as Clay held back tears.[2] Clay hung on and died less than two years later. It is fitting that a tablet within his crypt states:

"I know No South, No North, No East, No West."

A six-month debate followed and Mississippi Senator Henry Foote mentioned putting the resolutions into a single bill. Clay called it a "sort of omnibus" introducing a lot of things to everyone and the idea survived and became our nation's first Omnibus Bill. He believed it was fair to both the North or South and a compromise.

The Senate rejected it, the North and South became further divided, and Clay went home to Kentucky. However, there was good news. Stephen Douglas of Illinois, who later debated Lincoln for a United States Senate seat, put it back together again, introduced five separate bills, and each one passed. The result was the Compromise of 1850. The war didn't start for another ten years and to his death, Clay believed his compromise bill did, in fact, save the union.

In the meantime, Clay, Calhoun, and Webster died. Now, without them, where was leadership for this nation? There was a mad-scramble to lead, when Stephen A. Douglas stepped forward once again. Douglas was a very important man. He ran against Abraham Lincoln and lost.

Douglas was from Illinois and wanted to lead the nation. Douglas thought he was unique because Illinois dipped into the south and bordered on slavery.[3] For example, Kentucky was a slave state or border state (that stayed in the Union during the Civil War), the Mississippi River was a natural border to the West (Missouri-slave), while the northern part bordered on free states such as Wisconsin and Michigan. He believed if he could continually be elected senator, he could compromise. Douglas went to Taylor and said since Clay's bill failed, the nation owed it to his legacy by breaking the bill into five parts and just maybe, it would pass. Taylor gave a resounding no.

As fate had it, Taylor, suddenly died of Gastroenteritis or the Stomach Flu. Harrison died within 90 days but Taylor lasted about 16 months from March 1849 until July 1850. Vice President, Millard Fillmore became president. (1850-53). He was first of three presidents in 1850s who were poor leaders, (Fillmore, Pierce, Buchanan). They were northerners sympathetic to the South and called Doe Faces.

Douglas proposed the same thing of breaking up the bill to Fillmore who okayed it. Congress voted and the bill barely passed. However, there were enough moderates to support it. The Compromise of 1850, was born and there were a lot of angry people since the Missouri Compromise line was still in effect 36°. It settled nothing and delayed the inevitable, as the fundamental issue if free and slave could live side by side, was not settled. One element made everything worse and that was the new Fugitive Slave Law of 1850.

The Compromise of 1850 of five separate bills passed by the United States Congress temporarily calmed a four-year political debate between slave and free states on the status of territories acquired during the Mexican–American War (1846–1848). Once again, southerners were livid. They couldn't believe northerners had the guts to do this even though they themselves did the same thing. Our nation was deeply divided. This decade of the 1850s was volatile and presidential elections came every four years.

Why was the compromise such a big deal and what did it do? First, California was admitted as a free state and its boundaries remain the same today as they were in 1850. Texas gave up its claim to New Mexico as well as its claims to northern Texas but kept the Panhandle. The federal government took over the state's public debt, and in 1845 it became a state.

Then, the Utah-New Mexico Territory, sometimes called the Arizona Territory, was organized and there was absolutely no reference to slavery. Everyone assumed that the Californians would decide for themselves through popular sovereignty. The South previously prevented adopting the Wilmot Proviso which would have outlawed slavery in the new territories. Let's look at this in reality. Was this land really suited for plantation agriculture and were these settlers really interested in establishing slavery? They had bigger obstacles to worry about.

One of the things that bothered Northerners most was the slave pens and auction blocks in U.S. Capital. The compromise ended the slave trade in DC, but not slavery itself. The final point was based on extreme measures and was a matter of interpretation. Southerners claimed thousands of slaves escaped, went North or into Canada, and no one helped them get their property back and this cost them millions of dollars. To put a compromise in place, a federal fugitive slave law was enacted. It was very strict, powerful, and was meant to guarantee Southerners that the government would make sure slaves were returned.

One could interpret the law in stating that every man and woman in America, black and white, was a potential slave catcher. For example, if you were walking in the North and someone yelled, "look, there's a fugitive slave," you needed to react. Anyone, may be an enemy of yours, and could have you arrested or fined if you did nothing. The North didn't buy this law and in retaliation passed a series of laws, Personal Liberty Laws, which made it illegal to obey the Federal Fugitive Slave Law. Once again, there was a nullification of federal law.

How the law worked was very sneaky. It could forbid localities to incarcerate fugitive or alleged slaves in their jails. Slaves could go to court and plead for freedom. It could simply forbid local authorities to cooperate and capture slaves for return. Southerners who went North to get their slaves back weren't protected. Their slaves who made it into the North were often helped to get settled. The large result, however, was that many Yankees now became abolitionists. They had enough of Federal Law and didn't want the slave question in their territory.

***

The nation was divided and the decade before the war was volatile. Lots of other events were about to happen and Manifest Destiny was the belief that prevailed. White Americans had the God-given right to go across the continent and take what was rightfully theirs. If anyone or anything tried to stop it, God's wrath would come down upon them because Americans were the chosen people. People came by the thousands and by 1850, half of the population lived west of the Appalachians.

Southern soil was already depleted because of single intensive crops, such as cotton. Land out West was $2 or $3 an acre. Everyone came, Whigs, Democrats, all denominations, male and female. Women worked alongside the men as the land was cleared. Roads, canals, and the railroads opened huge new markets for farmers. There was new machinery. By the time the Civil War started, over 300,000 Americans had taken the long journey on the Oregon Trail.

Southerners went Southwest and were crazed with Alabama Fever or Texas Fever. This new short staple cotton was hardier, coarser, and could grow in any soil, and it was planted everywhere. Yeoman farmers, who were those without slaves, went Southwest.

The first obstacle was getting to the West and Europeans had the desire to immigrate also. There were not a lot of choices. If you got to Panama, you could go over the isthmus by land and encounter the usual Cholera, fevers, mosquitoes, and dysentery. You could go through the Mexican desert and pray banditos didn't finish you off. Or, the last option was overland, often starting in St. Joseph, Missouri.

Let's follow an imaginary family attempting to move west and find a whole new life. There's a gold rush going on in 1852 in Oregon and thousands more are joining them. Let's look back to 1804 when Jefferson commissioned Merriweather Lewis and William Clark to explore and map the newly acquired Louisiana Territory. This exemplified the lure of adventure, rugged individualism, and economic advancement continued.

We'll call our settlers the Hopeful Family. The Hopefuls could take one of many trails: the Oregon Trail or the Santa Fe Trail, or one of the lesser known. Their only desire was to head west to the land of opportunity. This was going to be an adventure and they knew they were going to own land once they got to that special "somewhere."

The Hopefuls believe that it should only take about six months to get there and get settled. The Hopefuls intend to go via a wagon train in a Prairie Schooner and are starting off in Independence, Missouri like thousands of others. Certainly, the trails are well-marked but just in case, Mr. Hopeful purchases the nineteenth century version of a guidebook. The guidebooks were published in a bunch of different languages! The book gave them a rough list of supplies, and personal and foods to carry.

Since Jane Hopeful is the woman, she is packing up cooking supplies, food, water, clothing and household goods, and the six children. She is really looking forward to cooking, minding the children, milking the family cow who is coming along, and helping other pregnant women in birthing. John Hopeful will take care of the oxen, mule, drive, protect the family, and hunt. They stock up on supplies using the last of their meager savings, and include a lot of guns and ammo to ward off those pesky Indians.

Although they are travelling with a heavy load, they know they can do it. Certain they'll find plenty of water and food for the animals, they begin the journey in early April. They start their approximate 2,200-mile journey early because the weather could change and they could end up stranded like the Donner Party. John hopes they will make it within five months but has heard tales of those taking a year to arrive. They cross the wide Missouri River and meet with other adventurers. Leaders are set-up and our family feels the safety in the company of others.[4]

Naïve as some were, the West was settled and groups such as the Mormons, settled the Utah Territory and prospered, without slavery. More on this shortly. Our family, has no language barriers and everyone is enjoying the trip for the first week or so. There have been a few downpours and they've had to wait them out and a few wagons have broken axles and slowed them down. The weight of carrying extra axles, wheels, and barrels is a burden but they estimate their travel is around 12 miles per day. So far, it's been good, even though little Joshua was frightened when confronted by a rattler. Thankfully, he was not struck and only broke a couple of fingers when he broke his fall. Maggie Jones, in the wagon behind them, is due any day and has been feeling ill so the women are watching her closely. After Mr. Poorfaith was accidently shot, everyone has been vigilant but thankfully he was not crushed by the wagon wheels when he struck the dusty terrain.

This lucky family made it to the West while many of their new-acquaintances did not. The party encountered heat over 100°F during the day while they didn't expect the dessert to get so cold at night. They were constantly thirsty and encountered dried-up rivers, desert, desert, and more desert with no water. After a sudden summer storm, one of the guides drowned in a river crossing and gossip spread that out of every ten who attempted the trail, only eight or nine survived. Jane Hopeful heard that a group had contracted cholera the previous year and many had perished.

The so-called trail was strewn with rotted food, rusty equipment, dead oxen, and unburied corpses. The settlers had no recourse other than push-on and force the animals to the point of collapse. Dysentery was common. There were episodes of people going crazy and committing suicide or just giving up. Many lost hope. Our family is safe and now they begin the journey to making this new life work.

Summary

We've had a lot going on and now America is as close as it is going to be expanded through all of the territories we've acquired. We had major issues and disputes, causing confusion amongst most Americans. The newspapers tended to report various versions of the same events. This period from 1800-1850 certainly was a time when events rolled quickly and the waves were continual until all were consumed in issues, wondering what this new country was coming to.

Sandi Ludwa

The Louisiana Purchase (1803) gave us land going up to the Canadian Border (states of partial Montana, Wyoming, North Dakota, South Dakota, Nebraska, Missouri, Arkansas, Kansas, and Oklahoma to name a few). What are we going to do with it?

The was the 54-40 or fight – Washington and Oregon and parts of Montana and Idaho going into present day Canada which we shared with the Brits for a while until the Oregon Treaty 1846 are ours. We now have conclusion and a treaty.

A war with Mexico settled the Texas territory issue land acquired from Mexico and our current states of California, Texas, Arizona, Utah, New Mexico, in the Treaty of Guadalupe Hidalgo 1848.

Our problem was free or slave states as these become territories. So, we had what was known as the Organic Laws, establishing how a territory was to be governed. The first were the Northwest Ordinances (1784, 85, 87).

We had the Missouri Compromise 36°30′, but was it unconstitutional? The South said slaves were movable property. The West was expanding and the belief was that its expansion would lessen the concentration on slaves in the East and there might be less of a chance of a slave revolt.

There was the Wilmot Proviso which was introduced that stated no slavery in any land taken from Mexico. There was an assumption that California and New Mexico would be free and Texas would become a slave state. Then there was the concept of Popular Sovereignty. Should the average American be given a right to choose? Lewis Cass, a Democrat from Michigan suggested it and ran against the war hero Zachary Taylor who went down to the Mexican Border to defend our rights in Texas. Five separate bills were passed resulting in the Compromise of 1850.

The North and South were divided over the new territories and states. This was the future of America. There was a gold rush going on in 1852 in Oregon and westward expansion was on the rise. Before the Civil War exploded, over 300,000 Americans had taken the Oregon Trail westward. In 1804, Jefferson had commissioned Merriweather Lewis and William Clark to explore and map the newly acquired territory. It began around St. Louis and was to find a route to the coast. Land was plentiful and there was a lure of economic advancement. They considered it Manifest Destiny. It was inevitable and ordained by God. Allow me to enter an interesting side-note about Merriweather Lewis. Lewis died in 1809 on a journey to Washington, DC, and there is presently a push to exhume his body to determine whether it was suicide or murder. He was depressed and speculation was he was either alcoholic or suffered from syphilis.

Population went through the roof, and by 1850, half of the population lived west of the Appalachians. Southern soil was already becoming depleted by planting, especially cotton which took from the soil. Land out west was $2 or $3 an acre. As Jefferson once said, "Those who labor in the earth are the chose people of God." Both Jefferson and Jackson considered a liberal land policy essential and by the 1850s this had become a reality.

Settlers out west were very diverse. Some were Whigs and some were Democrats. Women worked side by side with males as land was cleared. In the East, roads, canals, railroads opened markets for farmers and there was a lot of new machinery.

Southerners went westward to Alabama and Texas and the new short staple cotton was planted. Yeoman farmers went southwest. It was an exciting time in America. So much was going on, people began to think about their futures and making some changes, embarking on an adventure to form a new life, or were given hope to climb from their dire situation by any means possible. Optimism was in the air for many but the issue of slavery was foremost. This was mid-nineteenth century America!

Chapter 18

Approaching War
More Fuel is Added to the Fire

The United States has always been a nation of readers. Have you read Harriet Beecher Stowe's *Uncle Tom's Cabin*? Harriet lived in Cincinnati, Ohio which is situated on the northern bank of the Ohio River. Ohio was a free state. If we crossed the river in 1852, we would be in Kentucky, a slave state. Harriet did take a three-day trip to Kentucky, once.

One peaceful Sunday morning Harriet sat in church. She prayed, let her mind wander, and suddenly was overcome with spirit, inspiration, and soul. Harriet knew that she needed to write her book. Ohio was free, the Beecher's didn't own slaves, and they weren't acquainted with anyone who did own slaves, but Harriet believed it was her moral obligation to write about the peculiar institution of slavery.

Harriet's dad, Lyman Beecher, was a man of God who preached very powerful sermons, usually on slavery and temperance. If we attended one of his sermons, I'm certain we would believe our destiny already had us fated for hellfire and damnation. Since the Rev. Beecher's church in Massachusetts caught fire because a shopkeeper had been storing alcohol in its basement, he knew it was a message from God to preach against the vice of liquor, in addition to slavery.

Lyman had a huge following across the United States which he collected when he was spreading his beliefs in the East. When the family moved to Ohio, Lyman was an educator at Lane Theological Seminary but he moved back East after disagreements arose within the college on slavery.[1] Harriet had married and many of her siblings had become involved in the issue. Harried started writing about slavery, abandoning her other writings which were about religion and women's domestic roles.

Since most people didn't know anyone who was a slave, she added reality to the institution and brought the novel to life so you got to know the people personally. She humanized the people she wrote about. The evil, immoral, and foul malevolence were all immortalized in the institution of slavery and not the people themselves. Images were vivid and never to be forgotten.

Imagine Eliza running away with a baby, jumping from icy mass to icy mass across the mighty river in mid-winter. Make no mistake, anyone who read it, knew slavery was bad. The book sold 300,000 copies within the first eight months. In today's market, it would be exceeding Harry Potter books. The anti-slavery Northerners made the pro-slavery Southerners extremely defensive, angry, and ready to fight. It made matters worse and fueled the fire which in less than a decade would result in the American Civil War.

When the book was criticized, Beecher wrote, *A Key to Uncle Tom's Cabin* to verify to the public that the facts on which she wrote the story. She stated Tom was a real person, Josiah Henson. Henson also wrote memoirs in his later years, coming forward to the public. He never received any payment for this.[2] Harriet, her husband, and her seven children never became wealthy from the publications but she did achieve tremendous fame and popularity. Harriet continued writing as an activist until she died three decades after the war ended.

Ever since the 1852 election of Franklin Pierce, America was divided. This was not the same as the divide we experience today, but in the 1850s, it was a huge split in religion, philosophy, culture, and human nature. Harriet's book stoked the fire, adding more fuel, that became uncontrolled and spread, exploding in the Civil War. It was illegal to have a copy of *Uncle Tom's Cabin* in the South. When Lincoln met Harriet Beecher Stowe, he is recognized as stating to Harriet, "So you're the little lady who wrote the book that started this great war." [3]

The Nation was getting ready for the huge explosion of the Civil War, and matters got worst. At this time there were no real leaders. Franklin Pierce was not a strong trailblazer. He was viewed as someone who would not upset most people. Have you ever met someone who goes with the current vogue and doesn't want to make any waves? Pierce was this say-nothing person. It was one of the reasons Pierce was the president.

He had his share of misfortunes. Pierce did have a reputation for excessive drinking and had seen his third, only living son, die before his eyes in a train accident. Then, his vice president died about a month and a half after his inauguration. The man who emerged, during this time, as a strong leader was Stephen Douglas of Illinois. He got Clay's omnibus provisions passed by breaking it into parts, resulting in the Kansas-Nebraska Act in 1854 and popular sovereignty.

Did Douglas know what he was doing? He suggested that since the Compromise of 1850 was unsuccessful but some areas didn't cause problems because there weren't a lot of people, e.g., Utah, New Mexico, popular sovereignty would solve the rift. He put together a proposal and suggested that the Nebraska and Kansas Territories be organized on same basis of popular sovereignty. So, what was big deal?

The Nebraska Territory was above 36°30′ which still existed per the Missouri Compromise, so he suggested slavery be given a chance even though up until that point it was against the law. Douglas was trying to win over the Southerners because under the Missouri Compromise there was no chance of slavery, but under popular sovereignty it could happen. The Kansas-Nebraska Bill was put together but, there was only one thing that both the North and South agreed upon, and that was the building of a transcontinental railroad.

It's fine to build a railroad, but where will the lines be laid? Douglas suggested the rail lines be laid from Washington, DC north, to Chicago, then across the Rockies and into San Francisco. Southerners thought it should be routed from Washington, DC to New Orleans and across to San Diego or Los Angeles. It was important to Douglas that it go north because he was from Illinois and getting it to stop in Chicago meant big dollars. Southerners agreed for the time being and theoretically it would go north. It took a long time until it was finally completed. Douglas didn't live another 15 years to witness its completion.

Douglas sincerely believed that by organizing Kansas and Nebraska on popular sovereignty, there would be no problems. There was an issue, however. He didn't realize there were a number of ways to get a majority and this had to be acted upon quickly. Kansas was a magnet for people from both the North and South and huge groups were migrating.

Douglas told Pierce he would make his life a living hell if he didn't support the bill. Pierce did sign it and the Kansas-Nebraska Act was passed by our Congress in May 1854. It allowed people in the territories to decide for themselves whether to allow slavery within their borders. This was popular sovereignty at its best. The Act repealed the 1820 Missouri Compromise which prohibited slavery north of latitude 36°30′.

The Missouri Compromise was to preserve the balance of power in Congress between slave and free states, and admitted Missouri as a slave state and Maine as a free state. In 1854, it was repealed by the Kansas-Nebraska Act. In 1857, the Dred Scott decision made it unconstitutional.

Back to the Stowe Family and Harriet Beecher Stowe's dad, Lyman Beecher. His followers believed every word he said. He had created the New England Immigrant Aid Association to help those immigrating into Kansas. Sounds harmless? It wasn't. He enlisted the people in his congregation to contribute to the society and he shipped huge crates labeled as "Beecher's Bibles" out West. Sounds righteous enough? It looked good to others in the country, hoping for some agreement in the West. However, there were no Bibles. Beecher's Bibles were guns, ammunition, and supplies for all-out warfare. The NEAS was an unorganized, unofficial secret army. Southerners did same thing sending guns, ammo, and propaganda to make sure the territory became a pro-slavery land.

If that wasn't bad enough, the neighboring state of Missouri had pro-slavery people coming into Kansas called "Border Ruffians" The purpose was to injure and traumatize and let residents know how to vote, even though these Ruffians never lived there. This resulted in two disorganized armies, both with weapons, and destined for violence. Douglas didn't see it coming. This was a warning of about what would happen in the future, the Civil War.

Bleeding Kansas

Amazingly, no one in Washington realized what was going on. Kansas was now a magnet for crazies. The year was 1855 and "Border Ruffians" were crossing over into Kansas to vote illegally in the first territorial elections. Proslavery forces took over and established their legislature in Lecompton, Missouri. Everything was fraud. A person could be a legislator only if he promoted slavery and enforced fugitive slave laws. Lecompton was the zenith of corrupt politics.

When John Brown, an over-the-top Connecticut farmer, read that pro-slavers had attacked the folks in an anti-slavery town, he packed up anger, hate, four of his sons, and sought revenge by slaughter. Brown was a failure in everything he attempted: farming, business, and freeing slaves. He fathered 20 children, 13 by his second wife! He believed that GOD spoke to him and told him to kill God's enemies.

The night was dark in the village of Pottawatomie and the townspeople had gone to bed. Brown and his supporters dragged all men out of their homes along with their families. His four sons, who carried broad swords which they collected, then proceeded to slice the men to death in front of their wives and children. When anti-slavery people in Kansas decided that they didn't want slavery, they went to Topeka and established their own anti-slavery capitol. The Free-Soil Party, (1848–54), was established. It was a new political party opposed to extending slavery into any of the western territories. Lawrence Kansas became the seat of pro-slavers and Bleeding Kansas was appropriate. It was Americans killing other Americans over slavery. It was a preview of what was to come very shortly.

This was horrific and Americans were enraged and wanted the real story. They asked why Washington wasn't doing anything. Americans wanted to be educated and they read a lot. They read papers or they tried to witness things first hand before forming any opinions and were given every opportunity if they resided near the capitol. Every day outside of the national capitol, along Pennsylvania Avenue, there were long lines to hear the debates that went on daily. This was entertainment.

One of most outspoken anti-slavery senators was from Massachusetts. Charles Sumner. Like many of the leaders of the time, he also wanted to become president. He was never nominated because he had the reputation of being arrogant, underhanded, nasty, and extremely condescending, although he was Harvard educated. He didn't know it, but his arrogance and mouth were about to get him into the worst period of his life.

The Crime Against Kansas

Newspapers said that Sumner was scheduled to give a major speech in the Senate called "The Crime against Kansas." People lined up early. In 1855, the Senate was packed since Bleeding Kansas was a hot topic in the news. Sumner delivered an attack on the South for being responsible for Bleeding Kansas but he singled out in his speech the senior senator from South Carolina, Andrew Butler. What follows is the real story of what happened in "The Crime Against Kansas." It has four main characters: Preston Brooks, Laurence Keitt, Andrew Butler, and Charles Sumner, but it is Sumner who got the short end of the stick.

Strom Thurmond served 50 years in South Carolina Senate and died at age 100. He was a segregationist and very popular. He loved politics, women, and people in general. He was a fixture. Thurmond was charming and Andy Butler was the nineteenth century equivalent. Although Butler was a slave owner, rich, liked women, was courteous, and was loyal to the South, even the North found him charming. He was well-respected.

So, let's go inside. We've been standing in line for hours and are fortunate enough to be admitted. It's May 19, 1856. It's pretty hot in the Senate Chamber. Although only 1 p.m., it must be around 90°F. Senator Charles Sumner is getting ready to speak. I heard that he has memorized every single word of the speech because it took him months to get the time granted to delivery it. I'm excited and eager to hear what he has to say.

"Look, he's getting ready."

"Well, he's been talking for hours and we're going to have to come back tomorrow to hear the end of his speech. He sure is being pretty nasty talking about Stephen Douglas and even Andy Butler who is not even here today. I hate to even repeat it, but he is calling slavery, Andy's mistress and a harlot. He actually called Andy an imbecile. Just look around, people are really getting angry. That gentleman in front of us looks like he's ready to kill someone. Let's come back tomorrow and hear the end."

So, fellow companion, we'll go back to hear the ending. As we come back to the Senate Chamber the next day, thoughts race through our minds. Congressman Preston Brooks was listening today and he certainly was red-faced and angry. I know that he has good cause because he's from Edgefield, South Carolina and Andy Butler is his cousin. Laurence Keitt was also with him and they were both talking and appeared pretty riled up.

We soon learn that Mr. Brooks got angrier and angrier and told Keitt he had to avenge this (duel) for his kinsman. Keitt called Sumner a "rabid dog" not deserving a duel. Brooks came back on the 22nd to visit Sumner.

In those days, desks were bolted to thick hardwood floors. There was also the status of canes and walking sticks. A nineteenth century gentleman carried a walking stick. The wealthier you were, the larger the head became. It was also much easier to approach a senator or even the President of the United States because there was not the security there is in today's world.

Brooks and Keitt are coming back and making their way down to the floor of the Senate. It looks like they waited until all the ladies had left, but we'll stand in back so they won't see us. Brooks has his cane with him. He's approaching Sumner and beating him to a pulp with his cane! No one is doing anything. Sumner is desperately trying to get to his feet, and his knees are catching on the desk which is laying on the ground because it was yanked out of the floor. OMG, Sumner is collapsing, all 185 pounds of him. He's falling to the floor and the desk and cane are both destroyed. Sumner is lying on the floor unconscious and bleeding.

Why doesn't someone do something? Now, I see, because Lawrence Keitt has pistols in both hands defending Brooks. Wow, what a scene!

Sumner's physical injuries improved faster than his mental. He was out of the Senate for three long years and Massachusetts instructed the Sargent of Arms to leave the desk where it was, so no one would forget. It was to become a symbol. Massachusetts did not appoint an interim senator for the entire three years.

Northern news accounts were the opposite of the Southern, each believing they were right and justified in their opinions. Brooks was portrayed as both a hero or a bully. We were there. Which was he? In Ninety-Six, South Carolina today there stands a historical marker indicating a banquet attended by 10,000 to show their support for Brooks' act against Sumner.

Congress does not like to discipline their own so they only censured Brooks (censure is absolutely nothing to this day). Brooks delivered a speech and resigned because he would not accept any discipline for bringing down a mad dog. South Carolinians re-elected him unanimously to go back to House as they believed he defended their honor. He was never remorseful, repentant, or apologetic. For six to eight months he received walking sticks from all over the South with people saying "bravo" and giving him a list of other potential "hits."

When Sumner came back to his desk in the Chamber, he was even more enthusiastic, continued his writings and crusade against slavery, and did so throughout the Civil War. He delivered an extremely emotional speech in June 1860 called "The Barbarism of Slavery," which insulted everyone because it was considered to be a more violent attack on the South than the earlier "Crime Against Kansas" which was four years prior in 1856.[4] This kept the fire burning and continued the rift between North and South, moreover in Washington. Rapidly, the Northern and Southern Congressmen were moving to the opposite ends of the earth.

Stormy Waters

As president, Franklin Pierce, so desperate to please the South, put his name behind "filibustering." When someone keeps talking to hold the floor to prevent anything from happening, it's called filibustering. Even though they repeat the same things over and over, get off the topic at hand, and blah-blah for hours, they still have the floor and are delaying anything from happening. Thurmond did it. In the 1850s, however, filibustering meant an unauthorized military expedition, taking over countries that had peaceful relations with the United States. There were soldiers of fortune supported by Pierce attempting to find and rule territory which would enable the South to expand slavery. This was his number one goal and it was a delay tactic.

One of these Pierce-era soldiers was William Walker. Walker was a lawyer, physician, journalist, and extremely popular. He was from Louisiana, went to Nicaragua, and told people he would be the new dictator. They accepted him and he became president for a year, until he wanted to annex Nicaragua to the United States. A Statue of him still stands in the square. He went to Honduras but the Hondurans didn't want him so they executed him and his crew.

Sandi Ludwa

The best of all was the unofficial Ostend Manifesto, which was a message sent to Pierce from United States representatives to Britain, France, and Spain, meeting in Ostend, Belgium (1854). It stated the U.S. had a divine right to take Cuba from Spain by any means possible. Pierce rejected it because of the stormy waters over the Kansas-Nebraska Act.

Pierce was allowing this attempt at expansion to happen, in the hopes it would help the Southern expansion of slavery, even though it risked war with foreign nations. I believe it would be called "Imperialism."

1856 Rolled around for the next presidential election, and there was anger, blood, turmoil, but still no leader. We were five years prior to the war, the country was divided, Americans were killing Americans, and there was no one to control the nation.

Summary

How could one family have such a profound influence on a war? The Beecher family was just that, a major contributor to the war. When Harriet Beecher Stowe wrote *Uncle Tom's Cabin,* it was an overnight best seller. She brought her characters to life and showcased the disgrace of slavery.

Not to be overshadowed, her dad fueled revolution. Shipping Beecher's Bibles into Kansas, led to the murders between pro-slavers and anti-slavers. John Brown and company entered the picture and as a result Kansas was designated with the title of Bleeding Kansas. Border Ruffians, murderers, and folks on both sides of the fence, lived in this hostile territory.

Then there was Charles Sumner and his speech "The Crime Against Kansas," which separated politicians in Washington forever. It all came back to slavery and the economics of the system or Peculiar Institution as it was called in the South. President Pierce was having his share of problems and America was ripping herself apart.

Chapter 19

From Compromise to Secession

When the 1856 Presidential Election approached, the Whig Party inhaled its last breath, (Northern-Whigs) because of the slavery issue. Former Whigs needed a new party and found it in the birth of the Republicans (1854). One of their non-negotiable issues was absolutely no slavery in the territories. Yet, nothing was said about states. The bottom line, more Northerners became Republicans than Southerners. Since there was more education in the Northern states, Republicans were likely to have lucrative careers in fields such as business, education, the legal system, or medicine. The Republicans nominated John C. Fremont. He was a general, Mexican war hero, trailblazer, explorer, published author, good looking, and charismatic. The problem was, no one in South voted for him because of the slavery issue.

Democrats, (Southern Democrats) on the other hand, decided they were the only national party left and platformed that they were a national party and there were no sectionalism interests. Many Southerners were educated, but the tendency was that the men spent more time involved with the party and in careers involving the military and agriculture. The Democrats nominated James Buchanan who had been out of the country as a diplomat for the past two years. They wanted nothing to do with Pierce. There was no way that he could seek reelection!

The American Party, aka the Know Nothings, also came into being. They were a secret club more than a political party and they got the name because when someone asked them a question they said, "I know nothing." They were mostly Protestant males who stood up against immigration and Catholics. They believed Catholics were loyal to the Pope and intended to take over America. Slavery was not an issue for them. Whenever a candidate spoke they would always go to the topic of immigration and state that America had too many immigrants. Millard Fillmore ran under this party.

There were three candidates. This was the only election in history that a candidate (Buchanan) unseated a sitting president seeking nomination by his party to a second full term, then went on to win the general election. Isn't it also ironic that Buchanan got the nomination for being the worst president in history?

An aside to modern times: Polk, Buchanan, and Hayes did not seek a second term. Lyndon Johnson, Coolidge, and Truman served out the balance of a former president (dying in office's term) and then had another term so were considered two term presidents. There were others: William Taft, Herbert Hoover, Gerald Ford and George H.W. Bush that did not win re-election and the sole Democrat Jimmy Carter who did not win re-election, but they had their party's nomination.

When people voted, there was no contest and it was James Buchanan. He was the only bachelor to become president and his niece, Harriet Rebecca Lane Johnston, served as First Hostess."[1] Over the course of history, there have been various views of Buchanan. Did he lose an early love? Was he asexual, homosexual, or not interested? Once again, he is generally regarded as the worst president in American history. Did this have something to do with his lifestyle?

Perhaps, it did. Americans believe(d) in marriage and families, but Buchanan was unmarried. He was also from the Pennsylvania, and was the third Northern president in a row who was a Doe Face, a Northerner with Southern sympathies. When he assisted the South to gain the Kansas' admission to the Union as a slave state, he alienated both Republican abolitionists and Northern Democrats, who supported popular sovereignty. It all came down to the one fact and the main reason why he was remembered as the worst. He did nothing to stop our country's progression into the Civil War. Buchanan believed that slavery was morally wrong, but thought freeing slaves would cause worst problems. Was he weak and submissive or sneaky, conniving, and untrustworthy? There is another school of thought, however. He preceded Lincoln, a great president.

Buchanan battled Stephen A. Douglas for the nomination from Illinois but Douglas was really popular. Douglas and Lincoln would debate and run against each other in the next election, the important election of 1860. But, this was four years prior and in March 1857, Buchanan took office.

Dred Scott

Forty-eight hours after Buchanan was sworn in, the Supreme Court decided the *Dred Scott Case.* This gets complicated as it is our court system. Scott was enslaved and born in Virginia, but records are pretty iffy. His owner, Peter Blow, lived in Alabama and then moved to St. Louis, Missouri, taking all of his slaves with him. In 1832, Blow died and Scott was sold to army surgeon, Dr. John Emerson. Scott was a valet and house servant.

Scott accompanied Emerson on his transfer to Illinois. In 1818, when Illinois entered the Union, the state's constitution contained a phrase confirming that neither slavery nor involuntary servitude held, other than for punishment for crimes. The wording, however, allowed residents who already owned slaves to keep them as property. There was a big "but" because it circumvented the Ordinance of 1787, prohibiting slavery in that area which was then named the Northwest Territory. So, technically, Illinois was a free state, but ironically slaves remained enslaved into the nineteenth century.

In 1836, Emerson was reassigned to a fort in the Wisconsin Territory, again taking Scott with him. Scott fell in love, was allowed to marry a slave named Harriet Robinson, and her ownership was transferred to Emerson. When the army transferred Emerson again to St. Louis and then Louisiana, he left his slaves behind. Love was in the air. In Louisiana, Emerson married Eliza Irene Sanford, who was visiting from St. Louis. The couple decided to settle in St. Louis, and Emerson sent for Scott and his wife. He did something which was unheard of at the time. The journey down the Mississippi was a thousand miles but yet Emerson allowed the couple to travel unescorted. Neither attempted to escape.

All stayed in Illinois for a couple of years, then to the free territory of Wisconsin, and finally back to Missouri. In Missouri, Emerson died and his wife Eliza inherited Scott and his family. Since Scott had saved money over the years, he offered $300 to buy his freedom. Eliza Emerson refused, decided she wanted to move to New York, and left Scott and his family to an army captain who hired him out.

Anti-slavery groups approached Scott and convinced him to sue for freedom and become a test case through the court system. He started the process and then the mess really began. There were several trials. One trial declared the Scotts to be free but it was overturned because of technicalities. The question was, "Who owned Scott because Mrs. Emerson was in New York?"

Finally, the Missouri Supreme Court said he was a slave. It wasn't over yet and the case went to the U.S. Supreme Court. During this period, the court was doing nothing significant but it was about to embark upon a monumental decision. The chief justice was Roger Taney. He was from Maryland, owned slaves at some time in his life, and was 80 years old in an era when people lived to be half that age. Taney had a long career and had a healthy ego. In a 7-2 vote, he handed down the decision that Scott did not get freedom and was a slave without any constitutional rights. Therefore, as property, he was not a citizen. The year was 1857.

Taney wanted to resolve the issue once and for all before he died four years later. He added an addendum to his decision. The Constitution guaranteed a man a right to his property and said nothing about where a man could take his property. A slave could be taken anywhere and no one could prevent the owner from doing that. That's the part that did it. By saying it, the Northwest Ordinance, Missouri Compromise, Compromise of 1850, and Kansas-Nebraska Act, were all unconstitutional. Any congressional act excluding slavery from any territory was unconstitutional. Southerners were elated because no one could exclude slavery from anywhere in our nation.

It wasn't over yet. Recently, historians recovered some new information on Buchanan. Right before his inauguration, Taney gave Buchanan a heads up on the case before the decision was reached. Also, Buchanan jumped on Northern Justice, Robert Cooper Greer and told him he had to support decision so it didn't look like Southerners only supported it. Was this unethical as well as unconstitutional since Buchanan was not even supposed to know about the case? Here is where Buchanan got his reputation for being sneaky and manipulative. This time it was the Yankees who were incensed beyond belief. They felt the Declaration of Independence had been violated.

Here is the end of the story. What goes around comes around, as the old saying goes. Scott and his family were finally freed. Remember his original owner, Peter Blow? Well, Blow's sons had been paying for part of Scott's attorney fees. They arranged for transferred ownership to them and then to the former Eliza Emerson and her new husband who was a Massachusetts congressman and abolitionist. The connection with the case was not helping his political career so they freed Scott after receiving $750 from the Blow family. Scott stayed in St. Louis after his emancipation, and he found employment as a hotel porter.

Freedom was short-lived and a year later, Scott died from tuberculosis. Scott was buried in the Calvary Cemetery in St. Louis. Harriet died 18 years later. Putting pennies that display President Lincoln's face on Scott's headstone became a local tradition. The commemorative marker next to the headstone reads: "In Memory of A Simple Man Who Wanted To Be Free."

Honest Abe

The year was 1857 and Abraham Lincoln, a successful lawyer in the one-horse town of Springfield, Illinois, couldn't keep his mouth shut. He would talk to anyone who would listen, repeating over and over again that the *Dred Scott* decision was unfair. Lincoln did become a leader of the Republican Party in Illinois, but remember the Spot Resolution, when in the House of Representatives, he was called Spotty and thought his career was over?

In the 1858 senatorial election, Democrats nominated Stephen Douglas and no Republican wanted to run against him because they knew Douglas would win. Lincoln's dream was to become a United States Senator, but never president. He was the sacrifice. Lincoln delivered a speech at the Republican National Convention, called "The House Divided Speech." It set the stage for what thought and would eventually write in the Emancipation Proclamation.

He said, "In *my* opinion, it *will* not cease, until a *crisis* shall have been reached, and passed. A house divided against itself cannot stand."[2]

Douglas had everything to lose while Lincoln had nothing to lose and everything to gain. Consequently, Lincoln challenged Douglas to a series of seven debates all over the state of Illinois. Illinois dips down into the South wherein Southern Illinois approved of slavery. Douglas should have said no because Lincoln got a lot of publicity but his big ego won and the debates began. The debates ran from August to October 1858.

Once again, let's go to the last debate to witness it first-hand. So far, Douglas has come out ahead of Lincoln because of his long experience and good speaking voice but Lincoln seems to be getting better and better. The last one should be interesting and a challenge.

We are standing in a crowd of hundreds and there seems to be no order. The crowd is loud, animated, and some have already had something more than water to drink. Again, it's out in a field, hot and dusty. It's nice though because I can see lots and lots of vendors and we can purchase some drinks and snacks to keep us going. Let's sit down on our blanket near the platforms they've set up for the men, and see what happens as I've heard these things last about three hours, at least. The band that Mr. Douglas hired is certainly something to lift spirits. It reminds me of a circus.

Mr. Douglas has already arrived in his private personal railroad car. (I'm thinking ahead and relate this to an early Airforce One)! Look, some people have signs welcoming him by his pet name, "The Little Giant." But where is Mr. Lincoln? Look, there's Mr. Douglas, he is sure short, I'd say shorter than me, probably 5'4". Why is he off-balance and flushed?

The gentleman next to me blurted out, "Because he drinks a lot and is drunk! He's debated the best and isn't concerned about this Lincoln chap."

Thanking him for the insight, we look towards the horizon and see in the distance a man, 6'4" or so arriving by horseback. As he dismounts, one of you comments how dirty, dusty, and unkempt he appears. I totally agree.

Lincoln climbs the platform and then Douglas starts to speak. Isn't there anyone here to moderate and introduce? I guess not. Then Lincoln says a few words and everyone is stunned by his high pitched and shrill voice. Lincoln lost the first debate, and did better as they went on, winning, so we are anxious to hear the words.

We listen for hours and Douglas is clearly drunk. I think Lincoln won this one because the newspaper guys are talking very positively about him. I can't get over how that one gent is taking notes and the other keeps running back and forth so the proceedings can be telegraphed immediately. He must have run back and forth hundreds of times. The papers must have sent their whole office out to cover this one! I can't wait to read the accounts.

Once the debate was over, the newspapers reported. The accounts were different but they came down to the same conclusion that Lincoln was a pretty sharp individual and tied the Little Giant in knots. Douglas may have been victorious in many of the debates winning this battle, but he lost the war. Lincoln got his name out and people knew who he was then and there.

Shortly after, 1859, another major act of violence or prelude will occur and John Brown's name will be known. A volcano was about to erupt.

Summary

Another Doe Face became president in 1856, and was immediately faced with the *Dred Scott Decision*. Dred Scott's freedom was elusive and for well over half of a century, he was enslaved only to finally receive emancipation and die a year later. The decision, however, had far reaching complications. It seemed that former compromises and acts were now unconstitutional. The country was in an uproar as events beginning as trickles were now cascading across the country, leading towards total war. Yet, President Buchanan did nothing to stop the disintegration of our nation.

As the last years of the 1850s rolled along, both parties were searching for a front-runner for the 1860 election. The event at first seemed insignificant, then drew a lot of attention, but the impact of the outcome reverberated throughout the world. The Little Giant, Stephen A. Douglas from Illinois was challenged to a series of seven debates for the United States Senate race, by little a known back-woods attorney, also from Illinois, Abraham Lincoln. It was not a presidential debate but was a first step towards the Lincoln presidency. Lincoln never wanted to become president and being a senator was good enough for him. As the debates progressed, Lincoln's confidence grew and his name became known throughout America, thanks to the news media. The Lincoln-Douglas Debates became some of the most well-known in history.

Chapter 20

So, What Exactly is this Peculiar Institution?

We've been involved in enslavement for the past thousands of years, but a discussion on America is warranted. Our forefathers have been involved since 1619 when the captain of the *Battista* sold the first indentured servants to colonists. How bad was it? Some authors have compared it to the New England factory system and state that it wasn't that bad. If you've seen or read, *Gone With the Wind,* it is portrayed as "not so bad." I'll let you judge for yourself. Look at the issue morally, physically, and ask yourself, "How would you feel if you yourself became enslaved?"

The enslaved worked 24/7 and not just sun-up to sun-down. They were property, at their owner's disposal, and life and death depended upon their masters. By 1860, 4,000,000 had been brought to this country. Have you ever been to an auction? People were placed on auction blocks just like cattle and were bought and sold at any time the owner chose. Slavery was based on fear and this is the reason why there weren't more rebellions. There was isolation between plantations, punishment if caught, nowhere to go, fear of being turned in by a fellow slave, and the hope staying together as a family.

Some were branded with what were called "estate marks" which insured they could not escape. The question is, "Where would they have gone?" After all, no one could be trusted. The Underground Railroad was a long and perilous journey. There were no maps or Global Positioning Systems for directions to safe havens. People would be leaving family and friends. Those in the lower South had little hope of making it into the North because of the long distances and little support involved. Was there an alternative?

There were both house and field slaves and there were two forms of slave labor, Gang Labor and Task Labor. Both were clearly defined.

Gang labor was a team, everyone worked together, and left to go back to their quarters together. The task system could be specialized with tasks like cooking, child care, and house cleaning. These people usually had better food, clothing, and quarters. It could also involve field labor with a task to be completed and then, regardless of time, the worker was freed to leave the site. For example, an assigned task could be to pick so many acres of cotton. The down side was that these enslaved were on call seven days a week.

Slaves did jobs no one else would do in cultivating crops such as rice, cotton, and tobacco. If someone were unfortunate enough to be enslaved in South, Central America, or the islands where sugar cane was cultivated, life-spans were short. The work was perilous.

House slaves worked 24/7 and were always at the disposal of their masters. Women nursed the children. They cooked, cleaned, cared for the sick, and did all of the work the masters would never consider doing. Despite this, many people retained spirit, survived, passed along the old traditions and cultures, and chose life rather than death.

Field slaves were ruled by the seasons, depending upon which crop was grown. They were responsible for preparing the soil, the cultivation, the harvest, and any milling, or curing that was necessary. Only babies or toddlers, the very old, or the sick, could escape the painful day-to-day existence. Women and men worked side by side. Some jobs were year-round. There were always enclosures to be repaired, livestock to be fed, carpentry to be completed, blacksmithing chores, and the perennial day-to-day jobs to be handled.

A very small percentage of the enslaved worked in an industrial setting, being hired out by their masters or working for their masters who owned more than just plantations. Some worked in small companies and some in large factories, while certain industries, e.g., railroads and steamboats, used people routinely. Usually, work quotas were assigned and if the quotas were surpassed, credits could be issued. These credits could be redeemed for luxuries which could be coffee, sugar, clothing, or sometimes actual cash. Sometimes slaves were hired out for agricultural work, depending upon the season and the need. When slaves were hired out, the person hiring provided clothing, food, and medical care.

Even a smaller percentage were allowed to hire themselves out, although illegal. It was the master who benefited. This was the case for skilled workers who would then pay their masters a predesignated sum at the end of the week.

The average price of a slave was $500-850. There was some manumission wherein slaves were freed upon a master's death.

Sunday was usually a day off, except for essential chores such feeding the livestock. If slaves worked on Sundays, they were usually paid. Saturday nights were free and slaves could congregate. Owners did try to Christianize and the promise of an afterlife presented some hope to those who embraced the concept. Bibles were the rock and foundation upon which scripture was interpreted. Teachings repeatedly hammered one concept, and it was to be obedient to the white master. Many kept their resilient African origins and incorporated both teachings into their own methods and styles of worship.

One primary way that heritage was preserved was through oral traditions. Stories, songs, dances, poetry, and plain talk prevailed. There was never enough time for any family life but Sundays afforded time when people could attempt to relax and socialize. It was then they obtained news and socialized. Families were often broken up; but some owners allowed weekend visits to neighboring plantations. This stopped once slave codes became stricter. Procreation was encouraged so more slaves could be born.

Some owners kept strict records, such as Gist Family at South Carolina's Rose Hill Plantation in Union County. For some, plantations were the only home people ever knew. There were slave quarters, a blacksmith shop, fields, and the owners home, all on the same property. Slaves were not allowed to learn to read or write. Only a small minority were trusted to handle plantation matters. Some masters, such as Thomas Jefferson, allowed their slaves, or "family" as Jefferson called them, to become literate.

Although marriages were allowed, they were voided once a spouse was sold. Some slaves, however, were allowed time to visit a nearby plantation to meet with a spouse if feasible. Any resulting children were the property of the mother's master. Masters did encourage families for the procreation and in order to make life a bit more tolerable for the enslaved.

Sex between masters and slaves was not uncommon. The term is "miscegenation." There was no regard for the enslaved and most masters did not acknowledge their children who would often be sold once they were of value. Mary Boykin Chesnut, who was born to wealth and privilege, kept a dairy which later became a book. She wrote about mixed-race children who resembled the plantation owners, and the masters who frequently visited the slave quarters in the dark of night.

The typical diet was corn, salt pork, and vegetables, if the masters allowed. Sometimes slaves were allowed to cultivate personal gardens in order to supply additional food for themselves and their families. Traditional crops were okra, collards, corn, yams, and maybe some tomatoes. Malnutrition was uncommon and the diets of both blacks and whites were similar, other than the enslaved received the discarded parts of livestock, e.g., hams and chops went to the masters, while the hocks and bacon were delegated to the enslaved. Overall, diet depended on the master's livelihood during given periods. It would not be considered unusual for both master and slave to have an inadequate diet during periods of poor agricultural conditions.

Shelter or slave quarters could be a single family or group residence. Quarters could be in an attached building, single home, or cabin without paved floor. It usually contained a fireplace for warmth and cooking and perhaps a window. Sleeping was usually on the ground with a little straw and a blanket for warmth.

Medical aid was usually provided by the mistress or doctors. Slaves were an investment and masters had every reason to keep slaves healthy. Although the medicines of the day were used, the enslaved often used their own folk medicines which they believed were more favorable.

The mistress of the household did not live in the glory portrayed by many books and movies. Women, although still without the rights of white males, ran the household. These women were responsible for the management of the household and knew the enslaved much better than their male-counterparts. They furnished medical care, understood needs such as additional clothing, food, and the importance of participation in weddings or funerals. Since plantations, many of which were large farmhouses and not of the grandeur portrayed, were in remote areas, existence could be lonely with long periods of solitude.

When it came to discipline, the overseer was the authority, but in the labor system often a slave was appointed to be the gang boss or slave driver. Whipping, torture, imprisonment, or being sold were consequences. If you were a slow worker, late in getting to the field, defying authority, running away, you were punished. Slaves did have their own means of revenge, however, and often played along with the fact that masters believed the enslaved were inferior. Tools were broken, people faked illness, or pretended to not understand.

The overseer had to be an expert in agriculture and understand the land, planting, cultivation, and harvesting. Turnover was high and the average tenure was usually one year. Slaves were an investment and it didn't make sense to abuse the workers and have them become useless to the plantation. The overseer had a low social status and usually were younger men who hoped to someday own land.

The slave driver usually supervised his gang of less than one-dozen workers. He was given instructions by the overseer and had the responsibility of carrying out the work with his workers. He was given assignment and some additional privileges, but he was still a slave.

There was the Underground Railroad which helped as many as 100,000 escape over a period of 50 years. The goal was to make it North, preferably to Canada. Abolitionists, Quakers, and various churches were involved. However, most who helped were either freed blacks or those who had escaped prior. Most people were caught and returned to their masters.

The trip North was strewn with obstacles. Usually no help was provided until they reached the North, after hiking hundreds of miles. Most who escaped were from the Upper South because distances made it difficult to flee from the Deep South from states such as Alabama and Mississippi. Harriet Tubman and Frederick Douglass were two of the most successful in helping the enslaved reach freedom. John Brown (Bleeding Kansas and Harpers Ferry) was also a "conductor" on the railroad which was a secret organization providing aid to escaped slaves. It was not a railroad.

Investment and money spent was the bottom line. An owner needed to provide adequate food, clothing, shelter, and keep people well. Remember, that people who owned slaves were a very small part of the population in the South. Three-quarters of Southern whites owned no slaves and of those who owned them, 88% owned twenty or fewer. These small yeoman farmers worked side by side with their slaves and families to eke out a meager existence. Owning slaves and land was the symbol of status. Slaves were more important and worth more than land. Poor whites impowered themselves with the belief that although they were poor, they were not slaves and there was power simply by being white.

Prior to the war, unending arguments and discussions about the pros and cons of slavery existed. Many Northerners were still undecided or unconcerned, being involved in their own everyday struggle for survival. Albert Taylor Bledsoe, who was a Professor at the University of Virginia, an Episcopal priest, an attorney, and later an officer in the Confederate Army, wrote *An Essay on Liberty and Slavery*. It is a lengthy book, written in 1856, five years before war erupted. It discusses civil liberties, the fallacies of abolition, arguments from the old and new testaments, and fugitive slave laws. Long out of print, I found an original copy at my university library. He leaves it to the reader to decide and presents questions such as:

"If slavery were abolished today, would the North take responsibility and take-in the poor blacks?" He asserts that although "we" which meant the South he represented, desire harmony, we shall never seek it by surrendering the Constitution or Supreme Court decisions. The reader should decide and if he agrees that the arguments are "correct and well-grounded," and hopes the reader would concur that "the institution of slavery, as it exists among us at the South, is founded in political justice, is in accordance with the will of GOD and the designs of his providence, and is conducive to the highest, purest, best interests of mankind."[1] Bledsoe continued his Lost Cause writing until his death which coincided with the end of Reconstruction in 1877.

Summary of What Went Before Us

In 1860-1861, the South had the best cotton crop in American history. The hostilities grew to the point that the South didn't care for the central government and its tariffs, federal subsidies to railroads, etc. and the planters were doing well. They were capitalists and understood one thing, profit.

The cotton gin and the westward movement were the only routes to success. Migrate west and buy more land and slaves. The novo-rich did just that and expansion of slavery into the territories was a matter of life and death. Find cheap land. Cotton was king and global consumption doubled every decade from 1820-1860. It became the most valuable American export. By 1825, the South was the world's largest cotton supplier and the South became greedier.

In 1860, the planter holding 50 or more slaves had a net value of $22,350, (that was 85% of the per capita income of the time). They were the richest men in the world. Owners felt paternalistic and they knew what was best. The South made one big mistake, however, and that was letting the North handle their money and finance and industry.

The Yankees were always saving and counting their riches. They were bankers, capitalists, industrialists and liked to think of themselves as humanitarians. Slavery wasn't going away. This chapter of history describes the bold facts about slavery as it existed in the South. There is no way to sugar-coat the conditions that existed and it all boiled down to investment, money, profit, and survival, through the enslavement of others.

The American story is not all misery; nor is it all glory. We must have the courage to face the facts of what went prior. We did not cause these injustices, nor are we ourselves responsible for the great people who did cause tremendous change. The injustices that came before, e.g., black slavery, exploitation of Native Americans, ethnic group exclusion, both Christian and non-Christian religious persecution, continued and cannot be ignored as part of the American story. We can only live in the present and make changes that will enhance the future for ourselves, our children, and all who consider themselves Americans.

Let us move on to one of the most written about eras in our history, our Civil War. As we travel through four long years of war, observe, analyze, and keep an open mind.

Chapter 21

Over the Edge to War

Harpers Ferry

Another act of violence put the South over the edge. John Brown returned after murdering innocent people in Kansas. He went to Canada to formulate an idea for an enormous slave rebellion. Even though Brown would have been branded as a terrorist today, he accumulated quite a large group of supporters who were radical abolitionists and believed in freedom for slaves at any cost. Some followers were very prominent, wealthy, and gave him financial assistance. He also had many enemies after Bleeding Kansas became national news.

Brown planned to take his sons and his small army to attack a federal arsenal in the United States. A federal arsenal is a fort which stores weapons, guns, and supplies, until they are needed by the United States Army. He chose

Harpers Ferry, Virginia which was not yet the state of West Virginia. It was the perfect location: secure, up against a mountainside, and the government would not expect an attack. George Washington himself, a century ago, designated Harpers Ferry as the site for an armory.

Brown believed that once he controlled the arsenal, all slaves in Virginia and Maryland would revolt, kill masters, and join his army at Harpers Ferry. He was surprised how easily he had overtaken the guards and now controlled the armory. However, there was one problem. Many of Brown's supporters were having second thoughts and the locals were not enamored with Brown either. Brown did succeed in overtaking the armory and holding some local citizens as hostages, but no slaves showed up for the insurrection.

The locals took matters into their own hands and killed one-third of his army of two dozen and contacted the Virginia State Militia. The Commander of the militia was Cornell Robert E. Lee. Accompanying Lee, was a history professor from the Virginia Military Institute, Thomas J. Jackson, aka Stonewall Jackson. There was a battle between the militia and Brown's army. Two of Brown's sons and soldiers were killed, but Brown and his army were captured. Brown was wounded, brought back to Washington, and given one of the quickest trials for treason that ever occurred in the United States.

During the trial, Brown was emotionless but terror struck those witnessing the event. When sentenced to hanging, he said nothing and stared. In those days when taken to execution, the prisoner sat on his own coffin, shackled, and was taken by cart to the spot where he would be executed. Even soldiers were haunted by Brown's demeanor and wrote of it. When Brown finally spoke, he talked about the beautiful Virginia countryside and said he wished he would have been able to enjoy it. His last words were:

"I John Brown, am quite certain that the crimes of this guilty land will never be purged away accept with blood."

He spoke of rivers of blood, widows, and that he foresaw the end of what could have been a peaceful land. He was then hooded and hung. So afraid of a possible rebel attack to save Brown, over 1,000 soldiers surrounded the site and prohibited the public and press from attending.[1]

What happened after that put the South over the edge? Brown, a loser when alive, became a hero. Church bells were rung, ministers compared him to Christ saying that he sacrificed his life, and poems and ballads were written. Children learned the song, "John Brown's body lies a mouldering in the grave," the tune of the song which was to become the Battle Hymn of the Republic. Southerners found it unbelievable that he was a hero. Emotions flared and anger grew from hostility to radical-violence. They knew that their beliefs were the polar- opposite of their northern counterparts and that their future was not in the Union.

Although there was a great deal of drama, still everyday life went on in America. Textile mills thrived, slaves labored, and people moved West. Thomas Edison was busy perfecting his new inventions, machines that electrocuted rats and cockroaches. The Pony Express started delivering mail out West, even though the company survived for only a year. Immigrants still came in large numbers, hoping for a better life. However, most of America contemplated the 1860 election and tension was building.

It was the eve of the presidential election and the result could affect the fate of the entire United States of America. There was only one national party, the Democrats, and Stephen A. Douglas was setting himself up for the presidency. Buchanan was still the president. Southerners didn't want Douglas and didn't vote to nominate him so the Democrats met again in two weeks but the Southerners stormed out of the meeting hall. There were two separate conventions.

It ended up with four persons running for president. The Northern Democrats nominated Douglas on his popular sovereignty platform. The Party was split and Southerners needed someone who was level-headed, prominent, and who believed in slavery. They wanted an amendment guaranteeing them the right to take their slaves into the territories. There was no debate and they nominated Buchanan's Vice President, John C. Breckenridge. He owned slaves, a plantation, was from Kentucky, believed in the right to take slaves into U.S. territory, and was a military hero. He was the perfect candidate, so they thought.

The Republicans, on the other hand, had many contenders. On their first and second ballots no one had enough votes, so negotiations began. Lincoln's name came up since he did so well debating Douglas and he was a moderate.

He didn't buy full rights for slaves. He became the nominee and the platform was consistent, no slavery in the territories.

The Constitutional Union Party nominated John Bell. They decided to do what the constitution said, but they really didn't strongly advocate anything or know what the constitution advocated. They were pro-Union.

Another crazy election occurred. Lincoln was not on ballot in nine southern states. He had only 39% of the popular vote but still became President. No president received a smaller percentage of popular votes than Lincoln. Keep this in mind, when you view our modern-day results! Remember, popular vote doesn't count – the Electoral College decides. Lincoln got support from northern states so had more than enough votes, 180.

Lincoln's election lit a Southern fuse. It was December 1860, less than 30 days after the election and four months before he came to Washington, when South Carolina called a convention to discuss secession. This time South Carolina knew they would be followed out of the Union quickly. Let's look back to 1832 and John C. Calhoun days when there was the Nullification Crisis.

Six weeks later, six states abruptly left the Union along with South Carolina. They were Alabama, Florida, Georgia, Louisiana, Mississippi, and Texas. They created the independent nation of the Confederate States of America and created a constitution similar to that existing in the Union, but there was one amendment, slavery.

Who Was Lincoln?

Who was Abe Lincoln? We learned in the early grades that he was born in a log cabin in Kentucky in 1809. He grew to 6 feet and 4 inches, was long-limbed, angular, and physically strong. What early education doesn't tell us follows. The Lincolns were squatters and were forced to move into Indiana, until his father could afford to buy land. Young Abe would walk miles to borrow a book but formal education totaled about 18 months. When the family moved to Illinois, 22-year-old Lincoln, like most young adults, left the homestead to begin his own adult life.

He worked in many jobs, e.g., a shopkeeper, postmaster. He learned people-skills and loved to tell entertaining stories.

Lincoln could never outgrow is high-pitched and nasal voice. He married Mary Todd after a long courtship, which he had broken off. There were other women in his life, one being Ann Rutledge who died of typhoid; but, nevertheless, he ended up with Mary.

He became a lawyer, served one-term in the House of Representatives, and seemed to be an ordinary guy, with no outstanding accomplishments, so far. Lincoln served in the Illinois Legislature as a Whig and formulated his early ideas on slavery. Slavery was evil because it was impeding economic growth. When the Republican Party took shape, he joined it. After the Dred Scott Decision (*Scott v. Sanford*), he decided to challenge Douglas for his congressional seat. We have already attended the debates and know what happened. The rest is history. A word on his personal life....

The Lincolns had four children; three died young and were thought to be influential in the melancholy which encompassed both Mary and Abe throughout the years. Mary was diagnosed with mental illness. She was an extravagant spender and Abe had to curb her purchases (before credit cards existed), when she went overboard with expenditures on the White House and her wardrobe. He scolded her for her overindulgences when soldiers didn't have blankets to keep warm and the American public didn't care about the White House, which he referred to as "this damned old house." One author states in a one-month period she purchased 400 pairs of gloves.

The worst part was that her family owned slaves and many were fighting for the Confederacy. Ironically, growing up the Todd's had an enslaved-housekeeper that not only served in that household, but that of the Davis'. Mary said she was being followed by evil, and at one point of her life was temporarily in an asylum.[2]

Who was Jefferson Davis?

Jefferson Davis was appointed President of the Confederacy. The exact opposite of Davis was his Vice president, Alexander Stephens. In those first seven states that seceded, things went very smoothly. Politicians resigned from the federal government and went back to their home states accepting positions in the new Confederacy. There were no problems when the United States flag came down and the Confederate flag went up, until February 1861, when Virginia, North Carolina, and Tennessee voted against secession. The Confederacy was now only the Lower South. Look at a map and their location explains it. Virginia is not the lower South.

There were three places where the commander did not give up and would not allow the Confederate flag to be flown. Two were in Florida and one was in South Carolina at Fort Sumter. If we were to look at our time line to get things into perspective as we are travelling quickly through the years, it would be as follows.

Time Line:
November 1860 – Election of Abraham Lincoln
December 1860 – South Carolina secedes
January 1861 – Mississippi and five others by February join the Confederacy
March 1861 – Lincoln takes the oath of office
April 12, 1861 – Fort Sumter – the first shots of the Civil War

This is a short scoop on what the Buchanan administration did before Lincoln took office. Don't forget that March was the official inauguration. Try to put yourself in Lincoln's position. The Buchanan administration had appointed Robert Anderson to Fort Sumter since he was from the South and owned slaves, but he would not surrender. Running low on supplies he telegraphed Buchanan for food or he would be forced to surrender. Buchanan dispatched a ship and some eager beavers from the Citadel fired on the ship which turned around and went back to Washington. Buchanan said it was Lincoln's problem and washed his hands of it. More to come.

We're standing among the crowds on inauguration day March 4, 1861. It is cold and has been raining all morning. The streets are muddy and our shoes are covered with it. There are so many people here, I'd guess about 30,000, and we're getting muddier as the horse drawn carriages come by in the roadway. It is an extremely dismal day. It's almost high noon when Lincoln will be inaugurated. We wait with our primitive Victorian umbrella that is meant to shield the sun and isn't doing any justice in the rain.

Look, here he is now! We witness a miracle. As Lincoln is stepping up on the podium, the rain has stopped and the sun is out! He is delivering a conciliatory speech but telling Southerners that he will not mess with them, they can keep their slavery. All they must do is reconcile with the North. Our new president is telling us that if they choose not to do this, it won't be a peaceful separation. He's saying we're all friends, not enemies and is referring to the "mystic chords of memory."

Our America

Summary

Important People and Events that led to and Fueled the Civil War:

Abolitionists started to convince the population that slavery was evil, immoral, and against God's will. John Brown, Frederick, Douglass, Harriet Tubman, Harriet Beecher Stowe were in the spotlight, to name a few.

The Dred Scott Decision (1857) strengthened the law that slaves were property and had no rights.

Election of Abraham Lincoln – (1860) Lincoln, a Republican and a Yankee, put questions about the future in the minds of Southerners.

Emancipation Proclamation – (January 1863). Did it free the enslaved?

Harpers Ferry (1862) John Brown attempted to incite a slave rebellion once he overtook the federal arsenal.

Kansas-Nebraska Act – Allowed popular sovereignty, which resulted in Bleeding Kansas when John Brown and his following murdered pro-slavers (1854). The Reverend Stowe shipped Beecher's Bibles, which were guns and ammo, to the territory.

Missouri Compromise (1820) was Henry Clay's creation which passed, placing Missouri as a slave state and Maine coming into the Union as free. Slavery forever banned north of the 36°30′ and was criticized by both North and South.

Nat Turner's Rebellion (1831) struck more fear of slave rebellions into the minds of owners.

Nullification Crisis – South Carolina (1832) was a foreshadowing of what was to come.

Southerners worried that their habits, traditions, and practices would soon come to an end.

Stono Rebellion (1739) which occurred in South Carolina was a failed slave rebellion but caused stricter slave codes.

Tariffs favoring the North were abundant.

Uncle Tom's Cabin -- Harriet Beecher Stowe humanized slaves and put the issue in the forefront to the American public.

Unequal representation in Congress and new territories divided the country even more.

Vesey's Rebellion (1822) was unsuccessful rebellion. However, it took federal troops to come to Charleston, South Carolina to restore law and order.

Sandi Ludwa

***

One of the biggest questions is why did the poor white yeoman farmer who owned no slaves, support the war in the South? It was called the "rich man's war but the poor man's fight." Two-thirds of the population owned no slaves and the richest were one percent of the entire population. There are many answers, pride, homeland, loyalty, history, aspiration to one-day own slaves and become rich.

Are you from somewhere that you are not living now? Myself, I'm a Yankee who embraces the South. However, there are days when I still long for my roots in the cold, cold, North. Putting myself in the situation, if I were a white male living in the South during antebellum times, there would be several ways to look at my own situation and it would be a tough decision.

Where would I go if I didn't support the cause? The South would be the only life I knew and the thought of living in some cold and hostile unknown area, frankly, would scare me to death. Not fighting, would shame the family. Even though I didn't own slaves, I would be expected to contribute to the cause, even if it cost me my life. It would be the southern way of life I was fighting for and protecting, not necessarily that I agreed or disagreed with slavery.

When there was a United States draft, (which was eliminated in 1973 when Vietnam War was ending), men went to war. It was expected. Few fled the country in comparison to those who fought, were wounded, or died in far-off lands. As an additional burden, those who returned after doing their duty in Vietnam, were disrespected by many Americans. Fighting was duty and honor and the majority did not question.

That's only my opinion. It isn't wrong nor is it right. It is not racist. As I said at the beginning of our journey, walk in someone else's shoes and understand their reasoning. Let's move on and talk about Southern culture and beliefs because most Southerners just wanted to be left alone without Northern influence.

What made the South so different or distinctive? The Peculiar Institution was distinctive but when we compare the nation, there were more similarities than differences. The land was one, on one continent. Everyone spoke the same language, discounting regional accents. They both shared history and appreciated the heroes from the American Revolution and the War of 1812 who fought for American freedom. The Constitution still held the one nation together. Both had a desire to explore and improve their lot, own land, and most embraced Manifest Destiny. The dominant religions all worshipped one Protestant Christian God and yet we were not all Protestant or necessarily praying to a Christian God. Was it easier to make your way in the North than the South because of the slavery issue?

When Southerners were criticized, they felt the need to defend and insults were taken personally wherein people defended what they knew. Northerners, Westerners, immigrants, and Natives did the same. Like Maslow's Hierarchy of Needs, everyone had their own self-interests and looked for their own survival first and foremost.

Of the traveling we have done so far, each of us has formulated our own opinions and we will never agree upon everything. The same holds true in today's world. Stop for just a moment and place yourself in various positions. Was there a right answer? Could the nation be one if there were no war? Do we argue about the petty incidents and not take stock of the whole picture? Aren't we all Americans living in a democracy?

Let's move ahead to the Civil War which destroyed a nation. According to the 1860 census, the United States' population was 27,233,198 who were free. Those who were enslaved amounted to an additional 3,950,528.[3]

Chapter 22

WAR!

"Any people anywhere, being inclined and having the power, have the right to rise up, and shake off the existing government, and form a new one that suits them better. This is a most valuable - a most sacred right - a right, which we hope and believe, is to liberate the world."

Abraham Lincoln

He also stated:

"Our Nation is splitting apart. In his Inaugural address, the last two paragraphs state: *"that the country's hands hold the event of Civil War. I will protect and defend the most solemn one. We are not enemies or friends, every heart will be touched by angels."*

Let's think about the above and let's examine several beliefs. There are numerous ways to look at government. John C. Calhoun and Jefferson Davis argued the Constitution was a contract between sovereign states with the inherent authority to withdraw from the agreement.

Lincoln and Northern leaders maintained that the Constitution was neither a contract nor an agreement between sovereign states. They concluded it was an agreement solely with the people, and once a state entered the Union, they were part of it and absolutely couldn't leave it.

The belief is that the Constitution is based upon a federation. It is a union of states and holds all rights that are not specifically mentioned in words in its script. These rights are given to the Federal Government. It's interesting, after we fought the Revolutionary War, people from the various colonies, that became states, still called themselves e.g., Virginians, New Yorkers. We had 13 original colonies who considered themselves separate and distinct. They were: Connecticut, Delaware, Georgia, Maryland, Massachusetts Bay, New Hampshire, New Jersey, New York, Pennsylvania, North and South Carolina, and Rhode Island/Providence Plantations, and Virginia. Today we might say we're from whatever state, but if asked by a person of another country, we usually are proud to identify ourselves as Americans or citizens of the United States of America.

To identify this issue when there were other groups separating us, Thomas Jefferson wrote in his inaugural speech, "We are all Republicans, we are all Federalists." He summed it up meaning, "We are all Americans."

Then there was John Locke's Contract Theory of Government. He said that when the government stops being responsible to people as a whole, the people have the right and responsibility to overthrow it. He didn't advocate immediate revolution but asserted it was a people's right to oust it. Isn't this the basis of the Declaration of Independence? What did Lincoln say on page 194? We had been arguing about how much power states should have since our Constitution, and Southern states saw it one way, the federal government was taking away their rights and they had every justification to do as they chose. What is your interpretation?

The Civil War

Fort Sumter was only the beginning. South Carolina adopted an Ordinance of Secession and on December 20, 1860, it was the first state to leave the union. Unlike the Nullification Proclamation in 1832, this time secession became a reality.

The 68 federal troops stationed in Charleston, South Carolina, moved into Fort Sumter, which is located on a small island in Charleston Harbor. There was no question that the North considered the fort to be the property of the United States government which was now the Union. The South Carolinians disagreed and asserted that the fort belonged to the new Confederacy. Nothing happened until four months later, when the first engagement of the

Civil War erupted at the fort. During this four-month period, both South Carolina and the Confederate government seized federal arsenals, forts, customs houses, and any national property within their jurisdiction.

By the time Lincoln was inaugurated on March 4, 1861, federal troops held little in the South. They still controlled Fort Sumter in Charleston Harbor, Fort Pickens off the Florida coast, and Forts Taylor and Jefferson in remote areas near the Florida Keys. Major Robert Anderson, commanded Fort Sumter. Although he was a former slave owner, he was, nevertheless, unquestionably loyal to the Union. When 6,000 South Carolina militia surrounded the harbor, Anderson and his troops were in a tight spot. There could be no reinforcements and resupplies. How long could they hold out?

In January 1861, one of the last things President Buchanan did before vacating office was to send soldiers with supplies on an unarmed civilian ship. Anderson realized the danger and tried to tell the president that they would be okay for a while. Nevertheless, the ship kept coming, was fired upon, and never docked. Unarmed, the ship departed when the South Carolinians started firing.

On March 4, 1861, Abraham Lincoln took his oath of office as President of the Union in Washington, DC. The fate of Fort Sumter was going to be determined by two men, Lincoln and Davis. Weeks passed, and Lincoln was under extreme pressure to do something. Lincoln thought the Southern secession could never be permanent. He believed that our American attempt of a government run by the people, if it failed, would show the world a democracy could never exist anywhere in the world. He didn't want to consider the consequences of failure.

Jefferson Davis sent a group of commissioners to Washington to negotiate for the transfer of Fort Sumter to South Carolina, but they were snubbed. Seven States had already seceded. They were South Carolina, Mississippi, Florida, Alabama, Georgia, Louisiana, and Texas. There were still mixed-feelings. Did states have the right to secede since they were already members of the Union?[1]

Lincoln was faced with a dilemma and had to react quickly. He had several things to consider. Fort Sumter was running out of supplies, but an attack would be viewed as Northern hostility. Virginia and North Carolina which had not seceded, could easily do so if he was not careful. Then there were those who were undecided both in America and Europe, who might just side with the South. He couldn't allow his troops to starve to death, nor could he allow them to surrender.

Lincoln was troubled, but finally he developed a plan. On April 6, he told the South Carolina Governor that he was going to send supplies to Fort Sumter. He would send no arms, troops, or ammunition unless, of course, South Carolina attacked. Lincoln telegraphed the commanding general, stating if he allowed the allow ship to drop off supplies, we're good, but if fired upon, it would be an act of war.

South Carolina had to make a decision. Fire at the ship and there would be war or let it dock and the other Confederates would say they were caving in. South Carolina decided to fire on the fort before the ship got there. Their thinking was that the Union would surrender and the ship wouldn't come. The problem was that Anderson didn't surrender until 36 hours later. It was too late.

Lincoln then asked for 100,000 volunteer troops and this pushed four more states out of the Union: Virginia, Arkansas, North Carolina, Tennessee, making it eleven states in the upper and lower south. Also, four slave states of Missouri, Kentucky, Maryland, and Delaware were hanging by a thread while Lincoln sat on the fence, attempting balance.

The Union of twenty, included Maine, New York, New Hampshire, Vermont, Massachusetts, Connecticut, Rhode Island, Pennsylvania, New Jersey, Ohio, Indiana, Illinois, Kansas, Michigan, Wisconsin, Minnesota, Iowa, California, Nevada, and Oregon. Abraham Lincoln was their President.

The Confederacy of eleven included the states of Texas, Arkansas, Louisiana, Tennessee, Mississippi, Alabama, Georgia, Florida, South Carolina, North Carolina and Virginia. Jefferson Davis was their President.

The five states of Maryland, Delaware, West Virginia, Kentucky and Missouri were called Border States. and did not leave the union although they had slavery. These states often had two governments and people fought on both sides.

The Civil War - What Was it? Many questions

Six weeks after Lincoln's inauguration, it was Fort Sumter. The first of Lincoln's goals was to restore the Union. The big problem was that he didn't have a fighting general. He went through several who didn't do much but talk when they visited the White House. General William Tecumseh Sherman visited before the war just to warn Lincoln the magnitude of what was ahead. Lincoln, was naïve at the time just like most of America, North and South, and thought this would be short, bloodless, and the family quarrel would be solved.

This was one point that Sherman nailed. He knew it would be a long and traumatic war affecting everyone living in America. The North was superior to South with more resources, and if you listened to your friends and neighbors, the war would be over in a couple of weeks. The North had money, people, and was stable and established. They had industry and factories. It wasn't because they had West Point or their geography was any better, but they had capacity. Whereas, the South had only home-court advantage and they thought once northerners were tired of fighting they would simply give up and go home.

There was the one initial scene in the movie "Gone with the Wind" in which Southern enthusiasm is displayed, confirming what I have just said. They were as persuasive as the War Hawks who had prodded President Madison to the earlier War of 1812. The actors in the scene call the Yankees cowards and display their allegiance to the South with no regard to the basics. Rhett Butler displays the only points of reason, but it was a lost cause. Both the North and the South entered this war with enthusiasm hope, and dreams.

The Southern troops were commanded by Robert E. Lee. Lee had been offered a command in the Union Army, refused it, resigned from the army, and became a major general for the Confederacy. This was an emotional experience for Lee who labored over the decision. He had had close ties to General Winfield Scott, graduated second in his class from West Point, and had dedicated over 25 years to the Army of the United States. Yet, he was faced with this choice once Virginia seceded from the Union.

When Lee left his home, he never returned to it. The home which had originally been the Custis-Washington family residence, was then occupied by the Lees when Robert E. Lee married Mary Anna Randolph Custis. The Secretary of War, who received the Lee's rejection to take the Union command, ordered burials close to the home, so that it would never be occupied again. Later, the United States government confiscated the land. It became Arlington National Cemetery.[2]

The war was Johnny Reb against Billy Yank. The Democratic Party dominated the South and its conviction was the continuation of slavery. The Solid South has had a lot of different meanings over the year but that it was:

solid. No publication could exist if it disagreed with the gentry, nor could preachers voice their opinions against the establishment. An editor with opposing views, would have no support and soon would be bankrupt. Political candidates could only be loyal to the South and never mention the word abolition. The government was still run by slave owners in the South. In comparison in the North, money was also the bottom line, and the large corporations and monopolistic institutions ruled.

Jefferson Davis was inaugurated provisional president of the Confederate States of America on February 18, 1861, and elected president of the CSA later that year. He did not want the position.

Major General Davis was in his garden at Brierfield when the telegram came announcing his election to the Presidency of the Confederate States of America. Varina Davis later wrote that she thought some family member had died when she saw his reaction. Davis was loyal, duty-bound, and considered himself, just as Jefferson did, a public servant. He abruptly left the next day for Montgomery, Alabama, and accepted the presidency. Davis was the only choice for president. There was no other southerner with a stellular military and political record that could come close to his.

His Vice President was Alexander Stephens. Stephens and Davis never agreed on anything, and didn't work together. This was a problem. Davis and most governors believed that the Confederacy existed to protect slavery and also to protect state's rights. Here we go again. We had the same problem when the Union was one and it was always the feds vs. the states, ever since George Washington. The Confederate Constitution guaranteed state's rights and prevented the government from enacting protective tariffs or supporting internal improvements. Davis, on the other hand, had the sole purpose to get independence from the North and if it was necessary, state's rights would be secondary.

We had two men: Lincoln whose purpose was to keep the Union together and Jefferson whose purpose was to secure independence. One thing I'll reiterate about Lincoln....initially, he did not want to ban slavery but just stop its spread into the new territories. However, from the very start of the war, the Radical Republicans probed Lincoln to adopt an emancipation policy. Look to black abolitionist Frederick Douglass.

Davis had to set up a new country, a challenge in little time. The first thing he did was set up a flag. The flag was the Stars and Bars. There were 5.5 million whites and 3.5 slaves, (9 million) as against 22,000,000 Northerners.

In railroads, the South had only 9,000 miles, while the industrial North 22,000. The South needed to set up a cabinet, military, money, and taxes. We'll talk about these first and then go on to the next issues which assailed them.

Was it a rich man's war and a poor man's fight? There was no military and conscription started in April 1862. As the war raged on and more and more were needed in the army and navy, the draft age was changed to 17 to men in their 50s. However, those that served ranged from children to anyone who would serve. There were exemptions for certain occupations: clergy to shoemakers and those who could afford it paid substitutes; the going rate was approximately $1000 in order to avoid the draft. You were also exempt if you owned more than 20 slaves. The majority could not afford a substitute.

There was no treasury. How did the Confederacy get money and taxes? They began issuing paper money. Two American presidents appeared on Confederate dollars. They were George Washington and Andrew Jackson! The Confederacy issued paper money worth $1 billion during the Civil War—more than twice the amount circulated by the United States. While it's not surprising that Confederate President Jefferson Davis and depictions of slaves at work in fields appeared on some dollar bills, so too did two Southern slave-holding presidents whom Confederates claimed as their own: George Washington (on a $50 and $100 bill) and Andrew Jackson (on a $1,000 bill).

The South would be faced with a boycott and blockade. Davis needed to assemble a quick and loyal cabinet. There were few factories. The southern agricultural tradition helped because the South could produce food but it had no steel mills and only two gunpowder manufacturers. Since they had little foreign contact and had allowed the North to take care of finances, they looked for loans. The South was ready to unite in battle and allegiance.

The Confederacy took out the Erlanger Loan and exchanged goods such as cotton, turpentine, and tobacco for $8.5 million and the only one to benefit was Erlanger, the French financier. The South also had a good base of trained officers. Seven of the eight military colleges in the country were in the South. Many of the war generals for the South came from West Point, such as Robert E. Lee, Jubal Anderson Early, Thomas Jonathan "Stonewall" Jackson, and George Anderson Pickett. The biggest advantage was fighting in southern territory.

Weapons: The most common weapons used were: Muskets, Rifles, Carbines (short barreled riffles), and hand guns (pistols and revolvers). Early in the war, most brought their own weapons.

Uniforms were make-shift. Unlike the movies, where we see spotless matching uniforms, the Confederates never had a standard issue. Many were from state militia outfits, which had their own state-issued uniforms. In the early battles, some Confederate units wore dark blue uniforms and were often mistaken on the battlefields for that of the enemy. Conversely, many Union units that were originally militia units went to war wearing gray. This was readily apparent at the First Battle of Manassas. If you want to read an interesting story, read about the Missing Women of Roswell, Georgia – they worked in factories making the Confederate Gray. More about them later. It became the war of the blue vs. the gray.

Shoes wore out quickly and usually didn't fit. If you carried 60 pounds of gear and walked more than 30 miles in a day through changeable weather, blisters, infections, and pain were common.

Food: As the war went on, there was little. Like the Revolutionary War, it usually was not very appetizing because insects and mold were commonplace.

At the start of the war, Lincoln's army got their butt's kicked. Every evening Lincoln would walk to the telegraph office and pace, waiting for information on battles, losses, and deaths. The news he received was all bad. He was faced with a bleak future. Initially, the Union Army only had about 16,000 troops and most of them were stationed in the West, keeping law and order. Approximately, one-third of its officers had already resigned and joined the Confederacy. Before the war erupted, there had been no draft and little money was allocated for the Army.

In September 1861, the first year of the war, Lincoln began to see this was not the quick and bloodless war that he had anticipated. Little did anyone, Union or Confederate, know the length of the aggression nor the losses involved. When the First Battle of Bull Run, aka Manassas, was fought in July 1861, two inexperienced armies met. The American public was also naïve as they arrived with picnic baskets, expecting to witness the show and enjoy the entertainment. They finally realized the encounter was real and were horrified by what they were really witnessing. There were casualties on both sides with 2,000 wounded, missing, or killed. The South claimed victory.

One of the plans the North tried was the Anaconda Plan, which was devised by General Winfield Scott, who was a Mexican American War hero. The Union's plan was to blockade the Southern coast and "snake" down the Mississippi. At first, it's estimated 90 percent of the Confederates got through the blockade but the Union tightened its snaky grip and only a few got through. Ultimately, it was a successful plan.

April 1862 – Shiloh. Another 23,000 Union and Confederate were casualties as-a-result of the battle. Everyone was involved in the war, even children. Here is the story of one such remarkable patriot. He was drummer boy, Johnny Clem, who participated in Shiloh and Chickamauga and became a symbol for the Union. He was called "Johnny Shiloh or the drummer boy of Chickamauga." Various sources indicate different ages, but we know he was either 9, 10, or 11.[3]

Young Clem ran away from home to join the army. He was rejected because of his age. Eventually, he was adopted as a drummer boy with the Michigan 22nd and followed them in the war. His drum was struck by cannon fire in Shiloh and Clem was close to death but managed to survive. He changed his name to John Lincoln Clem shortly after that and became a member of the troop. The soldiers even gave him a "shorter" rifle that he could handle. At Chickamauga in September 1863, he shot and killed a Confederate officer. When he was captured as a prisoner, the Confederates used him for propaganda and asserted that the Union was desperate and had to rely on a "baby" to fight their war.

Nevertheless, this baby quickly came up through the ranks and became the youngest noncommissioned officer in United States History. When Clem was discharged from the army in the fall of 1864 and General U. S. Grant tried to get him into West Point but he couldn't pass the entrance exam, although he tried several times. He reenlisted for a second term and Grant made him a brigadier general. When Clem retired in 1915, he was the last veteran of the Civil War still on duty and one-year later, he was given the honor bestowed upon him as major general. When he died in 1937, he was buried in Arlington National Cemetery.

The war dragged on, Jackson's Valley Battles and Second Manassas, (Bull Run) brought more casualties. Lincoln was despondent and thought he would change the goal and objective of the war. Initially he wanted to save the Union, but now it was about freeing all of the slaves. This was brought about because he worried that Europe would become involved. The countries of

England, France, or Germany could decide the outcome of the war. If they diplomatically recognized the Confederacy, the war could go on forever. Lincoln had to keep Europe out of it at all costs. In Lincoln's mind, the Confederacy didn't exist and he still called the war a family quarrel. He continued with his stance, much like Jefferson's, in which we were all Americans or we were all part of the same family.

It came down to the big change. During the first year and a half of the war, the objective was to restore the Union, but it wasn't working. It bothered Lincoln that when he looked across the Potomac to Arlington that the first thing he noticed was the Confederate flag in all of its glory, waving in the breeze. The new objective in 1862 was to put an end to slavery, not just in rebelling states. To do this, he wrote the Emancipation Proclamation. [4]

It was a difficult decision. Lincoln's cabinet told him that if he announced it immediately, that everyone would think the Union was desperate. Yes, Lincoln was desperate and melancholic as he went to the telegraph offices day-after-day always receiving tragic news from the war. Casualties were mounting daily. His closest advisors told him to wait for a huge military victory to announce the proclamation. He didn't have to wait very long before the bloodiest day of the war erupted and a huge battle ensued.

September, 1862 – Antietam. Both armies met and this was the largest loss of people in one day, 12 hours. Most books say it was the most bloodiest day of war. 25,000 Americans lost their lives. It wasn't just bullets that killed, but when the forests caught fire, there was smoke, causing asphyxiation, and limited visibility. When you can't see, you can shoot your own. We now call it, "friendly fire." There were 13,000 Confederates and 12,000 Union losses. Antietam was called a "draw" but there was the story of the "Lost Orders," and some say it was a change of fate.

A copy of Robert E. Lee's Battle Plans, Special Order 191 were found either in an envelope containing several cigars, wrapped around a case of cigars under a locust tree, or whatever the various authors choose. The United States National Park Service states that it was from an envelope with 2-3 cigars in it. How could this have happened? The plan was found on September 13, 1862 and told about the Confederate movements, which enabled General George B. McClellan to know Robert E. Lee's plans and react to what the Union was planning in the future. Historians state it could have changed the events, had it not occurred. The Union claimed victory, but what was victory and at what cost?

Despite Clara Barton's efforts, who founded the American Red Cross, to tend to the troops after the surgeons attempted miracles, the carnage was horrific. Following the battle, dead Confederate soldiers were placed in a ditch. Hospitals were set-up anywhere they could in homes, barns, churches, and tents. The *Hagerstown Newspaper* printed that the whole area was one huge hospital.[5]

Lincoln grew increasingly despondent and told his cabinet that the outcome of Antietam would be God's will. If the Union lost, then maybe God willed that slavery was a reality and was meant to last. When the Union claimed victory, Lincoln announced the Emancipation Proclamation. Great Britain was becoming more involved with the war, but the Emancipation Proclamation made them reconsider having any relationship with the South.

The Emancipation Proclamation, was it practical? Did it free slaves in the South or only in areas the Union controlled? It pushed the border states towards emancipation. Blacks joined the Union army. This had been one of the worst of Confederate fears.

In the meantime, women formed the Women's National Loyal League (Susan B. Anthony, Elizabeth Cady Stanton), demanding freedom for slaves, which was important in what was to become the Thirteenth Amendment. Petitions could make a difference but the war continued.

Spies and Smuggling

In *Gone with the Wind,* sorry, I'm a junky, Rhett Butler was a smuggler and ran contraband into the South. Yes, this really existed, and so did spies and espionage. There are dozens of stories of both men and women who sacrificed themselves for the cause in the military or as civilians, whether it was North or South. I will relate several stories of those who worked for their cause.

Keep in mind that although most women supported the cause, there were those who went above and beyond. Women worked as nurses and aides but some disguised themselves as men in order to actively participate. Often they weren't discovered unless there was injury and they were taken to the medics. If discovered. they bore the additional chance of being raped or abused.

Maria Isabelle Belle Boyd spied for the Confederacy.[6] Belle was born to a slave-holding family in Virginia. She was lovely, not beautiful, well-endowed, charming, and could handle herself well, especially in the company of men. It didn't take her long to show her loyalty to the Confederacy. At 17, she shot and killed a Union soldier after he had broken into the family home and verbally assaulted her mother. She was cleared but watched. Spying ran in the family and three others in the Boyd family were also convicted at various times.

Apparently Belle had a tremendous amount of 'charm and charisma' because she was very friendly with Union troops. She got a reputation, and was often compared to Joan of Arc or Cleopatra. Belle knew how to use her feminine traits and was intelligent. She figured out that in her era women were thought of as the weak, harmless, and their female opinions should not be taken seriously. Belle certainly played the role. While officers enjoyed her youthful teasing and chitchat, little did they know the thoughts passing through her mind. She was a great actress, knew what she needed to do, and how to get it.

After Belle was arrested repeatedly, the soldiers advised her to stop all of her activities or there would be serious consequences. The family moved to Front Royal, Virginia and Belle wasn't done yet. She befriended Stonewall Jackson and P.G.T. Beauregard, both Confederate generals and helped in the Shenandoah Valley Campaign. Belle was caught.

The Feds deported her to Richmond, Virginia. This time she was again apprehended trying to get papers to England! Belle liked to carry papers, weapons, and whatever materials were needed for the cause, in her large hoop skirts! She was never a model-prisoner. She waved Confederate flags out of windows, sang Dixie, and like many incarcerated today, maintained close ties with those on the outside. She was given "special" privileges. Belle lived well and was given many gifts by the officers who befriended her.

When released, she went to England and married the Union naval officer who had interrogated her! She later wrote a book and remarried after her husband died, divorced her second husband after giving birth to four children, and married much younger men twice after her husband died. She toured our country and made a career out of her experiences during her lifetime.

Even though the British were neutral in the war, blockade runners were numerous. Huge profits were in the forecast, if successful, and the adventure was worth the risk. There were a good number of British manufacturers that entered into the lucrative practice on British owned ships or in partnership with the South. They brought muskets, cannons, and machinery into the South. Nonetheless, luxury items brought in more money. Taking off one machine and substituting material, fine furniture, liquor, or perfume could be much more lucrative. One auction could increase your profit tremendously. One round-trip could yield a $200,000 profit and the crew would be paid in gold. States such as North Carolina and Georgia as well as the Confederacy itself bought their own ships. The North was well-aware of the running and whenever a vessel was captured, their newspapers placed the good news in their headlines.

Officers and crew were needed and readily available and they could be those who already lived in the South, officers from the Royal Navy, or those without any other means of support seeking a get-rich-quick opportunity. The most important person was the 'pilot' who steered and maneuvered the ship through enemy waters. One of the most successful was the CSS *Robert E. Lee* which made over 20 trips before being put out of commission. This 642-ton ship was built in Glasgow, Scotland and was originally named the *Giraffe*.

Here's how it worked. The materials were brought to neutral ports outside of the united States, e.g., Hamilton, Bermuda or Havana, Cuba. The cargo was then placed upon the blockade-running vessel which would attempt to reach either the Carolina coast, or the Gulf of Mexico. In return, cotton was loaded to go back to England.[7]

Summary

The first shorts were fired at Fort Sumter and our Civil War began. Jefferson Davis' Confederacy was faced with the huge task of setting up a new nation, quickly. There were advantages to both the North and South. The North had more expendable soldiers, factories, and railroads. The South had home-field advantage, strong generals, resources to grow food, and strong spirit.

The first years did not go well and Lincoln was in a constant state of despondency. The deaths and destruction were huge in a war that both sides thought would be quick, painless, and reunite the nation quickly and easily.

The onset of the war was a learning experience for both sides and pitted families against each other, brother vs. brother, Johnny Reb vs. Billy Yank. It continued for four years.

Our America

The Confederates adopted many flags but nothing was exactly official. The following became a symbol of the South. In today's world, many view it as a symbol of racism, while others view it as history. It existed and cannot be erased.

Chapter 23

The War Continues: 1863-1865

The Emancipation Proclamation was to become effective on New Year's Day, 1863. It was to free all of the slaves that were currently in the areas under rebellion. On paper, they would be free, but in reality, it did nothing. Freedom was a long way off and elusive.

The Proclamation was a statement meant for Europe. It implied that if Europe entered the war, they would be fighting to keep slavery and would become enemies to the North. No countries outwardly supported slavery. After the proclamation nothing changed. Lincoln went through numerous generals because he still could not find effective leadership on the battlefield. Many could be compared to our current publicity agents. They gave Lincoln a good sales pitch. The candidates would secure good uniforms, make the troops look good, issue news which stretched the truth, but most were inadequate on the battleground. Many were untrained in tactical warfare and commanding large numbers of troops. Unlike movies we watch, troops were not clean-shaven, handsome, well-fed, and happy-go-lucky. This was a long and dirty war.

There were battles where people lost lives, as many as 25,000 in two to three-day battles, and the numbers grew. However, the Union could replace any loss while the South could not. Many strategies were employed to gain replacements. The Union had immigrants of every nationality which consisted of approximately one-third of the army, and under the Homestead Act promised 160 acres of land to any citizens or would-be citizens. Bounty was to increase enlistment. This often resulted in the unscrupulous who would enlist in a regiment, collect the bounty, disappear, and re-enlist in another for additional bounty. Seldom were they given severe sentences if, in fact, they were ever caught.

Lincoln had his share of problems and one was immigration. Immigration had a two-way streak. He welcomed immigrants but he was constantly thinking about the fact that many offered no support for the Union. They arrived in America, and taking no steps to citizenship, they lost the right to vote but gained the right of not being drafted. On the other hand, immigration slowed down during the war and industries faced labor shortages with so many men off to war. Businesses were constantly complaining to Lincoln. Then, when Lincoln announced the Emancipation Proclamation, many groups were less enthusiastic about supporting the war believing their jobs would be gone if blacks were freed. There were riots in various areas consisting of numerous nationalities. It was not until 1864, however, that new laws were passed to attract more immigrants.[1]

Lincoln then allowed blacks to enlist because he knew he had to. By his General Order 143, he established the United States Bureau of Colored Troops (USCT). Estimates vary from 100,000-200,000 who came, but the fact was they were subjected to inequity in both their pay and rations. Eventually, even the North allowed "stand-ins" which had been going on in the South for a long time.

The mix of nationalities, races, and cultural differences caused disunity in the battlefields. Human nature is such that there is always an "underdog" to be criticized regardless of traits. Not only were Americans fighting against Americans, but they were fighting within their military families, which didn't help either cause.

The Battle of Gettysburg

Gettysburg, Pennsylvania was a quiet town in southern Pennsylvania. although the battle lasted three days, from July 1, 1864 through July 3, the world has never forgotten the events that occurred here. It was part of the 35-day Gettysburg Campaign. Robert E. Lee was moving North and this was his second strike. However, it was different from the prior battles because he was bringing the war into Pennsylvania. Lee was driven by recent victories in both Fredericksburg and Chancellorsville. The major players were Lee, Grant, and Jeb Stuart. This battle turned the tide for the North in its aftermath.

Estimates on the losses are 50,000 on both sides, but southern casualty count was difficult to estimate. The battle took place in an area with divided loyalty. Often families were split apart because members fought on both sides and some regions were under martial law. To give you an idea of how horrific this battle was, information from "Maryland Civil War Trails" describes the carnage.

Soldiers "biting on a bullet during surgery and amputating limbs" was a myth and doctors provided good care despite conditions in our nineteenth century America. Germs and infection were always the negative factor. Six hundred Catholic nuns became nurses during the war, and the Daughters of Charity were the first to reach Gettysburg.

This Independence Day was far from joyful. The once black soil around Gettysburg, Pennsylvania was now red with blood. When the Battle was over, a seventeen-mile long wagon train carried over 10,000 Confederates back into Virginia and there was still another fifty miles to travel. Horses had difficulty moving over the ground because of the human and animal carnage strewn about. Of the 11,000 dead, most Union soldiers were hastily buried; but Confederate bodies lie where they had fallen. As the rain poured down, the thunder roared, and lightning lit the morbid parade, the cries of the wounded and dying could be heard across the land.

General John D. Imboden's troops protected the caravan. Imboden stated when he heard the cries of the wounded and dying,

"I realized more of the horrors of war than I had in all the preceding years."[2]

The realities of this war became known to every man, woman, and child as conflict moved across our land. Less than a week after Gettysburg, a third invasion of the North occurred at Monocacy, which is south of Frederick, Maryland. There were few casualties but Monocacy was important. The Union delayed the Confederates, allowing reinforcements to reach Washington and repel General Early's army. It redeemed Union Major General Lew Wallace, who had failed to obey orders at the Battle of Shiloh, and had cost 23,000 Union and Confederate casualties.

Historians are still divided about when the tide turned in the war. Was the Confederate cause hopeless from day one or was Gettysburg the turning point? Could it have been Lincoln's re-election or Sherman's brutal "total war" philosophy?

Nevertheless, while the fighting went on in Gettysburg, another event occurred in the small city of Roswell, Georgia. Roswell was a textile center-factory town. Tents, camping necessities, rope, material, and the cloth for Confederate uniforms or Roswell Gray, were manufactured here. Mostly young women, some black, were employed. They heard Union soldiers were coming to Atlanta but kept working while most Roswell residents abandoned their homes and left. The factory women kept their children with them because there was no such thing as a nanny, daycare, or babysitter.[3]

Sherman told the commander to arrest all of the women, take them to Marietta, Georgia, load them into rail cars, and send them up North. He said that the women would "howl" but nevertheless to do it. They were sent to Louisville in boxcars and eventually released. There were already refugees, and lack of lodging and food. What would you do as a southerner, perhaps with your children, no money, semi-illiterate, with only the clothes on your back, being dumped in a strange northern city with other refugees?

Few somehow made it back to Georgia, but the majority just disappeared. There were accounts of women coming back years later, only to find their husbands remarried, dead, or having moved away. The men, having no word, deduced their wives had been killed.

In October 1864, there was a battle we hear little about. It was the Battle of Cedar Creek in Virginia. It was one of the bloodiest days with 8,600 Union and Confederates killed, wounded, or captured. It was General Jubal Early vs. General Philip Sheridan. The Union was victorious because it destroyed food sources and the Confederates had nothing for their troops. The battle's importance is that it helped Lincoln's re-election three weeks later. The North quickly replaced troops to prepare for the next battle while the South suffered.

The only way the South could increase troops would be to allow 3.9 million slaves to bear arms. This was unheard of. Southerners asserted that arming slaves to fight with whites would be confirming they were equal. The War had been going on for years. Finally, in this 1864 presidential election year, Lincoln was convinced he would not be re-elected. A-number-of people told him that the election should be suspended. Lincoln said no, and emphasized that politicians needed to follow all constitutional responsibilities.

Sandi Ludwa

Lincoln knew Pennsylvania was going to be a swing state and wasn't certain that he wanted to give a speech. The Gettysburg Address became one of the best-known speeches in History. In November 1863, he was invited to deliver remarks, at the official dedication ceremony for the National Cemetery of Gettysburg in Pennsylvania. The cemetery was yet incomplete but it was the site of one of the bloodiest, decisive, and remembered battles of the Civil War. Lincoln was not the featured orator that day. Let's go to Gettysburg and witness the speech.

The Gettysburg Address

It's Thursday, November 19, 1863 and four and a half months after the Union defeated the Confederates at Gettysburg. We see the main speaker for the event, Edward Everett, who is considered one of the nation's foremost orators. He is a former senator, President of Harvard, and has every reason to believe he'll steal the show. Everett speaks Greek and Latin! Of course, Lincoln is on the agenda as well but I don't think the crowd is thinking he'll say anything that hasn't already been said. He's not a historian. We're lucky though to be able to witness the president's speech.

Everett is introduced and is speaking. It's been almost two hours, and I'm enjoying the beautiful words, logic, and his explanation of the significance and the tragedy of the Battle of Gettysburg. Do you agree with him that it was the turning point of the war? It appears that he's doing the whole speech from memory.

Oh look, President Lincoln is going to speak, but I think he's only doing some remarks about the cemetery. He's slowly rising to the planform.

"Four-score and seven years ago….." I think a score is 20 years plus 7 and that would equal 87 years. I've timed him, two minutes. We soon learn that Lincoln's speech was only 273 words, but oh what power in them!

One of the men in the crowd comments, "Look, he read the whole thing from a sheet of paper, but he really emphasized the words. It was very powerful! He's finished and it's so quiet. He's sitting down and looks really sad!"

We learn that when he finished his speech, he thought it was a failure because the crowd was so still. The initial reaction was "wait, he's setting down?!!? What happened?" People were expecting a full several hour speech since speeches were the entertainment of the day. This was the culture at that time when the crowd gathered for the dedication and most didn't think it was a very good speech for the occasion. Even though Everett spoke for two hours, everyone was ready for more.

Lincoln carefully thought about each and every word as he wrote the speech, even though he knew his appearance was secondary to the famous Everett. We know that it was one of the greatest and most influential declarations of our American purpose. Lincoln also asserted that the Civil War as a struggle not just for the Union, but more so for the principles of human equality. He reiterated on the principles that formed the pillars of our Declaration of Independence. When he stated that the war was a struggle to preserve the Union in-spite-of secession, I shuttered. His "new birth of freedom" called for a new beginning and equality for everyone, male, female, free, and formerly enslaved.

Sometimes people are not remembered for their accomplishments until they pass on. It was the case for Lincoln. It wasn't until after Lincoln's assassination, that he was martyred in the press and little did he know the significance of the Gettysburg Address.

Sandi Ludwa

The Horrors of War
Prisons

Andersonville, Georgia

Andersonville could be called a concentration or death camp. It was bad. Andersonville was a Confederate Prison on the Georgia plains close to a railroad away from fighting. It was still under construction when the first inmates arrived in February 1864. The prison was necessary when prisoner-exchanges between the North and South stopped in 1863 over disagreements on the handling of black soldiers. Slaves hastily constructed the stockade which had a capacity of 10,000. Nevertheless, within six months there were 30,000.

Conditions were deplorable, especially since there was no access to clean water. Clothes were taken from dead bodies as soon as men died. The imprisoned froze to death or succumbed to scurvy, diarrhea, hookworm, or dysentery. Those that survived were walking-skeletons. 13,000 Died out of the 45,000 sent there.[4]

Camp Douglas, Illinois
Andersonville of the North

It started as a training facility, but by the end of the war, 18,000 were incarcerated. Filth, disease, and the smell of human rot were the norm. Akin to Andersonville, Camp Douglas had the additional disadvantage of long and cold Chicago area winters. Leadership in the camp was blamed for greed, inferior and few rations, and causing disease, scurvy, and starvation. One in seven died.

Camp Hoffman (Point Lookout)

Camp Hoffman, the largest prisoner of war camp in the North, came into being under the same situation as Andersonville, when prisoner-of-war exchanges ceased. It was located at the confluence of the Chesapeake Bay and Potomac River and its construction began after Gettysburg. Its capacity was 10,000 but numbers quickly grew to 20,000 being confined. By the end of the war, the poor sanitation contaminated its wells. There were few comforts for the prisoners. Blankets and materials to sustain the prisoners, as well as wood for heating, were virtually nonexistent.

Salisbury Prison
North Carolina

Established early on in 1861, only 120 men were effectively housed. By 1864, the numbers soon reached 10,000. Filth, starvation, disease, and death followed with one-quarter of the population dying.

You get the idea. Neither North nor South had adequate facilities and these camps could be called "death camps." Others include: Alton, Illinois, Belle Isle, Virginia, and Elmira, New York. This is not a conclusive list; there were more, about 150.

The war dragged on. The election of 1864 was coming around. Soldiers voted as battlefield ballot boxes came out to the field. It was interesting, because Lincoln was convinced he would not being re-elected, but then he found a powerful soldier, Ulysses S Grant. Grant was not a fan of the war, but was realistic and knew that the only way to win was to beat the enemy everywhere. You had to be relentless and pound them into the ground. His colleague, William Tecumseh Sherman, shared this view. Grant decided to go from Washington DC South and Sherman would go from the West from Georgia, Mississippi, and Alabama east. Grant hoped to capture the South in a vice.

Summary

Lincoln had seen better days. After Antietam, he issued the Emancipation Proclamation which had little effect upon the South. There were labor shortages in the North and people become worried about both immigration and the effect an end to slavery would have upon their own economy. As the war dragged on and on, more troops were needed when Gettysburg became the turning point. The carnage was unbearable and the short war had become a lengthy one. The war camps were death sentences themselves.

Before the National Cemetery was completed, Lincoln gave his Gettysburg Address. The horrors of war were upon everyone. Death, disease, broken dreams, and the battles continued. The only hope to end the war was General Sherman's plan for total war.

Chapter 24

The Tide Turns and It's Total War

Sherman and Grant had a plan that there would be a march to the sea. They introduced the concept of "Total War." It's just like it sounds, it's making sure everyone knows a war is taking place through their own suffering. When food ran out and private homes and possessions were burned, people got the message. When entire villages were forced to evacuate, only to find their bridges and railroads destroyed they knew it couldn't get any worse. People lost possessions, didn't have the means to travel, would remain homeless, and lost faith in their country. Add to that to the news of those lost in battle or the uncertainty of their whereabouts, and people were terrified.

By 1864, soldiers fighting for the Confederacy included boys as young as 12 as well as older-middle-aged men. Everybody and anybody fought against the Union Army which was like a group of locusts, relentless. When Sherman took Atlanta and Savannah, it completely changed morale and Lincoln easily won the election of 1864. The whole purpose of Sherman's March to the Sea in November and December 1864, in his total and all-out war, was to inflict damage, misery, and devastate the South. This would cause morale, confidence, and the once fierce optimism to completely disintegrate and the war would be won.

Four years earlier, Lincoln won with 39 percent of the popular vote. In 1864, he was re-elected with 53 percent of popular vote. This time the soldiers overwhelmingly supported Lincoln. All knew they had to finish the work that waited to be done. Many believed that if they voted for George C. McClellan, who was on a peace platform, that those who sacrificed and died, would have died in vain. In the Electoral College, Lincoln won by a landslide.

There is the story of Lincoln's second inauguration, 42 days before his assassination, which gives us an idea of what our next president was like. Remember, the only way a vice president becomes the president, is when the president dies.

Andrew Johnson, the vice president-elect was in Washington still suffering from typhoid fever. Nevertheless, the night before the inauguration, he went to a party given by the secretary of state. Inauguration day had typical March weather and was bitterly cold, damp, and windy. Johnson, already hung-over from the night before, said he was weak and drank a few more whiskies. Flushed and showing the effects of the liquor, but feeling better, he went into the crowded and warm Senate chamber. After the introductions, Johnson rose and went to the podium.

He spoke to the crowd about his modest upbringing and his victory over the rebel aristocracy. The audience was shocked and Lincoln looked really disgusted and depressed. Remember Senator Charles Sumner? He covered up his face with his hands while the former vice president tried to cut Johnson's remarks short. When Johnson finally finished, he took his oath, kissed the Bible, and then tried to swear in new senators. Johnson was confused and had to relegate this duty to a Senate clerk.[1]

Soon it was 1865, and the Confederacy was failing. Its army to the West of the Mississippi couldn't do anything to stop the inevitable loss. The Union controlled the entire Mississippi River and in states such as Alabama, Georgia, and Mississippi, the South was powerless. Near Petersburg, Virginia, Grant had overtaken Lee and by that time Sherman's army was already in Savannah. Many Confederates wanted to fight to the last and continue the war, but Robert E. Lee knew it was time to quit. He watched the South die a slow death through starvation, lack of clothing, especially shoes, shelter, and moreover, witnessed the thousands of deaths. The End came at Appomattox Courthouse, Virginia when Grant and Lee met. Envision the scene on April 9, 1865.

It was Palm Sunday, Lee wore his best dress uniform which included a scarlet-red silk sash, a jeweled-sword that had been given to him by women in England, his red-stitched boots which included spurs, and long gray gloves. He wanted to look his best if Grant took him prisoner. Lee knew, if he didn't surrender and the war continued, thousands more would die. Lee arrived on his horse, Traveller, at Wilmer McLean's parlor Appomattox Court House, Virginia, looking elegant, while Grant was covered with mud and in disarray. They shook hands. It's been an old belief that Lee surrendered his sword to Grant, but current historians believe it never occurred.

Grant told Lee, if Lee's men stopped the fighting and took an oath to the Union, they could take food, horses, and weapons. He authorized supplies to feed them because the men were starving. Lee departed and rode to advise the men of his surrender. He told them to simply, go home and try to rebuild their lives. For four long years we fought and over 750,000 had suffered and died. Americans had killed other Americans.

Lincoln was relieved. During the endless conflict Lincoln struggled with his old demon of melancholy which was intensified from the day he took office. Now, the war was over and he could dwell on peace, for the few remaining days of his life. He wanted the South back into the Union quickly, compassionately, and painlessly and everyone to be one happy family again. It could have happened had he not been assassinated six days later. Even Southerners were distraught because they knew all possibilities of any peaceful reconstruction were gone. The war was officially over, but people kept fighting. For some, it never ended.

The Assassination

On the day of Lincoln's assassination, Lincoln had what some call a premonition. He told his cabinet:
"Gentlemen, something serious is about to happen. I have had a strange dream, and have a presentiment such as I have had several times before, and always just before some important event....But let us proceed to business."[2]

The assassinator was John Wilkes Booth, but Booth and his conspirators spent months engineering the perfect plan. The play, *Our American Cousin,* at Ford's Theatre in Washington, DC was perfect. Originally, they planned to kidnap Lincoln and do a prisoner exchange but when the Confederacy began to fall, they changed their plans. Not only was Lincoln in the assassination plan, but so were Vice President Andrew Johnson, General U. S. Grant, and Secretary of State William Seward. Others were invited that night but turned down the invitation. The Grants, for instance, declined because Julia Grant despised Mary Todd Lincoln. The Lincolns were accompanied by one other couple not on the "hit" list.

At 10 p.m., Booth walked into the theater and was allowed to come in because he knew the staff. Booth was an actor. Now-a-days presidents have ample security; but, this was not the case in 1865. Lincoln had no security. Booth shot Lincoln in the back of his head with a small single-shot derringer. Booth escaped but broke his leg. Lincoln was carried to a home across from Ford's, and declared dead at 7:22 a.m., the following morning. Booth was caught, shot, and killed. Another seven conspirators were arrested, found guilty, hung, or given life imprisonment.

Lee warned Jefferson Davis and his cabinet to leave Richmond when he knew Union troops would soon be entering both Richmond and Petersburg. Hastily, they took more than $500,000 in gold, Confederate bank notes, bonds, jewels, and boarded a train for Danville, Virginia. A day later, Union troops entered Richmond and Petersburg. Looting, fire, riots, and chaos took the city. However, Davis was not defeated and he still hoped to establish a new Confederate capital in Danville. Even when Lee surrendered on April 9, Davis and his officials kept moving, seeking sanctuary in the South.

There are diaries, letters, and journals that tell of their actions. These documents reveal a stories of the allegiance for the Confederate cause. The existence of these documents could be research enough to write several books or novels explaining the beliefs in a lost cause. Davis was captured in Irwinville, Georgia the following month. He was imprisoned, shackled, and jailed for two years. The Confederate treasury was minus $120,000. Where did it go?

Summary

Lincoln was assassinated and there was surrender at Appomattox. Everyone had enough and the war was finally over, or was it? Sometimes, it feels like we are still fighting a civil war between us.

What do you think? Was the Civil War inevitable, justified, and were the causes valid? Do you think it could happen again today or is it happening in its own way? I often wonder if U.S. Grant and his wife, Julia had gone to Ford's Theatre with the Lincolns, would something different have happened? What if Lincoln had lost the election and Stephen A. Douglas became president?

What kind of man was Sherman? Barbarian or liberator? Should there be rules of war?

There are so many questions yet never to be answered and agreed upon. Our final journey ends soon and we can examine our impressions of America so far. A lot of history, wins, losses, heartache, and joy, but this was and is America. We've been through new beginnings, endings, and learned about the people themselves who have come to life for us as we lived our vicarious experiences. Relax, I'll summarize, and you can contemplate about all of the things we have experienced together in our America.

Chapter 25

A Broken Nation – Where do we go from here?

Gone – Hopes and Dreams to be Rebuilt from the Ashes and We Will Start Again.

The Civil War was a total of approximately 10,500 military actions. Under various titles: there were major battles, clashes, engagements, sieges, and bombardments which were fought in 23 states and occurred in our own back yards, small towns, large cities, and in the countryside. The events propelled our nation, once separated, into one inseparable entity.

Likened to the Old West and the Dime Novel which portrayed the West as a land of romance and wealth, the "lost cause" was also romanticized, especially by those in the South who longed for the good old days. Jefferson Davis, Stonewall Jackson, and Robert E. Lee were placed on pedestals and revered as icons of what heroes should be. The South placed monuments in many town squares. Today, many are being removed. This sense of loss reinforced the resolve of a substantial portion of the white population to protect, restore, and strive to teach others, of what little remained of their "Gone with the Wind" world. We need to read, study, and research. I wonder myself, "Did it ever exist at all?"

The Elite Planter Class was gone. These were the slave traders, merchants, politicians, and middle class. Gone too was the slave class or caste. Before the War, the planters were the persons paying 95 percent of the taxes. However, now the taxes fell upon the poor yeoman. Slaves were taxed property before the war. Now the planters were gone, and this created a big problem. Taxes skyrocketed and the North came in and took control.

Before he died, Abraham Lincoln signed a bill that was passed by Congress. It became known as The Freedmen's Bureau. It was only to be a temporary measure to help freed men and women handle the immediate transition to freedom and stop any long-term government dependency before it started. The Act expired in March 1865 but was renewed for three years. General O.O. Howard (Howard University was named after him) was in charge and he was to organize and arrange these relief actions which would provide such things as medical help and schools. A Civil Rights Act (1866) was passed over a Johnson veto, but soon the Fourteenth Amendment was ratified.

The Situation in the American South:

Towns were gutted and gone. Burnt buildings, decaying debris, and bits and pieces of people's prior lives lay in the ashes.

Plantations were burned and little left of their past grandeur and majesty.

Fields were abandoned and overgrown with weeds and insects.

After the Revolutionary War there was a phrase, "Not worth a Continental," and such was the case with Confederate money. Confederate money was worthless.

The loss of personal property was huge. Most of the time, families were headed by females because the males were the casualties of the war. Twenty percent of the white male population, approximately 258,000 from the South, died as well as 38,000 blacks. People were homeless. Women often wore mourning clothes for more than two years.

Andrew Johnson was now president. he South was inhabited by Scalawags and Carpetbaggers. A Scalawag was a Southern white, mainly small farmers as well as merchants and planters, who supported the Northern Republicans during Reconstruction. A Carpetbagger were the Northern transplants to the South who stayed South after the War. Many were ex-Union soldiers and committed to rights.

The North was victorious and its generals and politicians became wealthy and famous. General Sherman wrote his memoirs and showed his frustration at the snail's pace both the North and South were working to record, preserve, and educate future generations. He believed the war was necessary and worth fighting. Sherman soon traveled in high social-circles and bragged of his status. He said, "Let the Astor's, Vanderbilt's and Gould's take a back seat for I am the richest man in New York."[1] He believed his job was well-done and seemed to display no remorse.

You may ask, what happened to all of the ex-Confederates? Jefferson Davis was imprisoned, charged with treason and complicity in Lincoln's assassination. Varina kept up her pleas and got Horace Greeley, founder of the *New York Tribune* to be a consigner of a bail bond for $100,000. He was able to get other Northerners to do the same, so Jefferson was released. Two years later, still free on bail, he was free. Varina was 16-years younger than Davis, but their marriage had been a happy one, despite the griefs they endured together. They retired Beauvoir in Biloxi, Mississippi.

Davis wrote a two-volume memoir, *The Rise and Fall of the Confederate Government* in 1881. In his book, he makes it very clear in his ending statements as to why he wrote the book. He stated that the truth, as he saw it, must be known. Davis addressed Fort Sumter as defense caused by the "hostile descent of the fleet," meaning the Union. This was his first point, that the South was in defense mode. He justified secession and praised Southerners for their "gallantry and devotion." Even though it was an unequal struggle, their conviction was justified. His final statement was that even though the war was "impracticable, but not wrong," it was necessary and "esto perpetua" (to endure or live forever), should be placed on the arch of the Union. He is buried in Richmond, Virginia.[2]

Prologue

Our journey is over and our nation did and continues to rebuild. The Civil War was not our last and final war. Sure, we're not perfect, no country can claim that virtue. I hope you have enjoyed our trip together and perhaps we can embark upon another journey into the future and understand more about our country. One thing is for sure, our nation is enduring, and we hope and pray it will live forever. It is Our America and we are all in this together. We are not just New Yorkers or Virginians or Alaskans but all Americans. I don't

Sandi Ludwa

quite know what the American Dream is supposed to be, but we are all living in Our America and need to take comfort and pride in this great country of ours –

The United States of America.

Bibliography

Abraham Lincoln Online." Collected Works of Abraham Lincoln. Ed. Roy P. Basler. http://www.abrahamlincoln.org/Lincoln/. Speeches/house.htm. Accessed September 11, 2018.

Abdill, George B., *Civil War Railroads.* New York: Bonanza Books, 1961. This is my recommendation for those who desire to learn more about the state of transportation during the war.

Akerman, Bruce. *The Failure of the Founding Fathers.* Cambridge: Belknap Press of Harvard University Press, 2005.

Adams, Randolph Greenfield, *Political Ideas of the American Revolution.* Durham: Trinity College Press, 1922.

"America's Story, From America's Library. Jump Back in Time, Colonial Period,1492-1763." Library of Congress. http://www.americaslibrary.gov/jb/colonial/jb_colonial_jamestown_2.html. Accessed September 4, 2018.

"Andrew Johnson, 16th Vice-President, 1865." United States Senate website. https://www.senate.gov/artandhistory/history/common/generic/VP_AndrewJohnson.htm. Accessed September 12, 2018.

"Antietam." National Park Service brochure to Antietam, obtained August 2018. National Park Service U.S. Department of the Interior. Antietam National Battlefield Maryland.

Bancroft, Frederick *Slave-Trading in the Old South*. Baltimore: J. H. Furst Co., 1931.

Barr, A. University of Virginia. *Remember The Alamo* [e-book]. Charlottesville Virginia: Generic NL Freebook Publisher; n.d. Available from: eBook Collection (EBSCOhost), Ipswich, MA. Accessed August 1, 2018.

Bennett, John D., *The London Confederates*. Jefferson, NC: MacFarland & Co., 2008.

Beringer, Richard E., Herman Hattaway, Archer Jones, William N. Still, Jr., *Why the South Lost the Civil War*. Athens: University of Georgia, 1986.

Bledsoe, Albert Taylor, LL.D. (Professor of Mathematics in the University of Virginia). *An Essay on Liberty and Slavery*. Philadelphia: J. B. Lippincott & Co., 1856.

"Blockade of Confederate Ports." Office of the Historian, Bureau of Public Affairs, United States Department of State. National Park Service, United States Department of the Interior. https://history.state.gov/milestones/1861-1865/blockade. Accessed August 2018.

"The Boston Tea Party," This Day in History: December 16, A+E Networks, History.com 2009. http://www.history.com/this-day-in-history/the-boston-tea-party, Accessed June 9, 2018.

Bovine Tuberculosis, Fact sheet on TB: APHIS Veterinary Services. United States Department of Agriculture. https://www.aphis.usda.gov/publications/animal_health/content/printable_version/faq_bovine_tb_.pdf. Accessed September 23, 2018.

Boyle, Christopher, *Mansfield Plantation, A Legacy on the Black River*. Charleston: The History Press, 2014. This publication provides an overall view of one rice plantation in the Carolina lowcountry.

Bramen, Lisa. "The Food that Fueled the American Revolution," Smithsonian.com, July 5, 2011. https://www.smithsonianmag.com/arts-culture/the-food-that-fueled-the-american-revolution-25701053. Accessed June 10, 2018.

Brooks, Rebecca Beatrice Brooks. "History of the Salem Witch Trials," August 18, 2011. http://historyofmassachusetts.org/the-salem-witch-trials/. Accessed September 6, 2018.

Bunch III, Lonnie G., Spencer R. Crew, Mark G. Hirsch, Harry R. Rubenstein, *The American Presidency,* (Washington: Smithsonian Institution Press, 2000).

Bryant, William Cullen, and Sydney Howard Gay, *A popular History of the United States,* Vol IV, New York: Charles Scribner's Sons, 1886 "Gettysburg Invasion & Retreat." Maryland Civil War Trails, Brochure. Further information www.civilwartrails.org.

Burnett, Edmund Cody. *The Continental Congress*, NY: MacMillan Co., 1941.

Caffrey, Kate. *The Mayflower*. New York: Stein and Day, 1974.

Campbell, Jacqueline Glass, *When Sherman Marched North From the Sea,* Gary W. Gallagher, ed., Chapel Hill: University of North Carolina, 2003.

Capers, Gerald M. *Stephen A. Douglas, Defender of the Union*. Boston: Little, Brown and Co., 1959.

Chesnut, Mary Boykin. 1961. *A Diary from Dixie: As Written by Mary Boykin Chesnut, Wife of James Chesnut, Jr., United States Senator from South Carolina, 1859-1861, and Afterward an Aide to Jefferson Davis and a Brigadier-General in the Confederate Army.* Edited by Isabella D Martin and Myrta Lockett Avary. Gloucester, Mass: Peter Smith.

"Christopher Columbus, The Sailor who gave us the New World," *National Geographic,* November 1978, Vol. 148., No. 5.

Civil War Home Page, Dedicated to the participants, both North and South, in the great American Civil War 1861 – 1865," http://www.civil-war.net. Accessed December 19, 2018.

"Confederate Spy Belle Boyd is Captured." This Day in History. https://www.history.com/this-day-in-history/confederate-spy-belle-boyd-is-captured. Accessed August 25, 2018.

Cooke, Allister. *Allister Cooke's America,* (New York: Alfred A. Knopf), 1973.

Cooper, William J., Jr. and Thomas E. Terrill, *The American South, A History,* Vol. I, Second Edition. New York: McGraw-Hill Companies, 1991

Coss, Stephen. "What Led Benjamin Franklin to Live Estranged From His Wife for Nearly Two Decades?" *Smithsonian Magazine*, September 2017 https://www.smithsonianmag.com/history/benjamin-franklin-estranged-wife-nearly-two-decades-180964400/#2AAekOqRxoshHprp.99. Accessed June 11, 2018.

"The Crime Against Kansas." May 19, 1856. Senate Stories. https://www.senate. gov/artandhistory/history/minute/The_Crime_Against _Against_Kansas.htm. Accessed July 30, 2018.

Crosby, Alfred W. *The Columbian Exchange: Biological and Cultural Consequences of 1492.* Connecticut: Greenwood Press, 1972.

"CSS Robert E. Lee." ConfederateNavy.com. http://www.confederatenavy. com/CSS_Robert_E_Lee.htm.Accessed August 27, 2018.

Current, Richard N., *The Lincoln Nobody Knows.* New York: McGraw-Hill Book Co., Inc., 1958.

Davis, Cyprian, *History of Black Catholics.* New York: Crossroad Publishing, 1996.

Davis, Jefferson, *The Rise and Fall of the Confederate Government.* New York: Appleton & Co., 1881.

Diamond, Jared, *Guns, Germs, and Steel: The Fates of Human Societies.* New York: W. W. Norton & Co., 2017.

Ecenbarger, William. "Ben Franklin's Dangerous Liaisons, That Kindly Old Kite Flyer Was Also A High-flying Ladies' Man," *Chicago Tribune,* May 6, 1990, http://articles.chicagotribune.com/1990-05-06/features/9002070774_1_poor-richard-lucy-mercer-franklin-delano-roosevelt. Accessed June 11, 2018.

Ellet, E. F. *Women of the Revolution,* Available Petus Archives at Winthrop University. 1850.

Eschner, Kat. "The Midnight Ride of Paul Revere and Some Other Guys," April 8, 2017, Smithsonian.com.https://www.smithsonianmag.com/smart-news/midnight-ride-paul-revere-and-some-other-guys-18096286. Accessed June 10, 2018.

Fellman, Michael. *Citizen Sherman. A Life of William Tecumseh Sherman.*(New York: Random House, 1995.

"The First American Factories." U.S. History online Textbook. Independence Hall Association of Philadelphia. http://www.ushistory.org/us/25d/asp. Accessed August 28, 2018.

Fisher, Mary Pat. *Living Religions.* 6th Ed. Upper Saddle River, New Jersey: Prentice-Hall, 1991.

Fisher, Sydney George, *The Struggle for American Independence Vol I* Philadelphia: J. B. Lippincott Co., 1908.

Fiske, John. *The Critical Period of American History 1783-1789.* Boston: Houghton Mifflin Co., 1888, by Abby M. 1916.

Flavion, Gary, "Civil War Prison Camps." Civil War Overview. American Battlefield Trust. https://www.battlefields.org/learn/articles/civil-war-prison-camps. Accessed August 25, 2018.

Franklin, Benjamin. "Benjamin Franklin on the Great Awakening, from His Autobiography," Digital History ID 1278 Website, Date: 1771. http://www.digitalhistory.uh.edu/disp_textbook_print.cfm?smtid=3&psid=1278.

Franklin, Benjamin. *Autobiography of Benjamin Franklin,* Ed. Frank Woodworth Pine, E-Book December 28, 2006, Project Gutenberg's Autobiography of Benjamin Franklin, by Benjamin Franklin, from New York: Henry Holt & Co., 1916, www.gutenberg.org.

Gillis, Chester. *Roman Catholicism in America.* New York: Columbia University Press, 1999.

Gelb, Norman, "Francis Scott Key: The Reluctant Patriot," Smithsonian Magazine, September 2004, Smithsonian.com; Accessed November 29, 2018.

"The Gettysburg Address." National Park Service brochure, obtained August 2018. National Park Service U.S. Department of the interior.

"Gettysburg Invasion and Retreat." Maryland Civil War Trails, Brochure. Further information www.civilwartrails.org.

Gordon-Reed, Annette. *The Hemingses of Monticello.* New York: W.W. Norton & Co., 2008.

Grady, Timothy P. "Contact and Conquest in Africa and the Americas," from *The Atlantic World: 1450-2000,* Ed. Toyin Falola and Kevin D. Roberts. Bloomington: Indiana University, 2008.

Green, Paul. *The Lost Colony: A Symphonic Drama of American History*. Roanoke Island Ed. ed. Chapel Hill: University of North Carolina Press, 1954.

"The Grounds, The White House Building," The White House. https://www.whitehouse.gov/about-the-white-house/the-white-house. Accessed December 24, 2018.

Hadlow, Janice, *The Strangest Family: The Private Lives of George III, Queen Charlotte and the Hanoverians*, UK: Harper Collins, 2014. https://www.harpercollins.co.uk/9780007165209/the- strangest-family. Accessed June 9, 2018.

Hall, Alice J. "Philosopher of Dissent Benjamin Franklin." *National Geographic* Magazine, July 1975, Vol. 148, No. 1.

"Harpers Ferry." National Park Service brochure to Harpers Ferry, obtained August 2018. National Park Service U.S. Department of the Interior. Harpers Ferry National Park.

"Harriet Beecher Stowe," History.com Staff, History.com, A+E Networks. 2009 https://www.history.com/topics/harriet-beecher-stowe. Accessed August 16, 2018.

"Harriet Beecher, Stowe" National Women's History Museum. https.//www.womenshistory.org/education-resources/biographies/harriet-beecher-stowe.

"Harriet H. Robinson, "Early Factory Labor in New England" 1883. Primary Sources, Workshops in American History. https://www.learner.org/workshops/primarysources/lowell/docs/factory2.html. Accessed August 28, 2018.

"This Day in History, Harrison Dies of Pneumonia." History.com Staff. 2009.

History.com. A+E Television Network. https://www.history.com/this-day-in-history/harrison-dies-of- pneumonia. Accessed August 19, 2018.

Hemings, Madison "The Life of Sally Hemings," ("drawn from the words of Madison Heming"), Thomas Jefferson Foundation. https://www.monticello.org/sallyhemings/. Accessed July 27, 2018.

Henderson, Bruce. "Lost Colony Clues found on coast will become a North Carolina Natural Area," *Charlotte Observer,* September 13, 2017.

Historic Jamestown, *Jamestown Rediscovery,* 2018. http://historicjamestowne.org/history/history-of-jamestown/the-starving-time/.Accessed June 12, 2018.

"Historic Jamestowne: A Short History of Jamestown." National Park Service. Last Updated February 26, 2015. www.nps.gov/game/learn/ /historyculture/a-short-history-of-jamestown.htm. Accessed September 4, 2018.

History.com staff. "Great Awakening," 2018. Published A+E Networks https://www.history.com/topics/great-awakening. Accessed July 31, 2018.

Hitsman, J. MacKay. *The Incredible War of 1812, A Military History.* Toronto: University of Toronto, 1965.

Horn, Joshua. "Charles Sumner: Crime Against Kansas." Discerning History. January 6, 2015. http://discerninghistory.com/2015/01/charles-sumner-crime-against-kansas/ Accessed July 30, 2018.

Howland, Louis. Stephen A. Douglas. New York: Charles Scribner's Sons, 1920.

Huddleston. Scott "Myths surround Alamo Mystery." By Scott Huddleston /shuddleston@express-news.net. San Antonio Express News. https://www.mysantonia.com/150years/leaders/article/Unknown-facts-about-the-Alamo-defenders-6169878.php Published 12:29 am

CST, Thursday, March 3, 2011. Accessed August 2, 2018.

"The Inauguration of President Andrew Jackson, 1829," EyeWitness to History, 2007, http://www.eyewitnesstohistory.com/jacksoninauguration.htm. Accessed July 31, 2018

"Isabelle Belle Boyd." https://www.womenshistory.org/education-resources/biographies/isabelle-boyd. Accessed August 25, 2018.

Jackson, Maurice, "The Rise of Abolition," Falola, Toyin and Kevin D. Roberts Edited, *The Atlantic World 1450-2000.* Bloomington, Indiana University Press, 2008.

John Brown's War, "Purged away with Blood," American Battlefield Trust.https://www.battlefields.org/learn/articles/purged-away-blood. Accessed August 17, 2018.

Johnny Clem 'Drummer Boy of Chickamauga,' August 13, 1851-May 13, 1937. Article from ACWS Newsletter, Summer 2010. American Civil War Society. https://acws.co.uk/archives-biography-clem. Accessed August 27, 2018.

"John Lincoln Clem" Updated March 28, 2007. Arlington National Cemetery Website. http://www.arlingtoncemetery.net/jlclem.htm. Accessed August 27, 2018.

"John Wilkes booth: Escape of an Assassin." Maryland Civil War Trails. Brochure, obtained August 2018. More information at www.visitmaryland.org.

Johnson, Gerald W. *An Epic in Homespun.* New York: Minton, Balch & Co., 1927.

Jordan, Don and Walsh, Michael, *The King's Bed: Sex, Power and the Court of Charles II.* New York, Pegasus Books, 2015.

Kidd, Thomas S. *George Whitefield : America's Spiritual Founding Father*. New Haven: Yale University Press, 2014.

Kupperman K. *The Jamestown Project* [e-book]. Cambridge, Mass: Harvard University Press; 2007. eBook Collection (EBSCOhost), Ipswich, MA. Accessed September 4, 2018.

Kupperman, Kareen Ordahl. *The Atlantic in World History*. Oxford: Oxford University Press, 2012.

Langguth, A. J. *Patriots, The Men who Started the American Revolution*, New York: Simon & Schuster, 1988.

Lassieur, Allison, and Peter McDonnell. *The Voyage of the Mayflower*. Graphic Library. Graphic History. Mankato, Minn.: Capstone Press, 2006. Accessed June 12, 2018.

Last public speech before his death (4 March 1799); as quoted in *Patrick Henry: Life, Correspondences and Speeches* (1891) by William Wirt Henry, Vol. 2. (New York: Charles Scribner's Sons), 1891. 609-610, from http:/www.archive.org/stream/pathenrylife02henrrich#page/608/mode/2up. Accessed August 26, 2018.

Lemay, J. A. Leo, *The Life of Benjamin Franklin, Vol 1*. Philadelphia: University of Pennsylvania, 2006.

Leyburn, James G. *The Scotch-Irish, A Social History*. Chapel Hill: University of North Carolina Press, 1962

Lossing, Benson J. *Our Country. A Household History,* Vol one., New York: Henry J. Johnson, 1878.

Lossing, Benson J., *War of Independence: A History of the Anglo-American Reprint*. Detroit: Singing Tree Press, 1970.

Lyman Beecher." Ohio History Connection. http://www.ohiohistorycentral.org/w/Lyman_Beecher. Accessed August 22, 2018.

MacLeish, William. "A Whimsical View of the Indian World in 1492-1991," *Major Problems in American Indian History.* Documents and Essays Ed. Albert L. Hurtado and Peter Iverson. Lexington, MA: D. C. Heath and Co., 1994.

"Malaria." CDC, Centers for Disease Control and Prevention. Last update December 19, 2017. https://www.cdc.gov/malaria/about/history/index.html. Accessed September 23, 2018.

"Mansa Musa's Golden Empire," National Geographic Videos. http://www.nationalgeographic.com.au/videos/quest-for-gold/mansa-musas- golden-empire-3540.aspx. Accessed June 1, 2018.

Mansfield, Edward D. The Mexican War: History of its Origin. New York: A. S. Barnes & Co., 1848.

"Maria Belle Boyd." American Battlefield Trust. National Women's History Museum.https://www.battlefields.org/learn/biographies/maria-belle-boyd. Accessed August 25, 2018.

Matthews, Richard K. *The Radical Politics of Thomas Jefferson, A revisionist View.* Lawrence KS: University of Kansas, 1986.

"The Mayflower Story," 1620-2020, Mayflower 400. https://www.mayflower400uk.org/website-privacy-policy/. Accessed June 12, 2018.

"The Mayflower," History.com Staff, A&E Network, 2010. https://www.history.com/topics/mayflower. June 12, 2018.

McMaster, John Bach, *A History of the People of the United States, From the Revolution to the Civil War.* Vol. I. New York: D. Appleton and Co., 1888.

McWhiney, Grady. *Cracker Culture,* Tuscaloosa: University of Alabama, 1988.

"Mexican American War and the Treaty of Guadalupe Hidalgo," National

Park Service, U.S. Department of the Interior. https://www.nps.gov/cham/learn/historyculture/mexican-american-war.htm. Accessed August 20, 2018.

Mitchell, Margaret, *Gone With the Wind.* Garden City: International Collectors Library, 1936.

"Monocacy." National Park Service brochure, obtained August 2018. National Park Service U.S. Department of the Interior. Provides details of the Monocacy battle.

Morais, Herbert M., *The Struggle for American Freedom, The First Two Hundred Years.* New York: International Publishers, 1944.

Morgan, Edmund S. *The Meaning of Independence.* Charlottesville: University of Virginia,1975.

Peeples, Lynn, "The Origin of Human Malaria." August 18, 2009. Scientific American. https://www.scientificamerican.com/article/origin-human-malaria-chimpanzees/. Accessed September 23, 2018.

People & Events: "Nat Turner's Rebellion 1831." PBS On-Line. https://www.pbs.org/wgbh/aia/part3/3p1518.html. Accessed August 1, 2018.

Nicolay, Helen. *Andrew Jackson The Fighting President.* New York: The Century Co., 1929.

Nofi, Albert A. *The Alamo and the Texas War of Independence, September 30, 1835 to April 21, 1836 : Heroes, Myths, and History.* 1st Ed. Ed. Conshohocken, PA: Combined Books, 1992. Accessed August 1, 2018.

Onuf, Peter S. *Jefferson's Empire.* Charlottesville: University of Virginia, 2000.

"Patrick Henry Biography." Biography.com Editors. A&E Television

Networks. Last updated April 27, 2017. www.biography.com/people/ patrick-henry-9335512. Accessed August 26, 2018.

"Patrick Henrys Red Hill," Patrick Henry National Memorial Brochure. Obtained August 2018.

Paul, Lee. "The Alamo: 13 Days of Glory," from "The Battle of the Alamo," Facts, information and articles about Battle Of The Alamo, an event of Westward Expansion from the Wild West. Originally printed in "Wild West Magazine, February 1996. ttp://www.historynet.com/battle -of-the-alamo#articles. Accessed August 2, 2018.

Peterson, Merrill D. *The Jefferson Image in the American Mind.* New York: Oxford University Press, 1960.

Petite, Mary Deborah, *The Women Will Howl.* Jefferson, NC: McFarland & Co., Inc., 2008.

"Pilgrim History," General Society of Mayflower Descendants. https://www. themayflowersociety.org/the-pilgrims/pilgrim-history. Accessed June 12, 2018.

Pillsbury, Albert E., *Lincoln and Slavery.* Boston: Houghton Mifflin Co., 1913.

Porphyia in the Royal Family" English Dynasties, Hanover Index 2004- 2018. http://www.englishmonarchs.co.uk/hanover_15.htm. Accessed June 9, 2018.

"President Lincoln's First Inaugural Address, 1861._Gilden Lehrman Institute of American History, Gilden Lehrman Collection, https://www.gilderlehrman.org/content/president-lincoln%E2%80%99s-first-inaugural-address-1861. Accessed August 17, 2018. This source provides the primary source Senate recordings of the event.

Price, David A. *Love and Hate in Jamestown : John Smith, Pocahontas, and the Heart of a New Nation*. 1st Ed. ed. New York: Knopf, 2003.

Price, Mark, "Outer Banks wild horses shot with birth control." *Charlotte Observer*, September 10, 2018.

"The Real Story of Revere's Ride," Paul Revere House, Paul Revere Memorial Association, 2017. https://www.paulreverehouse.org/the-real- story. Accessed June 10, 2018.

"Religions, Muslim Spain." BBC. Updated 2009. http://www.bbc.co.uk/ /religion/religions/islam/history/spain_1.shtml. Accessed August 23, 2018. This site provides an interesting narrative of life as it existed during the Muslim domination of Spain.

Remini, R.V. *Andrew Jackson.*. New York: Twayne Publishers, 1966.

Remini, R. V. *The Legacy of Andrew Jackson. Essays on Democracy, Indian Removal, and Slavery.* Baton Rouge: Louisiana State University Press, 1988.

Richards, Laura A. *Abigail Adams and Her Times*, New York: D. Appleton & Co., 1917.

Rogers, Joseph M., *The True Henry Clay*. Philadelphia: J. B. Lippincott Co., 1905.

Rosenhek, Jackie. "First Lady of Lunacy." November 2006. http://www.doctorsreview.com/history/nov06-history_medicine/. Accessed August 27, 2018.

Ryerson, Egerton, *Loyalists of America and their times*. Vol II, 2nd Ed., Haskell House Publishers, Ltd., New York: Haskell House Publishers, Ltd., 1970. First publication was 1880.

Schnirring, Lisa, "FAO: World on Verge of riderpest eradication." Center for Infectious Disease Research and Policy. University of Minnesota. http://www.cidrap.umn.edu/news-perspective/2010/10/fao-world-verge-rinderpest-eradication. October 14, 2010. Accessed September 23, 2018.

Shaw, Peter. *The Character of John Adams.* Chapel Hill: University of North Carolina Press,1976.

Sherman, William Tecumseh. *Memoirs of General W. T. Sherman,* Ed. With intro and notes Michael Fellman, New York: Penguin books, 2000.

Silverman, Jason H. *Lincoln and the Immigrant.* Carbondale: Southern Illinois University Press, 2015.

"Slave Labour." History Extra, owned and published by Immediate Media Co., Ltd. https://www.historyextra.com/period/slave-labour/. Accessed August 28, 2018.

Smith, Helen Ainslie, *The Thirteen Colonies,* Part I, New York: G. P. Putnam's Sons/Knickerbocker Press, 1901.

Smith, John, and James P. P Horn. *Writings : With Other Narratives of Roanoke, Jamestown, and the First English Settlement of America.* Library of America, 171. New York: Library of America, 2007.

Smith, Mark M., *Mastered by the Clock.* Chapel Hill: University of North Carolina, 1997.

Smith, Richard Norton: "The surprising George Washington: Part IV."*Prologue Magazine,* Spring 1994, Vol 26, No. 1, National Archives. https://www.archives.gov/publications/prologue/1994/spring/george-washington-4.html. Accessed September 24, 2018.

Snyder, Michael T. *Journal Register News Service,* "Battle of Gettysburg, How Area Residents Dealt with the Carnage," *The Pottstown Mercury,* July 7 ,2013, https://www.pottsmerc.com/lifestyle/battle-of-Gettysburg-how-area-residents-dealt-with-the-carnage/article_ _e8f06330-d547-523b-b4b8-23f484c26c94.html.

"Soldier, Statesman, Dog Lover: George Washington's Pups," 2018 George Washington's Mount Vernon, Mount Vernon Ladies' Association.https://www.mountvernon.org/george-washington/biography/washington-stories/solider-statesman-dog-lover-george-washingtons-pups/.Accessed June 15, 2018.

"Something About Everything Military, Blockade Runners." Reprint of David A. Norris. Hide and Seek on the High Seas. *History Magazine*. April / May 2007. http://www.jcsgroup.com/military/war1861fringe/runners.html. Accessed August 27, 2018.

South Carolina, City Population, https://www.citypopulation.de/USA-SouthCarolina.html.*2000 Census: US Municipalities Over 50,000 :Ranked by 2000 Population, 1994-2005*, Wendell Cox Consultancy, http://demographia.com/db-uscity98.htm. Accessed May 11, 2018.

"The Story of Josiah Hensen, the Real Inspiration for 'Uncle Tom's Cabin." Smithsonian.com.https://www.smithsonianmag.com/history/story-josiah-henson-real-inspiration-uncle-toms-cabin-180969094/. Accessed August 24, 2018.

Stout, Harry S., *Upon the Altar of the Nation, A Moral History of the Civil War.* New York: Penguin Books, 2006.

Stowe, Harriet Beecher, *Key to Uncle Tom's Cabin. Presenting the Original facts and Documents upon which the story is founded.* Together with corroborative statements verifying the truth of the work. Public-domain. Google Book Search.https://archive.org/strea/akeytouncletoms01stowgog, djvu.text. Accessed August 24, 2018.

Street, James, *The Revolutionary War.* New York: Dial Press, 1944.

Sumner, Charles, *The Barbarism of Slavery,* Library of Congress Collection,
New York: Young Men's Republican Union. https://archive.org/details/barbarismofslave00lcsumn. Accessed September 4, 2018.

"Ten Facts About Martha Washington," "Death Defied." George Washington's Mount Vernon. https://www.mountvernon.org/george-washington/martha-washington/ten-facts-about-martha-washington. Accessed July 26, 2018

"31e, Canefight!. Preston Brooks and Charles Sumner. U.S. History Pre-Columbian to the New Millennium. Independence Hall Association. http:www.ushistory.org/us/31e.asp. Accessed July 30 2018.

Thomas, J. P. Ed. *Carolina Tribute to Calhoun*. Columbia: Richard L. Bryan, 1857.

Toppin, Edgar A., *A Biographical History of Blacks in America since 1528,* New York: David McKay Co., 1971.

"USS Fort Donelson-Confederate Blockade Runner Robert E. Lee" American Civil War.com. https://www.americancivilwar.com/tcwn/civil_war/Navy_Ships/USS_Fort_Donelson.html. Accessed August 27, 2018.

Voyages Database. The Trans-Atlantic Slave Trade Database. Emory University, 2013. http://www.slavevoyages.org/2013. Accessed May 11, 2018.

Wallace, Willard Mosher. *Sir Walter Raleigh*. Princeton: Princeton University Press, 1959.

Washington, George. *George Washington Papers, Series 2, Letterbooks – 1799: Letterbook 24,*
April 3, 1793 – March 3, 1797. 1793. Manuscript/Mixed Material.

https://www.loc.gov/item/mgw2.024/. Accessed July 27, 2018.

Weaver, Robert B. *The Struggle Over Slavery*, Chicago: University of Chicago Press, 1938.

Webb, Garrison, *Amazing Women of the Civil War,* Nashville: Thomas Nelson, 1999.

Werner, Emmy E. *Reluctant Witnesses, Children's Voices from the Civil War.* Boulder: Westview Press, 1998.

Whitefield, George, *Sinners in the Hands of an Angry God, Ipswich, MA: Great Neck*

"What was the truth about the madness of George III?" April 15, 2013, BBC News Magazine, https://www.bbc.com/news/magazine-22122407. Accessed June 9, 2018.*Publishing, Primary Source Document). Accessed on-line through Winthrop University, MAS—Ultra School Edition, EBSCO, June 8, 2018.*

"Wild Horse and Burro Program." Bureau of Land Management. https://www.blm.gov/programs/wild-horse-and-burro. Accessed September 21, 2018.

"Wild Horses as Native North American Wildlife." Animal Welfare Institute. 2018. https://awionline.org/content/wild-horses-native-north-american-wildlife. Accessed September 21, 2018.

Wiltse, Charles M., *John C. Calhoun, Nullifier, 1829-1839*. Indianapolis: Bobbs-Merrill Co., Inc., 1949.

Wish, Harvey, edited with an intro by Harvey Wish. *Ante-bellum.* New York: Capricorn Books, 1960.

The Wives and Children of John Brown," Harpers Ferry National Historical Park National Park Service, U.S. Department of the Interior.

https://www.nps.gov/articles/wives-and-children-of-john-brown.htm. Accessed July 30, 2018.

"Women Spies of the Civil War." Special Report Smithsonian Institution. Smithsonian.com. https://www.smithsonianmag.com/history/women-spies-of-the-civil-war-162202679/. Accessed August 25, 2018.

Young, Mary. "The Cherokee Nation: Mirror of the Republic." *Major Problems in American Indian History.* Documents and Essays Ed. Albert L. Hurtado and Peter Iverson. Lexington, MA: D. C. Heath and Co., 1994.

Sandi Ludwa

Endnotes

Chapter 1

*For in-dept discussion on man's needs and desires, I suggest A. H. Maslow's original *A Theory of Human Motivation,* aka, *Hierarchy of Needs,* published in 1943, which goes beyond basic needs of air, water, food, shelter, sleep, etc.

[1] Voyages Database. 2013 *The Trans-Atlantic Slave Trade Database.* http://www.slavevoyages.org/2013 Emory University. (accessed April 13, 2018).

[2] Fisher, Mary Pat. *Living Religions.* 6th Ed. (Upper Saddle River, New Jersey: Prentice-Hall, 1991), 38.

[3] It is commonly agreed that Santángel was responsible in convincing the throne to sanction Columbus and a very good account is given in "Christopher Columbus, The Sailor who gave us the New World," *National Geographic,* November 1978, Vol. 148., No. 5., 597.

[4] Grady, Timothy P. "Contact and Conquest in Africa and the Americas," from *The Atlantic World: 1450-2000,* Ed. Toyin Falola and Kevin D. Roberts. Bloomington: Indiana University, 2008). 3-6, 20; "Religions, Muslim Spain." BBC. Updated 2009. http://www.bbc.co.uk/religion/religions/islam/history/spain_1.shtml. Accessed August 23, 2018. This site provides an interesting narrative of life as it existed during the Muslim domination of Spain; Kupperman, Kareen Ordahl. *The Atlantic in World History.* Oxford: Oxford University Press, 2012). 20-21.

[5] Statistics taken from 2000 Census: US Municipalities Over 50,000: Ranked by 2000 Population, 1994-2005, Wendell Cox Consultancy, http://demographia.com/db-uscity98.htm, accessed April 20, 2018 and USA: South Carolina, City Population, https://www.citypopulation.de/USA-SouthCarolina.html, accessed April 20, 2018.

[6] "Mansa Musa's Golden Empire," National Geographic Videos. http://www.nationalgeographic.com.au/videos/quest-for-gold/mansa-musas-golden-empire-3540.aspx. Accessed June 1, 2018.

[7] Alfred W. Crosby, *The Columbian Exchange: Biological and Cultural Consequences of 1492,* (Connecticut: Greenwood Press, 1972).

[8] Jared Diamond, *Guns, Germs, and Steel: The Fates of Human Societies,* (New York: W. W. Norton & Co., 2017).

[9] Crosby, *The Columbian Exchange: Biological and Cultural Consequences of 1492,* 42.

[10] *Guns, Germs, and Steel* is best source. Following provide insight. Discussion on Riderpest: Lisa Schnirring,, "FAO: World on Verge of riderpest eradication." Center for Infectious Disease Research and Policy. University of Minnesota.

http://www.cidrap.umn.edu/news-perspective/2010/10/fao-world-verge-rinderpest-eradication. October 14, 2010. Accessed September 23, 2018; Fact sheet on TB: APHIS Veterinary Services. United States Department of Agriculture. https://www.aphis.usda.gov/publications/animal_health/content/printable_version/faq_bovine_tb_.pdf , Accessed September 23, 2018. " Offers a history: "Malaria." CDC, Centers for Disease Control and Prevention. Last update December 19, 2017. https://www.cdc.gov/malaria/about/history/index.html. Accessed September 23, 2018. The following presents a case for the chimp being a possible initial host instead of birds: Lynn Peeples, "The Origin of Human Malaria." August 18, 2009. Scientific American. https://www.scientificamerican.com/article/origin-human-malaria-chimpanzees/. Accessed September 23, 2018.

[11] William J. Cooper Jr. and Thomas E. Terrill, *The American South, A History.*, Vol. I, Second Edition. (New York: McGraw-Hill Companies, 1991).

[12] Mark Price, "Outer Banks wild horses shot with birth control." *Charlotte Observer,* September 10, 2018.

[13] "Wild Horses as Native North American Wildlife." Animal Welfare Institute. 2018. https://awionline.org/content/wild-horses-native-north-american-wildlife. Accessed September 21, 2018; "Wild Horse and Burro Program." Bureau of Land Management. https://www.blm.gov/programs/wild-horse-and-burro. Accessed September 21, 2018.

[14] Diamond, *Guns, Germs, and Steel,* 24.

Chapter 2

[1] For early history see: Wallace, Willard Mosher. *Sir Walter Raleigh*. Princeton: Princeton University Press, 1959; Smith, Helen Ainslie, *The Thirteen Colonies,* Part I, (New York: G. P. Putnam's Sons/Knickerbocker Press, 1901), 356 discussed first treaty with Indians; Green, Paul. *The Lost Colony: A Symphonic Drama of American History.* Roanoke Island Ed. ed. Chapel Hill: University of North Carolina Press, 1954.The following gives a possible answer to the disappearance: Bruce Henderson, "Lost Colony Clues found on coast will become a North Carolina Natural Area," *Charlotte Observer,* September 13, 2017.

Chapter 3

[1] Price, David A. *Love and Hate in Jamestown : John Smith, Pocahontas, and the Heart of a New Nation.* 1st Ed. ed. New York: Knopf, 2003; Kupperman K. *The Jamestown Project* [e-book]. Cambridge, Mass: Harvard University Press; 2007. eBook Collection (EBSCOhost), Ipswich, MA. Accessed September 4, 2018; Smith, John, and James P. P Horn. *Writings : With Other Narratives of Roanoke, Jamestown, and the First English Settlement of America.* Library of America. (New York: Library of America, 2007), 171.

[2] Historic Jamestown, *Jamestown Rediscovery,* 2018 https://historicjamestowne.org/history/history-of-jamestown/the-starving-time; For an account of Jamestown, with no mention of the starving time see "America's Story, From America's Library. Jump Back in Time, Colonial Period, 1492-1763." Library of Congress. Accessed September 4, 2018. http://www.americaslibrary.gov/jb/colonial/jb_colonial_jamestwn_2.html

[3] A wonderful account of the founding of the House of Burgesses is given by: Allister Cooke, *Allister Cooke's America,* (New York: Alfred A. Knopf, 1973), 67-68.

Chapter 4

[1] While the information that follows is considered common knowledge, I have listed several sources which furnish good studies with significant details for those wishing to learn more: Lassieur, Allison, and Peter McDonnell. *The Voyage of the Mayflower.*Graphic Library Graphic History. (Mankato, Minn.: Capstone Press, 2006). Accessed June 12, 2018; Lossisng, Benson J. *Our Country. A Household History,* Vol one., (New York: Henry J. Johnson, 1878). Winthrop University Library; "The Mayflower Story," 1620-2020, Mayflower 400 https://www.mayflower400uk.org/website-privacy-policy/. Accessed June 12, 2018; "The Mayflower," History.com Staff, A&E Network, 2010. https://www.history.com/topics/mayflower . June 12, 2018;"Pilgrim History," General Society of Mayflower Descendants.https://www.themayflowersociety.org/the-pilgrims/pilgrim-history. Accessed June 12, 2018.

[2] Lossing, Benson J. *Our Country. A Household History,* Vol one., (New York: Henry J. Johnson, 1878).

[3] *Our Country. A Household History,* Vol one., author Benson J Lossisng,1878: NY: Henry J. Johnson, 401; Second version: Brooks, Rebecca Beatrice Brooks. "History of the Salem Witch Trials," August 18, 2011. http://historyofmassachusetts.org/the-salem-witch-trials/. Accessed September 6, 2018.

[4] The following offer insight into ownership of slaves by religious organizations: Chester Gillis, *Roman Catholicism in America.* (New York: Columbia University Press, 1999), 54; Cyprian Davis, *History of Black Catholics* (New York: Crossroad Publishing), 36-37.

[5] For more information on slavery refer to the following: Bancroft, Frederick *Slave-Trading in the Old South.* Baltimore: J. H. Furst Co., 1931 and Slave Labour." History Extra, owned and published by Immediate Media Co., Ltd. https://www.historyextra.com/period/slave-labour/. Accessed August 28, 2018.

Chapter 5

[1] There are many sources which engage in lively stories about Charles II. I have listed several in the Bibliography. Many would certainly amuse the reader. Since this document is about American History, I don't want to get too far off track.

[2] George Whitefield. *Sinners in the Hands of an Angry God,* (Ipswich, MA: Great Neck Publishing, Primary Source Document). Accessed on-line through Winthrop University, MAS-ULTRA School Edition. June 8, 2018; To learn more about Whitefield see: Kidd, Thomas S. *George Whitefield : America's Spiritual Founding Father*. (New Haven: Yale University Press, 2014); Also see: History.com staff. "Great Awakening," 2018. Published A+E Networks. https://www.history.com/topics/great-awakening. Accessed July 31, 2018.

[3] Benjamin Franklin, "Benjamin Franklin on the Great Awakening, from His Autobiography," Digital History ID 1278 Website, Date:1771, http://www.digitalhistory.uh.edu/disp_textbook_print.cfm?smtid=3&psid=1278, Accessed June 9, 2018.

[4] Jackson, Maurice, "The Rise of Abolition," Falola, Toyin and Kevin D. Roberts Edited, *The Atlantic World 1450-2000.* Bloomington, Indiana University Press, 2008. Gives in-dept account of the Stono Rebellion, 221.

Chapter 6

[1] Numerous publications give an insight into further reading on Franklin: Coss, Stephen. "What Led Benjamin Franklin to Live Estranged From His Wife for Nearly Two Decades?" Smithsonian Magazine, September 2017 https://www.smithsonianmag.com/history/benjamin-franklin-estranged-wife-nearly-two- decades-180964400/#2AAekOqRxoshHprp.99. Accessed June 11, 2018; Franklin, Benjamin. *Autobiography of Benjamin Franklin,* Ed. Frank Woodworth Pine, E-Book December 28, 2006, Project Gutenberg's Autobiography of Benjamin Franklin, by Benjamin Franklin, from New York: Henry Holt & Co., 1916, www.gutenberg.org; Lemay, J. A. Leo, *The Life of Benjamin Franklin, Vol 1.*(Philadelphia: University of Pennsylvania, 2006); Alice J. Hall. "Philosopher of Dissent Benjamin Franklin." *National Geographic* Magazine, July 1975, Vol. 148, No. 1. 93-121; Ecenbarger, William. "Ben Franklin's Dangerous Liaisons, That Kindly Old Kite Flyer Was Also A High-flying Ladies' Man," *Chicago Tribune,* May 6, 1990, http://articles.chicagotribune.com/1990-05-06/features/9002070774_1_poor-richard-lucy-mercer-franklin-delano-roosevelt. Accessed June 11, 2018;

[2] A. J. Langguth, A. J. *Patriots, The Men who Started the American Revolution* (New York: Simon & Schuster, 1988),74.

³ Jordan, Don and Walsh, Michael, *The King's Bed: Sex, Power and the Court of Charles II*. (New York, Pegasus Books, 2015); "Porphyia in the Royal Family" English Dynasties, Hanover Index 2004-2018, http://www.englishmonarchs.co.uk/hanover_15.htm. Accessed June 9, 2018; "What was the truth about the madness of George III?" April 15, 2013, BBC News Magazine, https://www.bbc.com/news/magazine-22122407. Accessed June 9, 2018; Hadlow, Janice, *The Strangest Family: The Private Lives of George III, Queen Charlotte and the Hanoverians*, UK: Harper Collins, 2014. https://www.harpercollins.co.uk/9780007165209/the-strangest-family. Accessed June 9, 2018.

⁴"Patrick Henrys Red Hill," Patrick Henry National Memorial Brochure. Obtained August 2018; Edmund Cody Burnett. *The Continental Congress*, (NY: MacMillan Co., 1941), 13.

Chapter 7

¹Insight into the various political ideas of the time: Randolph Greenfield Adams, *Political Ideas of the American Revolution*. (Durham: Trinity College Press, 1922); Egerton Ryerson, *Loyalists of America and their times*. Vol II, 2ⁿᵈ Ed., Haskell House Publishers, Ltd). First publication was 880), 123. Discusses treatment of Loyalists.

²Numerous publications give more insight into the war: "The Boston Tea Party," This Day in History: December 16, A+E Networks, History.com 2009, http://www.history.com/this-day-in-history/the-boston-tea-party, Accessed June 9, 2018; Lossing, Benson J., *War of Independence: A History of the Anglo-Americans.* Detroit: Singing Tree Press, 1970; John Bach, *A History of the People of the United States, From the Revolution to the Civil War*. Vol. I. New York: D. Appleton and Co., 1888; Morais, Herbert M., *The Struggle for American Freedom, The First Two Hundred Years.* New York: International Publishers, 1944; "The Real Story of Revere's Ride," Paul Revere House, Paul Revere Memorial Association, 2017. https://www.paulreverehouse.org/the-real-story. Accessed June 10, 2018; Eschner, Kat. "The Midnight Ride of Paul Revere and Some Other Guys," April 8, 2017, Smithsonian.com, https://www.smithsonianmag.com/smart-news/midnight-ride-paul-revere-and-some-other-guys-18096286. Accessed June 10, 2018.

³Bramen, Lisa. "The Food that Fueled the American Revolution," Smithsonian.com, July 5 2011.https://www.smithsonianmag.com/arts-culture/the-food-that-fueled-the-american-revolution-25701053. Accessed June 10, 2018.

⁴James Street, *The Revolutionary War, (*New York: Dial Press, 1944), 144.

Chapter 8

[1] Morgan, Edmund S. *The Meaning of Independence.*(Charlottesville: University of Virginia, 1975). Gives the beliefs of John Adams, George Washington, and Thomas Jefferson very thoroughly in this 85 page book; Akerman, Bruce. *The Failure of the Founding Fathers.* Cambridge: Belknap Press of Harvard University Press, 2005. Provides a different view.

Chapter 9

[2] "Ten Facts About Martha Washington," "Death Defied." George Washington's Mount Vernon.https://www.mountvernon.org/george-washington/martha-washington/ten-facts-about-martha-washington. Accessed July 26, 2018.

Chapter 10

[3] The following offer insight into Washington's traits, beyond his political prowess and stamina: National Archives, Richard Norton Smith. "The surprising George Washington: Part IV."*Prologue Magazine,* Spring 1994, Vol 26, No. 1, https://www.archives.gov/publications/prologue/1994/spring/george-washington-4.html. Accessed September 24, 2018; Washington, George. *George Washington Papers, Series 2, Letterbooks – 1799: Letterbook 24, April 3, 1793 – March 3, 1797.* 1793. Manuscript/Mixed Material. https://www.loc.gov/item/mgw2.024/. Accessed July 27, 2018; Cooke, *Allister Cooke's America,* 111.

[4] Sydney George Fisher, *The Struggle for American Independence Vol I* (Philadelphia: J. B. Lippincott Co., 1908), 350.

[5] "Soldier, Statesman, Dog Lover: George Washington's Pups," 2018 George Washington's Mount Vernon, Mount Vernon Ladies' Association.https://www.mountvernon.org/george-washington/biography/washington-stories/solider-statesman-dog-lover-george-washingtons-pups/ . Accessed June 15, 2018.

[6] Richards, Laura A. *Abigail Adams and Her Times*, New York: D. Appleton & Co., 1917. Provides fascinating account of the first lady's life; The following provide insight into John Adams and his administration: Peter Shaw. *The Character of John Adams.* Chapel Hill: University of North Carolina Press, 1976; William Cullen Bryan and Sydney Howard Gay. *A popular History of the United States*, Vol IV, (New York: Chas Scribner's Sons, 1886), 127-154.

[7]McWhiney, Grady. *Cracker Culture,* Tuscaloosa: University of Alabama, 1988. This is a controversial study of social life in the old South comparative with the North; Leyburn, James G. *The Scotch-Irish, A Social History.* Chapel Hill: University of North Carolina Press, 1962.

[8]Last public speech before his death (4 March 1799); as quoted in *Patrick Henry: Life, Correspondences and Speeches* (1891) by William Wirt Henry, Vol. 2. 609-610, from http://www.archive.org/stream/pathenrylife02henrrich#page/608/mode/2up. Accessed August 26, 2018; Also see www.biography.com/people/patrick-henry-9335512. Accessed August 26, 2018. "Patrick Henry Biography." Biography.com Editors. A&E Television Networks. Last updated April 27, 2017. www.biography.com/people/patrick-henry-9335512. Accessed August 26, 2018; For overall short summary see, "Patrick Henry's Red Hill." Patrick Henry National Memorial, brochure, obtained August 2018. www.RedHill.org.

Chapter 11

[1]For more information on the White House, refer to Lonnie G. Bunch III, Spencer R. Crew, Mark G. Hirsch, Harry R. Rubenstein, *The American Presidency,* (Washington: Smithsonian Institution Press, 2000), 108; "The Grounds, The White House Building," The White House. https://www.whitehouse.gov/about-the-white-house/the-white-house. Accessed December 24, 2018.

[2]Gelb, Norman, "Francis Scott Key: The Reluctant Patriot," Smithsonian Magazine, September 2004, Smithsonian.com.

[3]The following provide in-dept analysis of Jefferson and his actions. Richard K. Matthews.. *The Radical Politics of Thomas Jefferson, A revisionist View.* (Lawrence KS: University of Kansas, 1986); Merrill D. Peterson. *The Jefferson Image in the American Mind.*(New York: Oxford University Press, 1960); Peter S. Onuf, *Jefferson's Empire.* (Charlottesville: University of Virginia, 2000); Annette Gordon-Reed, *The Hemingses of Monticello.* (New York:
W. W. Norton & Co., 2008.)

Chapter 12

[1] J. MacKay Hitsman, *The Incredible War of 1812, A Military History.* (Toronto: University of Toronto, 1965). 3. Canadian view of the war discusses the poor international boundary, return of property after the American Revolution, and reveals an interesting insight.

Chapter 13

[1] The following are excellent sources for good reading on Jackson's life: Gerald W. Johnson, *An Epic in Homespun*. New York: Minton, Balch & Co., 1927; Helen Nicolay. *Andrew Jackson The Fighting President*.(New York: The Century Co., 1929); Remini, R.V. *Andrew Jackson.*.(New York: Twayne Publishers, 1966); R. V. Remini, *The Legacy of Andrew Jackson.Essays on Democracy, Indian Removal, and Slavery.* Baton Rouge: Louisiana State University Press 1988).

[2] Rogers, Joseph M., *The True Henry Clay*. (Philadelphia: J. B. Lippincott Co., 1905.), 124.

[3] "The Inauguration of President Andrew Jackson, 1829," EyeWitness to History, 2007 http://www.eyewitnesstohistory.com/jacksoninauguration.htm. Accessed July 31, 2018.

[4] For insight into John C. Calhoun, see the following: Ed J. P. Thomas. *Carolina Tribute to Calhoun*. Columbia: Richard L. Bryan, 1857. Charles M. Wiltse, *John C. Calhoun, Nullifier, 1829-1839*. (Indianapolis: Bobbs-Merrill Co., Inc., 1949.), 11-15.

[5] Mary Young. "The Cherokee Nation: Mirror of the Republic." *Major Problems in American Indian History*. Documents and Essays Ed. Albert L. Hurtado and Peter Iverson. Lexington, MA: D. C. Heath and Co., 1994., 232.

[6] The following offers an in-dept study. People & Events: "Nat Turner's Rebellion 1831." PBS On-Line. https://www.pbs.org/wgbh/aia/part3/3p1518.html. Accessed August 1, 2018.

Chapter 14

[1] "This Day in History, Harrison Dies of Pneumonia." History.com Staff. 2009, History.com.A+E Television Network. https://www.history.com/this-day-in-history/harrison-dies-of-pneumonia. Accessed August 19, 2018.

Sandi Ludwa

Chapter 15

²The following are resources to learn more about the Alamo and subsequent Treaty: A. Barr, University of Virginia. *Remember The Alamo* [e-book]. Charlottesville, Va: Generic NL Freebook Publisher; n.d. Available from: eBook Collection (EBSCOhost), Ipswich, MA. Accessed August 1, 2018; Paul, Lee. "The Alamo: 13 Days of Glory," from "The Battle of the Alamo," Facts, information and articles about Battle Of The Alamo, an event of Westward Expansion from the Wild West. Originally printed in "Wild West Magazine, February 1996. http://www.historynet.com/battle-of-the-alamo#articles. Accessed August 2, 2018; Huddleston. Scott "Myths surround Alamo Mystery." By Scott Huddleston / shuddleston@express-news.net. San Antonio Express News. https://www.mysanantonio.com/150years/leaders/article/Unknown-facts-about-the-Alamo-defenders-6169878.php Published 12:29 am CST, Thursday, March 3, 2011. Accessed August 2, 2018; "Mexican American War and the Treaty of Guadalupe Hidalgo," National Park Service, U.S.Department of the Interior. https://www.nps.gov/cham/learn/historyculture/mexican-american-war.htm. Accessed August 20, 2018; Nofi, Albert A. *The Alamo and the Texas War of Independence, September 30, 1835 toApril 21, 1836 : Heroes, Myths, and History*. 1ˢᵗ Ed. Ed.(Conshohocken, PA: Combined Books, 1992). Accessed August 1, 2018; Edward D. Mansfield. *The Mexican War: History of its Origin.* (New York: A. S. Barnes & Co., 1848).

Chapter 16

¹Edgar A. Toppin. *A Biographical History of Blacks in America since 1528,* Edgar A. Toppin, (New York: David McKay Co., 1971), 92-93.

²For insight into factory life: "Harriet H. Robinson, "Early Factory Labor in New England" 1883. Primary Sources, Workshops in American History. https://www.learner.org/workshops/primarysources/lowell/docs/factory2.html. Accessed August 28, 2018; "The First American Factories." U.S. History online Textbook. Independence Hall Association of Philadelplhia. http://www.ushistory.org/us/25d/asp. Accessed August 28, 2018.

Our America

Chapter 17

[1] The stories are a series written by Senate historians revealing stories, many of which are unusual. "Senate Stories 1801-1850,Clay's Last Compromise, January 29, 1850," accessed 4/23/18, https://www.senate.gov/artandhistory/history/minute/Clays_Last_Compromise.htm, U.S. Senate Website.

[2] Ibid. "Senate Stories 1801-1850,Clay's Last Compromise, January 29, 1850," accessed 4/23/18, https://www.senate.gov/history/essays.htm, U.S. Senate Website; Rogers, Joseph M., *The True Henry Clay*. (Philadelphia: J. B. Lippincott Co., 1905), 342. This author also cites Clay's statement, "I know No North....." 372.

[3] For reading on the life of Douglas: Gerald M. Capers. *Stephen A. Douglas, Defender of the Union*. (Boston: Little, Brown and Co., 1959); Louis Howland. *Stephen A. Douglas*. (New York: Charles Scribner's Sons, 1920).

[4] The Donner Party set out from Illinois in 1846 and actually had a guidebook. They followed its advice and ended up in ice and snow in the High Sierras. Some of the party reached California but at a cost. They turned to cannibalism in order to survive.

Chapter 18

[1] Lyman Beecher." Ohio History Connection. http://www.ohiohistorycentral.org/w/Lyman Beecher. Accessed August 22, 2018.

[2] Harriet Beecher Stowe. *Key to Uncle Tom's Cabin. Presenting the original facts and Documents upon which the story is founded.* Together with corroborative statements verifying the truth of the work. Public-domain. Google Book Search. https://archive.org/strea/akeytouncletoms01stowgoog/akeytouncletoms01stowgog, djvu.text. Accessed August 24, 2018; "The Story of Josiah Hensen, the Real Inspiration for 'Uncle Tom's Cabin." Smithsonian.com. https://www.smithsonianmag.com/history/story-josiah-henson-real-inspiration-uncle-toms-cabin-180969094/. Accessed August 24, 2018.

[3] Harriet Beecher Stowe, History.com Staff, History.com, A+E Networks. 2009 https://www.history.com/topics/harriet-beecher-stowe.

[4] Three excellent sources: Sumner, Charles, *The Barbarism of Slavery*, Library of Congress Collection, (New York: Young Men's Republican Union. https://archive.org/details/barbarismofslave00lcsumn. Accessed September 4, 2018; Harvey Wish, *Ante-bellum*, (New York: Capricorn Books, 1960), 14; "31e, Canefight!. Preston Brooks and Charles Sumner. U.S. History Pre-Columbian to the New Millennium. Independence Hall Association. http://www.ushistory.org/us/31e.asp. Accessed July 30, 2018.

Chapter 19

[1] The only other bachelor when elected but married while in White House in was Grover Cleveland in 1886.

[2] Albert E. Pillsbury, *Lincoln and Slavery,"* (Boston: Houghton Mifflin Co., 1913)), 83-84; "Abraham Lincoln Online." Collected Works of Abraham Lincoln. Ed. Roy P. Basler. http://www.abrahamlincolnonline.org/lincoln/speeches/house.htm. Accessed September 11, 2018; For additional insight on Lincoln see: Richard N. Current, *The Lincoln Nobody Knows* (New York: McGraw-Hill Book Co., Inc., 1958.

Chapter 20

[1] Bledsoe, Albert Taylor , LL.D. (Professor of Mathematics in the University of Virginia).*An Essay on Liberty and Slavery* (Philadelphia: J. B. Lippincott & Co., 1856). 381-382 present the ending thesis and beliefs held by Bledsoe.

Chapter 21

[1] John Brown's War, "Purged away with Blood," American Battlefield Trust. https://www.battlefields.org/learn/articles/purged-away-blood. Accessed August 17, 2018; The Wives and Children of John Brown," Harpers Ferry National Historical Park, National Park Service, U.S. Department of the Interior. https://www.nps.gov/articles/wives-and-children-of-john-brown.htm. Accessed July 30, 2018; "Harpers Ferry." National Park Service brochure to Harpers Ferry, obtained August 2018. National Park Service U.S. Department of the Interior. Harpers Ferry National Historical Park.

[2] Jackie Rosenhek, "The First Lady of Lunacy." November 2006. http://www.doctorsreview.com/history/nov06-history_medicine/. Accessed August 27, 2018. Alludes to the 400 pairs of gloves, while the following details the lavish spending, insanity, and asylum, Webb Garrison, *Amazing Women of the Civil War,* (Nashville: Thomas Nelson, 1999), 226, 229.

[3] "The Civil War Home Page,"http://www.civil-war.net/pages/1860_census.html. Accessed December 19, 2018.

Chapter 22

[1] John Fiske. *The Critical Period of American History 1783-1789*. Boston: Houghton Mifflin Co., 1888, by Abby M., 344.

[2] Allister Cooke, *Allister Cooke's America*, (New York: Alfred A. Knopf, 1973), 214.

[3] Sources disagree on age and also membership in either Michigan 22nd or Massachusetts 22nd, but the remaining facts are agreed upon. "Johnny Clem 'Drummer Boy of Chickamauga,' August 13, 1851-May 13, 1937. Article from ACWS Newsletter, Summer 2010. American Civil War Society. https://acws.co.uk/archives-biography-clem. Accessed August 27, 2018; "John Lincoln Clem" Updated March 28, 2007. Arlington National Cemetery Website. http://www.arlingtoncemetery.net/jlclem.htm. Accessed August 27, 2018; Emmy E. Werner, *Reluctant Witnesses Children's Voices from the Civil War*. (Boulder: Westview Press, 1998), 26.

[4] Stout, Harry S. Stout, *Upon the Altar of the Nation, A Moral History of the Civil War*. (New York: Penguin Books, 2006). 168-171.

[5] "Antietam." Antietam National Battlefield, Maryland. National Park Service, U.S. Department of the Interior, official brochure.

[6] Confederate Spy Belle Boyd is Captured." This Day in History. https://www.history.com/this-day-in-history/confederate-spy-belle-boyd-is-captured. Accessed August 25, 2018; "Isabelle Belle Boyd." https://www.womenshistory.org/education-Resources/biographies/isabelle-boyd. Accessed August 25, 2018; For an overall view refer to: Women Spies of the Civil War." Special Report Smithsonian Institution. Smithsonian.com. https://www.smithsonianmag.com/history/women-spies-of-the-civil-war-162202679/. Accessed August 25, 2018; Also see "Maria Belle Boyd." American Battlefield Trust. National Women's History Museum. https://www.battlefields.org/learn/biographies/maria-belle-boyd. Accessed August 25, 2018.

[7] "Something About Everything Military, Blockade Runners." Reprint of David A. Norris. Hide and Seek on the High Seas. *History Magazine*. April / May 2007. http://www.jcs-group.com/military/war1861fringe/runners.html. Accessed August 27, 2018; "CSS Robert E. Lee." Confederate Navy.com. http://www.confederatenavy.com/CSS_Robert_E_Lee.htm. Accessed August 27, 2018; Blockade of Confederate Ports." Office of the Historian, Bureau of Public Affairs, united States Department of State. National Park Service U.S. Department of the Interior. https://history.state.gov/milestones/1861-1865/blockade. Accessed August 2018; "USS Fort Donelson-Confederate Blockade Runner Robert E. Lee" American Civil War. Com https://www.americancivilwar.com/tcwn/civil_war/Navy_Ships/USS_Fort_Donelson.html. Accessed August 27, 2018.

Chapter 23

[1] Jason H. Silverman, Lincoln and the Immigrant. (Carbondale: Southern Illinois University Press, 2015), 112-114.

[2] "Gettysburg Invasion & Retreat." Maryland Civil War Trails, Brochure. Further information www.civilwartrails.org; The following provided materials on estimates of casualties and conditions at Gettysburg: Michael T. Snyder, *Journal Register News Service*, "Battle of Gettysburg, How Area Residents Dealt with the Carnage," *The Pottstown Mercury*, July 7, 2013, The Mercury https://www.pottsmerc.com/lifestyle/battle-of-gettysburg-how-area-residents-dealt-with-the-carnage/article_e8f06330-d547-523b-b4b8-23f484c26c94.html.

[3] Mary Deborah Petite, *"The Women Will Howl."* (Jefferson, NC: McFarland & Co., Inc., 2008.

[4] Gary Flavvion, "Civil War Prison Camps." Civil War Overview. American Battlefield Trust. https://www.battlefields.org/learn/articles/civil-war-prison-camps. Accessed August 25, 2018. This publication provides good insight into the conditions.

Chapter 24

[1] "Andrew Johnson, 16th Vice-President, 1865." United States Senate website. https://www.senate.gov/artandhistory/history/common/generic/VP_Andrew_Johnson.htm. Accessed September 12, 2018.

[2] Pillsbury, *Lincoln and Slavery*. 96.

Chapter 25

[1] Michael Fellman, *Citizen Sherman. A Life of William Tecumseh Sherman.* (New York, Random House, 1995), 400; William Techumseh. Sherman. *Memoirs of General W. T. Sherman,* Ed. With intro and notes   Michael Fellman, (New York: Penguin books, 2000). For an overall view on the War refer to the following: Richard E. Beringer, Richard E., Herman Hattaway, Archer Jones, William N. Still, Jr., *Why the South Lost the Civil War.* Athens: University of Georgia, 1986; Jacqueline Glass Campbell, *When Sherman Marched North From the Sea,* Gary W. Gallagher, ed., (Chapel Hill: University of North Carolina, 2003).

[2] Jefferson Davis, *The Rise and Fall of the Confederacy.* Vol. I and II. (New York: D. Appleton & Co., 1881) 292, 764; Webb Garrison, *Amazing Women of the Civil War,* 273. Esto Perpetua is the motto of the State of Idaho.

www.ingramcontent.com/pod-product-compliance
Lightning Source LLC
Chambersburg PA
CBHW030311080526
44584CB00012B/519